PARLIAMENTARY SOVEREIGNTY AND THE HUMAN RIGHTS ACT

The Human Rights Act 1998 is criticised for providing a weak protection of human rights. The principle of parliamentary legislative supremacy prevents entrenchment, meaning that courts cannot overturn legislation passed after the Act that contradicts Convention rights. This book investigates this assumption, arguing that the principle of parliamentary legislative supremacy is sufficiently flexible to enable a stronger protection of human rights, which can replicate the effect of entrenchment. Nevertheless, it is argued that the current protection should not be strengthened. If correctly interpreted, the Human Rights Act can facilitate democratic dialogue that enables courts to perform their proper correcting function to protect rights from abuse, whilst enabling the legislature to authoritatively determine contestable issues surrounding the extent to which human rights should be protected alongside other rights, interests and goals of a particular society.

Parliamentary Sovereignty and the Human Rights Act

Alison L Young

·HART·
PUBLISHING

OXFORD AND PORTLAND, OREGON
2009

Published in North America (US and Canada) by
Hart Publishing
c/o International Specialized Book Services
920 NE 58th Avenue, Suite 300
Portland, OR 97213-3786
USA
Tel: +1 503 287 3093 or toll-free: (1) 800 944 6190
Fax: +1 503 280 8832
E-mail: orders@isbs.com
Website: http://www.isbs.com

Hart Publishing Ltd, 16C Worcester Place, Oxford, OX1 2JW
Telephone: +44 (0)1865 517530 Fax: +44 (0)1865 510710
E-mail: mail@hartpub.co.uk
Website: http://www.hartpub.co.uk

British Library Cataloguing in Publication Data
Data Available

ISBN: 978-1-84113-830-5

Typeset by Hope Services, Abingdon
Printed and bound in Great Britain by
TJ International Ltd, Padstow, Cornwall

Preface

The Human Rights Act 1998 was once described to me in a tutorial as an example of a 'typical English compromise' (although the author of the quote—who wishes to remain anonymous—failed to explain whether the Scots, Welsh and Northern Irish were either also as prone to making compromises, or as desirous of the need for such a compromise to be made). The compromise stems from its aim to reconcile a strong protection of human rights with the need to preserve parliamentary sovereignty. Yet, as with many compromises, far from providing an acceptable solution for all, the Act has been criticised for having made the compromise in the first place. For those wishing to move to a stronger, constitutional protection, where the courts can overturn legislation that contravenes human rights, parliamentary sovereignty seems an outmoded principle that does not deserve to be protected at the cost of human rights. For some supporters of parliamentary sovereignty, even the power to declare statutes to be incompatible with Convention rights is deemed too great to be placed in the hands of the courts.

This book aims to investigate the relationship between parliamentary sovereignty and the Human Rights Act. It begins by investigating the assumption that it is not possible to provide a constitutional protection of rights without undermining Dicey's conception of parliamentary sovereignty. It will argue that Dicey's theory is compatible with a stronger protection of rights than that found within the Human Rights Act. First, principles of interpretation can be used to produce an 'entrenchment effect'. This occurs when potential conflicts between statutory provisions are avoided through a creative use of principles of interpretation, rendering it practically impossible for later statutes to overturn the provisions of earlier statutes. Second, human rights principles could be entrenched through a modification of the rule of recognition, although this can be difficult to achieve in practice.

Having established the possibility of providing for a stronger protection of human rights, the book then investigates whether the Human Rights Act should be modified. It does so by investigating whether there is a justification for the model of rights protections found in the Act. It is argued that the Act can be defended as providing for a democratic dialogue model of rights protection. After setting out the model of democratic dialogue, the book establishes a method through which the powers of the legislature and the courts should be exercised in order to facilitate the dialogue required by the Act.

Finally, the book investigates the deeper issue—is there anything worthy of preservation in Dicey's theory of parliamentary sovereignty? It argues that, in a similar manner to democratic dialogue models of rights protection, Dicey's legal principle of continuing parliamentary legislative supremacy preserves a model of inter-institutional comity that provides greater legitimacy and stability to our model of parliamentary democracy than that provided by self-embracing parliamentary legislative supremacy.

There are many people to whom I owe a large debt of thanks. I am particularly indebted to Nick Barber, Vernon Bogdanor and Tomas Furlong, all of whom both read the entire penultimate draft and provided extremely helpful and inspiring comments and suggestions. Tomas Furlong, in particular, has gone above and beyond the call of duty, having had to endure listening to, and commenting on, my ideas in three years worth of tutorials, as well as being the perfect research assistant in the final editing stages of the book. I am also indebted to Richard Albert, Richard Danbury, Julie Dickson, Pavlos Eleftheriadis, Tom Hickman and Danny Nicol, all of whom have diligently read and helpfully commented on one or more chapters of the book at various stages of its incarnation. I have also benefited greatly from discussions of the ideas in the book with Alan Bogg, Aileen Kavanagh, Ian Leigh, Roger Masterman and Gavin Phillipson. I am also grateful to Alan Bogg for providing such a supportive environment and being the perfect colleague at Hertford, particularly in Trinity Term 2008 when book editing took over. I also owe thanks to the law students at Hertford and Merton and to participants on the BCL Constitutional Theory course (I would list all of their names, but then the preface would be longer than the book!), for their endurance, patience, criticisms and suggestions. I am also extremely grateful to all at Hart Publishing for answering my many questions and for their guidance and support from gestation to completion of the book.

Thanks are also due to Mr D Howard, Mr M Nicholls, Mr C Wolstenholme and especially Mr M Bellamy, without whom I would never have had the energy or enthusiasm to work late into the night, thereby allowing me to write a book without completely abandoning my family.

My biggest debt is owed to Duncan and Imogen, to whom this book is dedicated.

Contents

Table of Cases

Table of Legislation

Table of Statutory Instruments

Table of International Treaties and Conventions

1

Introduction

T
HE HUMAN RIGHTS ACT 1998 is designed, at least in part, to provide greater protection of human rights without compromising the fundamental constitutional principle of parliamentary sovereignty. This is made clear in the Government's White Paper, which served as a precursor to the Bill[1] and in the ministerial statements of both Lord Irvine[2] and Jack Straw[3] when the Bill was introduced for its second reading in the House of Lords and House of Commons respectively. The desire to preserve parliamentary sovereignty was not questioned throughout the Bill's legislative progress, including during its lengthy discussion at committee stage in the House of Lords. The importance of the preservation of parliamentary sovereignty stems from the manner in which it protects democracy. The legislature enjoys the electoral mandate, which legitimises the choices made by the legislature when enacting legislation. To allow the judiciary to overturn legislation would be to question democracy and challenge the democratic law-making process of the legislature: by ensuring that the judiciary cannot overturn legislation, parliamentary sovereignty and democracy are preserved.

The Human Rights Act therefore differs from other constitutional protections of human rights which empower the judiciary to overturn statutory provisions that contravene fundamental rights (for example, in the United States of America, or Germany) referred to as 'hard' as opposed to 'soft' protections of human rights. Hard protections of human rights entrench fundamental rights: fundamental rights cannot be overturned by legislative provisions, requiring instead a constitutional amendment, something that is in practice more difficult to achieve than the passing of normal legislation.[4] When proposing the Human Rights Act, the Government maintained that such entrenchment was neither possible nor desirable: it would require a major constitutional change, overturning the principle of parliamentary sovereignty.

---

[1] Secretary of State for the Home Department, 'Rights Brought Home: the Human Rights Bill' (Cm 3782, 1997) paras 2.13–2.16.

[2] Hansard HL vol 582, cols 1228–29 (3 November 1997).

[3] Hansard HC vol 306, cols 769–70 (16 February 1998).

[4] Eg, many constitutions require a two-thirds majority as opposed to a simple majority of votes cast in its legislative chambers in order to amend the constitution; some constitutions require that constitutional amendments are approved by a referendum.

The aim of this book is to question some common assertions. Is it true that it is impossible to entrench human rights without overturning the principle of parliamentary sovereignty? If not, should the Human Rights Act be modified in order to provide a strong protection of human rights, or should we preserve parliamentary sovereignty? To answer these questions, we need first to examine constitutional orthodoxies and unpick latent tensions within these orthodoxies, in order to reconstruct our understanding. This requires a general account of Dicey's theory of parliamentary sovereignty. Tensions evident in the orthodox account of sovereignty will then be explored, stemming from an exploration of arguments that the Human Rights Act itself could undermine parliamentary sovereignty. These tensions will be explored more fully in later chapters. An account will then be provided of the main argument of the book. It will be argued that it is possible, although difficult, to entrench human rights without undermining parliamentary sovereignty. Nevertheless, the protection of human rights found in the Human Rights Act will be defended, through the way in which this facilitates inter-institutional dialogue between the legislature and the courts. The facilitation of inter-institutional comity also provides a modest defence of Dicey's theory of parliamentary sovereignty.

I. DEFINING PARLIAMENTARY SOVEREIGNTY: DICEY'S CONCEPTION

Dicey's account of the sovereignty of Parliament is well known. It has become an unshakeable truism that parliamentary sovereignty is the key to understanding the English constitution:

> The principle of Parliamentary sovereignty means neither more nor less than this, namely, that Parliament thus defined has, under the English constitution, the right to make or unmake any law whatever; and, further, that no person or body is recognised by the law of England as having a right to override or set aside the legislation of Parliament.[5]

The sovereignty of Parliament contains two elements. The 'positive aspect': Parliament, as a matter of law, may enact primary legislation on any subject matter it desires. To cite the proverbial example, if Parliament wished to pass a statute requiring the slaughter of all blue-eyed babies, it could do so. This can be contrasted with the 'negative aspect': if Parliament were to pass a statute requiring the slaughter of blue-eyed babies, then neither the courts nor any other authority could question the legislation: once recognised as a valid statute, the courts can only interpret and apply the legislation.[6]

---

[5] AV Dicey, *An Introduction to the Study of the Law of the Constitution*, 10th edn (London, Macmillan, 1959) 39–40.

[6] But see Goldsworthy who states that the negative component automatically follows from the positive component, arguing that parliamentary sovereignty can be summed up by stating that 'Parliament has the legal right to make or unmake any law whatever': J Goldsworthy, *The Sovereignty of Parliament: History and Philosophy* (Oxford, Clarendon Press, 1999) 10.

Three further clarifications need to be made. First, for Dicey, the term 'Parliament' was coterminous with the 'Queen in Parliament'. Consequently, Dicey was not referring to the sovereignty of the Westminster Parliament or the House of Commons alone, but that of the Commons, Lords and the monarch acting together to enact legislation. Secondly, although Dicey asserted that there were no legal limits on the legislation that could be passed by Parliament, he was not arguing that Parliament's legislative powers were completely unlimited. Internal and external limits could restrict the subject matter of legislation. Internal limits were those limits stemming from the characteristics of the law maker. For example, it may be that the moral scruples of the Queen in Parliament would make it impossible to pass legislation authorising the slaughter of blue-eyed babies: such a statute could be legally passed, but it is very unlikely. External limits stem from those governed by Parliament. If Parliament were to pass a law authorising the slaughter of blue-eyed babies, the governed are likely to rebel, or refuse to obey the law. Consequently, aware of these possible challenges to its authority, Parliament would not pass such legislation.[7]

Thirdly, Dicey believed that Parliament's law-making powers are limited by the nature of sovereignty itself: namely that Parliament cannot pass a law which binds its successors. If Parliament in 1990 were to pass legislation purporting to bind a future Parliament elected in 1997, this future Parliament would no longer be free to pass law on any subject. Consequently, the Parliament in 1997 should be able to overturn the legal limitation placed upon its law-making capacity by the Parliament in 1990 to ensure that it too possessed legislative omnipotence.[8]

II. THE COMPATIBLITY OF THE HUMAN RIGHTS ACT 1998 WITH DICEY'S THEORY OF PARLIAMENTARY SOVEREIGNTY

The Human Rights Act was intended to provide for a protection of human rights that did not challenge Dicey's conception of parliamentary sovereignty.[9] This intention was meant to be achieved through section 3 and section 4 of the Act. Section 3 (1) provides that:

> So far as it is possible to do so, primary legislation and subordinate legislation must be read and given effect in a way which is compatible with the Convention rights.

Section 3(2)(b) states that any interpretation, 'does not affect the validity, continuing operation or enforcement of any incompatible primary legislation'. Where it is not possible to read and give effect to primary legislation in a manner compatible with Convention rights, section 4(2) provides that a court,

---

[7] Dicey, above n 5, at 76–84.

[8] *Ibid*, at 67–8.

[9] Hansard HL vol 582, col 1229 (3 November 1997). This view was reiterated by the Government in debates in the House of Commons. See in particular, Hansard HC vol 306, cols 771; 782; 790 and 858 (16 February 1998).

of the level of the High Court or above, 'may make a declaration of that incompatibility'. Section 4(6)(a) provides that any declaration of incompatibility 'does not affect the validity, continuing operation or enforcement of the provision in respect of which it is given'.

In short, although courts can interpret legislation to achieve compatibility, they cannot question or overturn legislation that is incompatible with Convention rights. Even where a court issues a declaration of incompatibility, the statute remains legally valid and is applied in the same manner as all other statutes. Furthermore, section 6(3)(b) expressly excludes Parliament and those performing functions 'in connection with a proceeding in Parliament' from the definition of a public authority: thus making it clear that Parliament has no legal duty to act in a manner compatible with Convention rights. To put it in Dicey's terms, Parliament remains legally free to legislate on any subject matter, even where this is contrary to Convention rights. Lord Irvine reiterated this conclusion when assessing the first two years of operation of the Human Rights Act.[10]

Despite these assurances, doubts have been raised as to the compatibility of the Human Rights Act 1998 with Dicey's conception of parliamentary sovereignty. There are three main sources of potential conflict. First, Lord Irvine's assurances only concern sections 3 and 4 of the Act. However, challenges to Dicey's conception of parliamentary sovereignty also stem from other sections of the Act: section 19, which could be interpreted as providing for a new manner and form requirement for enacting valid legislation; and section 10 which provides for a prospective Henry VIII clause, empowering a minister of the Crown to pass delegated legislation which amends primary legislation, even if that primary legislation is passed after the Human Rights Act 1998 came in to force.

Secondly, the Human Rights Act 1998 has been categorised as a constitutional statute. As such, the Human Rights Act is a different species of statute, with the implication that it is to be treated differently, particularly regarding the manner in which its provisions can be repealed. Thirdly, the Human Rights Act establishes a model of constitutional dialogue between Parliament and the courts concerning the compatibility of Convention rights with existing and future legislation, providing more evidence for the claim that, in reality, the English constitution is best described as a model of 'dual' or 'bi-polar' sovereignty—where sovereignty does not vest in Parliament, but is shared between Parliament and the courts.

This section will argue that these arguments provide both a direct and an indirect challenge to Dicey's conception of parliamentary sovereignty. Direct challenges stem from section 19 and section 10 of the Act as well as the classification of the Act as a constitutional statute. Each section may give rise to a situation in which courts do not apply the doctrine of implied repeal to the Human Rights

---

[10] Lord Irvine of Lairg, 'The Impact of the Human Rights Act: Parliament, the courts and the executive' [2003] *Public Law* 308, 309–10.

Act: this effectively entrenches *those* provisions by requiring that modifications can only be made through express (as opposed to implied) repeal.

Indirect challenges question the feasibility of classifying the United Kingdom constitution as one that does, or should, adhere to Dicey's conception of parliamentary sovereignty. The classification of the Human Rights Act as a constitutional statute may question Dicey's assumption that there is no hierarchy among statutes. Arguments based on dual or bipolar sovereignty question the reality of Dicey's conception of sovereignty given the growing role of the courts when interpreting legislation.

A. Section 19: the Manner and Form Challenge

Section 19 requires a minister, when proposing legislation, to 'make a statement to the effect that in his view the provisions of the Bill are compatible with the Convention rights'[11] or to 'make a statement to the effect that although he is unable to make a statement of compatibility the government nevertheless wishes the House to proceed with the Bill'.[12] Section 19 could be interpreted as providing a manner and form requirement as to the enactment of valid legislation.[13] Such requirements are problematic because they suggest that a previous Parliament has bound a future Parliament, by setting rules as to what constitutes valid legislation. The argument is that if legislation were to be enacted without a section 19 statement, then it could be regarded as invalid legislation. If this were the case, then courts would strike down as invalid those statutes enacted without a section 19 declaration. This is only a *potential* challenge to Dicey's conception of parliamentary sovereignty. It only undermines parliamentary sovereignty if courts are prepared to recognise that section 19 has modified the definition of validly enacted legislation and therefore were prepared to strike down legislation that fails to comply with section 19.

This interpretation of section 19 may also undermine another fundamental constitutional principle.[14] 'Parliamentary privilege' requires that proceedings in Parliament cannot be questioned by the courts.[15] As such, it restricts the extent to which courts can determine whether a purported statute is or is not validly enacted. Courts have the power to determine whether a purported statute is an Act of Parliament,[16] but are restricted to an examination of the Parliamentary

---

[11] Human Rights Act 1998 s 19(1)(a).
[12] Human Rights Act 1998 s 19(1)(b).
[13] D Feldman, 'The Human Rights Act 1998 and Constitutional Principles' (1999) 19 *Legal Studies* 165, 184–5 and N Bamforth, 'Parliamentary Sovereignty and the Human Rights Act 1998' [1998] *Public Law* 572.
[14] Bamforth, *ibid*, at 579–82.
[15] Bill of Rights 1689 art 9.
[16] *Prince's Case* 8 Cook Reports 1a, 77 ER 481 and *Jackson v Attorney General* [2005] UKHL 56, [2006] 1 AC 262.

Roll.[17] If a purported Act of Parliament contains a statement that it has been enacted following the assent of the Commons, Lords (or through the provisions of the Parliament Acts 1911–49) and the monarch, then it is recognised by the courts as a validly enacted statute. To inquire beyond this, for example to investigate allegations that the enactment of a statute was motivated by fraud, would question proceedings in Parliament, breaching parliamentary privilege.[18] Consequently, even if section 19 were interpreted as a manner and form requirement, the courts would be limited to merely determining whether a section 19 statement had been made, in order to preserve parliamentary privilege.

B. Section 10: the Henry VIII Challenge

Section 10 of the Human Rights Act provides a method for changing legislation that is both powerful and very convenient for the executive: it empowers the executive to use delegated legislation to amend primary legislation, so as to ensure its compatibility with Convention rights. Consequently, it is an example of a Henry VIII clause.

Henry VIII clauses can be both retrospective and prospective. A retrospective Henry VIII clause empowers the executive to enact delegated legislation that overrides or amends primary legislation passed *before* the statute containing the Henry VIII clause.[19] A prospective Henry VIII clause enables the executive to use delegated legislation to overturn or amend *all* Acts of Parliament, even those passed *after* the enactment of the legislation containing the Henry VIII clause.

Section 10 is best understood as a prospective Henry VIII clause. The wording of the section does not indicate that it only has retrospective effect. Instead the section gives a wide power to a minister to amend legislation that has been declared incompatible with Convention rights,[20] or which appears to be incompatible with a decision of the European Court of Human Rights,[21] whenever there are 'compelling reasons' to use the section 10 procedure.[22] Such situations could arise with regard to statutes enacted after the Human Rights Act 1998, as well as those that were validly enacted before the 1998 Act. This interpretation of the scope of section 10 is reinforced by an analysis of the purpose of the Human Rights Act 1998. Section 10 is intended to facilitate the amendment of legislation that is contrary to Convention rights, regardless of whether this

---

[17] *The Proprietors of the Edinburgh & Dalkeith Railway v Wauchope* (1842) 8 Cl & Fin 710, 8 ER 279.

[18] *British Railways Board v Pickin* [1974] 1 AC 765.

[19] So, for example, if s 10 of the Human Rights Act were to contain a retrospective Henry VIII clause, it would mean that s 10 could only be used to overturn legislation passed prior to 1998, when the Human Rights Act was passed, or prior to 2 October 2000 when s 10 of the Human Rights Act 1998 came into force.

[20] Human Rights Act 1998 s 10(1)(a).

[21] Human Rights Act 1998 s 10(1)(b).

[22] Human Rights Act 1998 s 10(2).

legislation is enacted prior to or after the Human Rights Act. Such a purpose would be frustrated were the section to be limited to amending those statutes passed prior to the enactment or coming in to force of the Human Rights Act 1998.

It is the classification of section 10 as a prospective Henry VIII clause that may cause problems for Dicey's conception of parliamentary sovereignty. This is because prospective Henry VIII clauses may conflict with another aspect of parliamentary sovereignty: implied repeal.[23] This is best explained by means of an example. For the purposes of simplification, let us imagine that section 10 of the Human Rights Act 1998 is a stand alone provision that merely states that a minister of the Crown may pass delegated legislation to amend legislation that is contrary to Convention rights.[24] In 2008, Parliament passes the Blue-Eyed Baby Act, authorising the slaughter of blue-eyed babies. Following the public outrage, subsequent dissolution of Parliament and a general election, the new Home Secretary wishes to use section 10 to pass delegated legislation to overturn the Blue-Eyed Baby Act 2008.

There are two ways in which prospective Henry VIII clauses might relate to implied repeal in our example. First, the Blue-Eyed Baby Act 2008 *impliedly repeals* section 10, to the extent that section 10 could no longer be validly used to amend the 2008 Act. By legislating contrary to Convention rights when passing the 2008 Act, a conflict has arisen between the Human Rights Act and the 2008 Act. In such circumstances, the later statute impliedly repeals the former.[25]

The second view is that *there is no conflict between the Human Rights Act and the 2008 Act*. Section 10 is therefore still valid and can be used to make the 2008 Act compliant with the Convention. The 2008 Act does not contradict the power of the minister to use a prospective Henry VIII clause, as there is nothing in the Blue-Eyed Baby Act that states that it is not capable of being amended through delegated legislation passed under section 10. Nor is there any provision in the Act regarding Henry VIII clauses. As such, on the second view, instead of being regarded as a statute that had placed a limit on the substance of the laws that can be modified by section 10, it would instead be regarded as an example of a law that contradicted Convention rights and that could be amended by the prospective Henry VIII clause found in section 10.

Section 10 only contradicts Dicey's conception of parliamentary sovereignty if these two views are confused. This would occur if the doctrine of implied repeal was interpreted so that the future legislation partially impliedly repeals the prospective Henry VIII clauses, while at the same time it was argued that

---

[23] See, NW Barber and AL Young, 'The Rise of Prospective Henry VIII Clauses and their Implications for Sovereignty' [2003] *Public Law* 112.

[24] This over-simplification avoids difficulties that arise due to the wording of s 3(1). The impact of s 3(1) and its implications for implied repeal will be discussed further in ch 2, pp 52–4.

[25] In a previous article, Barber and Young, above n 23, this was referred to as the contrast between a conflict of norms model (interpretation 1) and a conflict of subject-matter model (interpretation 2). For further discussion see ch 2, pp 45–9.

section 10 could be used to overturn legislation enacted after the Human Rights Act. This should be regarded as a logical impossibility. If the Blue-Eyed Baby Act 2008 is interpreted as partially impliedly repealing section 10 of the Human Rights Act, then section 10 could not be used to overturn its provisions.[26] Moreover, it is unlikely that the courts will interpret a conflict between the Blue-Eyed Baby Act and section 10 of the Human Rights Act in this manner, following the decision of *Thoburn v Sunderland City Council (Thoburn)*.[27]

Thoburn concerned the prospective Henry VIII clause found in section 2(4) of the European Communities Act 1972. The clause had been used to enact the Units of Measurement Regulations 1994, which required that goods sold in bulk be measured predominantly in metric as opposed to imperial measurements. This contradicted section 1 of the Weights and Measures Act 1985 which expressly stated that both imperial and metric measurements were legal measurements for the sale of goods in bulk. Counsel for the applicant (the trader) argued that section 1 of the Weights and Measures Act 1985 partially impliedly repealed section 2(4) of the European Communities Act 1972. It placed a substantive limit on the power of section 2(4), such that it could not be used to amend the recognition of imperial and metric measurements as legally valid weights and measures.[28] Laws LJ rejected this argument, stating that:

> there is no inconsistency between a provision conferring a Henry VIII power to amend future legislation and the terms of any such future legislation.[29]

He did so because counsel's interpretation of the potential conflict between the Weights and Measures Act 1985 and the European Communities Act 1972 challenged Dicey's conception of parliamentary sovereignty. It placed a restriction on the powers of Parliament by limiting the ability of Parliament to enact a prospective Henry VIII clause: it would allow the very legislation that should be modifiable using the prospective Henry VIII clause, to defeat that clause.[30] Parliamentary supremacy is only preserved if Parliament has the power to empower the executive to overturn future as well as past legislation through the Henry VIII clause.

By the same analysis, the prospective Henry VIII clause found in section 10 of the Human Rights Act 1998 does not undermine Dicey's principle of parliamentary sovereignty.[31] *Thoburn* concludes that future legislation does not impliedly repeal the provisions of prospective Henry VIII clauses and it is hard

---

[26] Feldman appears to adopt this position: see Feldman, above n 13, at 189.
[27] [2002] EWHC 195 (Admin), [2003] 1 QB 151.
[28] *Ibid*, at [37]–[49].
[29] *Ibid*, at [50].
[30] *Ibid*, at [51].
[31] Prospective Henry VIII clauses appear to pose a different challenge to Dicey's concept of parliamentary sovereignty, in that they empower the executive to question, suspend and amend legislation enacted by Parliament. However, this power is granted to the executive by Parliament and can be taken away by Parliament, by either express or implied repeal of the Henry VIII clause.

to see why this conclusion would be not reached when applied to section 10 of the Human Rights Act 1998.

C. A Constitutional Statute?

A further challenge to Dicey's theory of parliamentary legislative supremacy arises from the classification of the Human Rights Act 1998 as a constitutional statute.[32] Dicey's concept of parliamentary sovereignty implies that there is no hierarchy between statutes. All statutes can be overturned by future legislation, either expressly or by implication. The classification of some statutes as 'constitutional', however, appears to imply that these statutes are different from, and superior to, ordinary legislation. This is particularly the case if constitutional statutes cannot be overturned in the same way as other statutes. The strongest argument for distinguishing between constitutional and other statutes in this manner stems from the judgment of Laws LJ in *Thoburn*, when he asserted that constitutional statutes could not be impliedly repealed.[33]

Laws LJ described as 'constitutional' a statute 'which conditions the legal relationship between citizen and state in some general, overarching manner',[34] or which 'enlarges or diminishes the scope of what we now regard as fundamental constitutional rights'.[35] The Human Rights Act satisfies both of these criteria. It conditions the legal relationship between the individual and the state as it limits the extent to which public authorities can act contrary to Convention rights,[36] as well as the extent to which Parliament can legislate contrary to Convention rights.[37] It enlarges the scope of what we would regard as fundamental constitutional rights by providing for a legal protection of Convention rights, enabling individuals, in certain circumstances, to rely on Convention rights in English courts.[38]

If we accept the statement of Laws LJ, then it can be argued that the Human Rights Act is contrary to Dicey's conception of parliamentary sovereignty. Unlike other statutes it requires a special procedure for its amendment; express as opposed to implied repeal. This occurs because of the way in which courts interpret constitutional statutes and statutes purporting to amend their provisions. Due to the importance of constitutional statutes, Laws LJ argues that later statutes will only amend constitutional statutes when the courts are assured that it is Parliament's 'actual—not imputed, constructive or

---

[32] *Thoburn v Sunderland City Council*, above n 27, at [62].
[33] *Ibid*, at [63]–[67].
[34] *Ibid*, at [62].
[35] *Ibid*.
[36] Human Rights Act 1998 s 6.
[37] Human Rights Act 1998 s 3 and s 4.
[38] For a criticism of the breadth of Laws LJ's classification of constitutional statutes see G Marshall, 'Metric Measures and Martyrdom by Henry VIII Clause' (2002) 118 *Law Quarterly Review* 493.

presumed—intention'[39] to amend the constitutional statute. Laws LJ concludes that only 'express words in the later Statute',[40] or 'words so specific that the inference of an actual determination to effect the result contended for was irresistible'[41] would be capable of repealing a constitutional statute. 'The ordinary rule of implied repeal does not satisfy this test'.[42] Whether we accept Laws LJ's argument depends on the scope of the doctrine of implied repeal and its application to section 3(1) of the Human Rights Act. This issue will be discussed in more depth in chapter two.

D. Dialogue and Duality

Sections 3 and 4 of the Human Rights Act facilitate democratic dialogue between Parliament and the courts.[43] Dialogue takes place predominantly when courts issue a section 4 declaration of incompatibility. This provides a signal to Parliament that legislation, while remaining in force, contains provisions that are contrary to Convention rights. The declaration of incompatibility may prompt the legislature to debate if and how to respond to the actions of the courts. Parliament may respond either by amending legislation to ensure its compatibility with Convention rights, or by providing a justification for its maintenance on the statute books, despite its incompatibility. Dialogue may also be instituted when the courts use section 3 to read a statute in a manner compatible with Convention rights. Here, courts are sending a different signal to Parliament: that a statute appeared to be incompatible with Convention rights, but that the courts were able to remedy this incompatibility with a Convention-compatible reading of the statute. If Parliament objects, then it is open to Parliament to amend the legislation, ensuring that it uses clear wording that removes the ability of the courts to read the statute in a Convention-compatible manner.[44] Although the range of situations that can be correctly classed as democratic dialogue is controversial,[45] there is sufficient evidence from

---

[39] *Thoburn v Sunderland City Council*, above n 27, at [63].

[40] *Ibid.*

[41] *Ibid.*

[42] *Ibid.*

[43] See, R Clayton, 'Judicial Deference and "Democratic Dialogue": the Legitimacy of Judicial Intervention under the Human Rights Act 1998 [2004] *Public Law* 33 and T Hickman, 'Constitutional Dialogue, Constitutional Theories and the Human Rights Act 1998' [2005] *Public Law* 306.

[44] Clayton, *ibid*, at 46 and Hickman, *ibid*, at 326–8.

[45] See, eg the Hogg, Bushell and Manfredi exchange: PW Hogg and AA Bushell, 'The *Charter* Dialogue between Courts and Legislatures (or perhaps the *Charter of Rights* isn't such a bad thing after all)' (1997) 35 *Osgoode Hall Law Journal* 75; CP Manfredi and JB Kelly, 'Six Forms of Dialogue: a Response to Hogg and Bushell' (1999) 37 *Osgoode Hall Law Journal* 513 and PW Hogg and AA Thornton, 'Reply to "Six Degrees of Dialogue"' (1999) 37 *Osgoode Hall Law Journal* 529. See also L McDonald, 'New Directions in the Australian Bill of Rights Debate' [2004] *Public Law* 22 and J Waldron 'Some Models of Dialogue between Judges and Legislators' (2004) 23 *Supreme Court Law Review* (2d) 7.

Parliament's reaction to declarations of incompatibility to show that sections 3 and 4 generate an inter-institutional dialogue between Parliament and the courts.

By protecting Convention rights in this manner Dicey's conception of parliamentary sovereignty is maintained, as courts can neither question nor overturn legislative provisions, even if they are incompatible with Convention rights. However, paradoxically, the dialogue introduced by sections 3 and 4 may undermine the accuracy of Dicey's conception of parliamentary sovereignty. To see parliamentary sovereignty as the keystone of the English constitution is to misunderstand the way in which Parliament and the courts interact. This adds to the growing body of challenges made by commentators to the accuracy of Dicey's conception of parliamentary sovereignty, stemming from the relationship between English and European Community law since the *Factortame* decisions and the conventional limits placed on the power of the Westminster Parliament following the various devolution statutes.[46]

Concepts of dual or bipolar sovereignty[47] were first articulated prior to the enactment of the Human Rights Act and suggest that Dicey's conception of parliamentary sovereignty does not accord legal sovereignty to Parliament per se, but to the will of Parliament as expressed in the wording of the statutory provisions it enacts. Interpreting this legislation is the job of the courts, not Parliament, and consequently sovereignty is best understood as shared between Parliament and the courts. If Parliament wishes to express a particular intention, it must do so using words that will be recognised by the courts as expressing that particular intention.[48]

The Human Rights Act may provide further evidence for this conception of sovereignty. First, the Act establishes inter-institutional dialogue between Parliament and the courts, demonstrating the interrelationship between these two institutions. Secondly, the Act gives large powers of interpretation to the courts, reinforcing the way in which the will of Parliament is filtered through the interpretation of the courts.[49]

---

[46] M Elliott, 'Parliamentary Sovereignty and the New Constitutional Order: Legislative Freedom, Political Reality and Convention' (2002) 22 *Legal Studies* 340; V Bogdanor, 'Our New Constitution' (2004) 120 *Law Quarterly Review* 242, 249.

[47] Some commentators have gone further, suggesting that the term 'sovereignty' is inappropriate and that the relationship between Parliament and the courts is best understood as a 'collaborative enterprise': see PA Joseph, 'Parliament, the Courts and the Collaborative Enterprise' (2004) 15 *King's College Law Journal* 321, 333–5.

[48] S Sedley, 'Human Rights: A Twenty-first Century Agenda' [1995] *Public Law* 386, 389; S Sedley, 'The Common law and the Constitution' in MP Nolan and S Sedley, *The Making and Remaking of the British Constitution* (London, Blackstone Press, 1997) 36–7; TRS Allan, 'The Constitutional Foundations of Judicial Review: Conceptual Conundrum or Interpretative Inquiry' (2002) 61 *Cambridge Law Journal* 87, 102; TRS Allan, *Constitutional Justice: A Liberal Theory of the Rule of Law* (Oxford, Oxford University Press, 2001) 205–7.

[49] TRS Allan, *Constitutional Justice: A Liberal Theory of the Rule of Law*, *ibid*, at 225.

E. Evaluation

The potential challenges posed by the Human Rights Act to Dicey's theory of continuing parliamentary legislative supremacy indicate two elements of tension that will form the basis of further exploration in the book. First, there is a need to explore the connection between continuing parliamentary legislative supremacy and the doctrine of implied repeal, which itself depends on its relationship to principles of statutory interpretation. This analysis helps to determine the strength of the challenge posed by section 10 of the Human Rights Act, the classification of the Act as a constitutional statute and the challenge from dual or bipolar sovereignty. Secondly, we need to explore the way in which the United Kingdom constitution defines validly enacted legislation. This helps to evaluate whether section 19 challenges parliamentary sovereignty.

(i) Sovereignty, Interpretation and Implied Repeal

The investigation of the scope of the doctrine of implied repeal confirms that section 10 does not pose a challenge for continuing parliamentary legislative supremacy. It will be argued in chapter two that the doctrine of implied repeal only applies when a statutory provision in one statute is specifically contradicted by a statutory provision found in a later statute. A statute enacted after the Human Rights Act that is incompatible with Convention rights does not contradict section 10 as it does not limit the scope of legislation that can be modified by the executive. It is best understood as an example of a statute whose provisions can be modified by the executive using the prospective Henry VIII clause found in section 10.[50]

This does not mean that section 10 cannot be impliedly repealed. It merely explains that a later statute whose content is incompatible with Convention rights does not conflict with the power granted to the executive by section 10 to modify legislation whose provisions contradict Convention rights. Section 10 could be impliedly repealed by future legislation whose provisions did contradict the power granted to the executive by the prospective Henry VIII clause found in section 10. This would occur, for example, if a later statute included a section explaining that its provisions could only be altered by legislative amendment, as opposed to through delegated legislation, or if it included a section to the effect that its provisions were to take effect notwithstanding section 10.

The book will also argue in chapter two that the doctrine of implied repeal is best understood as a narrow exception to the presumption that later statutes are not intended to overturn the provisions of earlier statutes. The strong role of principles of interpretation will be used to explain how legislative provisions may benefit from an entrenchment effect. An entrenchment effect occurs when statutory provisions are capable of being impliedly repealed in theory, but

---

[50] See ch 2, pp 46–7.

where the wording of the provision makes it difficult to achieve implied repeal in practice.

This analysis explains why the classification of the Human Rights Act 1998 as a constitutional statute by Laws LJ in *Thoburn* does not undermine Dicey's theory of parliamentary sovereignty. Laws LJ states that constitutional statutes cannot be impliedly repealed. His statement implies that constitutional statutes are 'entrenched' as they can only be repealed in a specific manner; through express as opposed to implied repeal. A better understanding of Laws LJ's statement in *Thoburn* concerns the way in which courts interpret constitutional statutes. Principles of interpretation are used to remove potential conflicts between constitutional statutes and later statutes. In this sense it is rarely possible in practice to impliedly repeal a constitutional statute.

The role of interpretation also explains how a classification of some statutes as 'constitutional' need not challenge Dicey's conception of parliamentary sovereignty. A 'constitutional' statute is one containing constitutional principles that the courts will strive harder to protect from inadvertent modification by the doctrine of implied repeal. It is not an example of a statute that stands in a higher hierarchical relationship to other ordinary statutes. The difference between the two types of statute is merely a matter of degree, depending on the strength of evidence required to rebut the presumption that Parliament would not wish to legislate contrary to its previous legislative enactments.

Chapter four will argue that, far from contradicting Dicey's theory of parliamentary sovereignty, the classification of statutes as 'constitutional' corresponds to the way in which Dicey reconciled parliamentary sovereignty with the rule of law. Dicey advocated that courts should interpret statutes so as to preserve common law principles, even if such interpretations would not necessarily receive the approval of the legislature.[51] Those statutes classed as 'constitutional' are those whose content is more likely to contain those common law principles that the judiciary strives to protect. The classification of some statutes as 'constitutional' need not challenge, but may actually support Dicey's theory.

The broad ambit of the courts to interpret legislation in order to avoid conflicts between two statutory provisions also explains why theories of dual or bipolar sovereignty do not challenge Dicey's conception of sovereignty. Dicey's theory of sovereignty accepts that courts can interpret legislation in a manner different from the intentions of Parliament and, indeed, advocates that the courts should ensure that they protect common law principles when interpreting legislation.[52] However, the powers of the courts to interpret legislation so as to protect common law principles reaches a limit when the courts would be required to amend legislation in order to ensure its compatibility with common law principles. Courts cannot question the validity of the statute. Courts must also ensure that later legislation repeals contradictory provisions of earlier

---

[51] Dicey, above n 5, at 413–14. See also ch 5, pp 136–7.
[52] *Ibid.*

legislation. This recognition of the role of the courts would only challenge Dicey's conception if bipolar theories of sovereignty required courts to overturn legislation that contradicted common law principles, or to uphold the provisions of earlier legislation, despite their contradiction by later legislation. This would only occur if it were impossible to distinguish between interpretation and repeal, once the courts are empowered to look beyond the literal meaning of the words of the statute, or the intentions of the legislature. The book will argue in chapter two that this is not the case.[53]

(ii) Defining Legally Valid Legislation

Section 19 poses the strongest potential challenge to Dicey's conception of sovereignty. If we interpret section 19 as governing the manner and form in which legislation is passed, and if courts were to strike down legislation that was enacted without a section 19 statement, then this would appear to provide conclusive evidence of a challenge to Dicey's conception of sovereignty. Dicey's argument rests on the claim that Parliament cannot bind its successors. If later legislation were to be struck down for failing to comply with the requirements of section 19, then this would provide an example of where Parliament had successfully bound its successors.

Chapter three will argue that this conclusion misunderstands a key element of Dicey's theory. Dicey does not argue that it is impossible for future Parliaments to be bound by factors limiting their law-making capacity. Rather, he argues that it is not possible for future Parliaments to be bound by the actions of its predecessors, or to bind its successors. If Parliament acting alone through the enactment of legislation can modify the requirements of validly enacted legislation, then section 19 can be regarded as an example of a manner and form provision that binds future Parliaments. If, however, a mere legislative enactment is not capable of determining validly enacted legislation, then, even if courts were to strike down legislation for failing to make a section 19 statement, this may not be regarded as a breach of Dicey's conception of parliamentary sovereignty. The court's decision, failing to recognise legislation enacted without a section 19 statement, could also be interpreted as evidence of a partial modification to the rule of recognition.

A change in the rule of recognition occurs when there is evidence of a modification of the political facts that constitute the rule of recognition and evidence that officials in the system accept this new rule of recognition.[54] This evidence could be found in legislation purporting to change the rule of recognition, followed by judicial acceptance of this change. The legislature's enactment of section 19 itself, coupled with the executive's continued practice of making section 19 statements, could be interpreted as evidence of a shift in the political facts,

---

[53] In particular, see pp 49–61.
[54] See ch 1, pp 23–4.

accepted by the legislature and the executive, concerning the way in which valid legislation needs to be enacted. The judiciary's refusal to recognise legislation as valid were it to be passed without a section 19 statement could be interpreted as evidence of its acceptance of a change in political facts, accepting the need for valid legislation to contain a section 19 statement. When failing to recognise the legislation as valid, the courts would not be recognising the ability of the legislature in 1998 to bind its successors as to the manner and form in which legislation is passed. Instead, the courts would be recognising a shift in political facts, which, coupled with their legal decision, could be regarded as changing the rule of recognition.

III. SOVEREIGNTY EXPLORED

Dicey argues that, legally, there are no limits on the power of Parliament to enact legislation, but that it cannot bind its successors. Accordingly, the courts and other institutions cannot question or overturn validly enacted legislation. However, within this simple assertion of Dicey's conception of sovereignty lies a series of assumptions. It is only by exploring these assumptions, and delineating the various perspectives from which sovereignty can be analysed, that we can understand more fully whether it is possible to entrench Convention rights without undermining Dicey's conception of sovereignty and whether such entrenchment would be desirable.

A. Continuing Parliamentary Legislative Supremacy

This chapter has referred, so far, to 'Dicey's conception of parliamentary sovereignty'. This section will argue that Dicey's theory is best understood as a theory of 'continuing parliamentary legislative supremacy'. Sovereignty is assessed by determining the power ascribed to the institution deemed to be sovereign in a particular state or legal system. It implies absolute and unlimited power. As such, sovereignty cannot be shared. A body either is sovereign, or it is not. Christians ascribe sovereignty to God because, according to Christian belief, He is omnipotent and omniscient. There are no areas in which He cannot exercise His power and there is no entity with greater power than God.

Parliament is not ascribed the same omnipotence in Dicey's theory. Parliament's sovereignty is both confined and limited. Although Parliament could enact legally valid legislation to alter the laws of physics, require the UK to sever its ties with the European Union or require the slaughter of blue-eyed babies, it is at least arguable that Parliament would not be able to achieve these ends in practice. Among other things, nature, economics and politics limit the power of Parliament. To recognise these limits is not to contradict Dicey's conception of parliamentary sovereignty. Instead, it is to recognise that Dicey is describing the legal conception of parliamentary sovereignty. His theory examines the legal limits placed on Parliament's law making powers.

In addition to non-legal limits, Dicey's conception of sovereignty places a further limit on the powers of the sovereign legislature. Parliament cannot bind its successors. This limit does not challenge the absolute nature of sovereignty. Instead, it is one solution to a conundrum facing any sovereign entity. It is a restriction stemming from the nature of sovereignty itself. If Parliament is sovereign and can enact legislation on any subject matter it chooses, then it follows that it should enjoy the power to limit its own law-making power. Yet, if Parliament can successfully limit its law-making powers, it means, in turn, that there must be certain actions that it and future parliaments cannot perform. Future parliaments, therefore, no longer enjoy the power to enact legislation on any subject matter that they wish. To ensure that future parliaments remain free to enact any legislation they wish requires that a limit is placed on the current parliament. Under either analysis, there is a limit to the powers of the sovereign law-making authority. Either it cannot bind its successors, or it risks being bound by the limitations placed on it by its predecessors.

To argue that Parliament cannot bind its successors is to adopt a theory of continuing parliamentary legislative supremacy. This solution focuses on the law-making powers of each separate Parliament. Each Parliament is sovereign and faces no limits on its law-making power, but to achieve this it is itself limited and cannot bind its successors. Alternatively, to argue that Parliament can bind its successors focuses upon Parliament as a whole composed of a series of separate incarnations over time. Each separate Parliament may place limits on itself and its successors and may be bound by its predecessors. However, if the powers of each of these separate Parliaments were to be viewed across time, there would be no limits on that sovereign entity. To adopt this solution is to adhere to a theory of self-embracing parliamentary sovereignty.[55] Dicey adopts a continuing theory of parliamentary sovereignty. The restriction that Dicey places on Parliament—that it cannot bind its successors—maintains this conception of sovereignty.

Our analysis has explained that Dicey's conception is best understood as a legal conception of continuing parliamentary sovereignty. The absolute nature of *sovereignty* is contrasted with the more relative notion of *supremacy*. A body is sovereign when it has more power than all other institutions. It has the power to perform any action with no limits being placed on its powers. A body is supreme when it has the power to act within a certain set of boundaries, set by the body itself, but where its measures once enacted cannot be challenged by any other institution.[56] Dicey asserts that he is providing an analysis of

---

[55] This terminology stems from the analysis of HLA Hart, *The Concept of Law*, 2nd edn (Oxford, Oxford University Press, 1994) 146.

[56] P Oliver, 'Sovereignty in the Twenty-First Century' (2003) 14 *King's College Law Journal* 137, 138–9.

sovereignty,[57] yet his theory places limits on the power of the sovereign. First, Dicey recognises that Parliament cannot bind its successors. Secondly, Dicey recognises that Parliament faces political and practical limits on its powers, limiting his analysis to the lack of legal limits on the power of Parliament. Moreover, Dicey's theory is restricted to an analysis of only one of Parliament's powers—the power to enact valid legislation.

It is possible to classify Dicey's conception of sovereignty in two ways. First, his theory can be explained as one of continuing parliamentary legislative sovereignty, provided that we are restricting our analysis to the legal as opposed to the non-legal limits placed on the powers of Parliament. Secondly, Dicey can be classified as adhering to a theory of continuing parliamentary legislative supremacy. His theory is regarded as a theory of supremacy as it discusses the power of Parliament to enact legislation which cannot be questioned by the courts, within the confines set by practical and political realities.

The categorisation of Dicey as providing for a theory of 'continuing parliamentary legislative supremacy' will be the one adopted in the rest of the book. It provides a more realistic account, recognising that although Parliament has no legal limits on its law-making powers, this is balanced against other, non-legal limits on its powers. In turn, this provides an insight into the manner in which Dicey justified his conception of continuing parliamentary legislative supremacy.[58]

B. Perspectives of Parliamentary Sovereignty

Our discussion of the more precise categorisation of Dicey's conception of sovereignty touched on the fact that sovereignty can be analysed from different perspectives. Dicey drew a distinction between legal and political sovereignty, classifying his theory as a legal conception of sovereignty. His concern was to establish the existence of continuing parliamentary legislative supremacy as a legal fact.[59] Legal sovereignty was constituted by a legal rule determining that Parliament faced no legal limits on its law-making power, save the inability to bind its successors.

Political sovereignty is concerned with an analysis of political facts, seeking a justification for granting continuing parliamentary legislative supremacy to Parliament. Sovereignty is placed in Parliament, the body 'the will of which is ultimately obeyed by the citizens of the state'.[60] To place sovereignty in Parliament preserved the ultimate political sovereignty of the electorate. Legislation enacted through the Queen in Parliament would, at least in the long run, cohere with the wishes of the electorate. This occurred through the

---

[57] Dicey, above n 5, at 39.
[58] See, ch 4.
[59] Dicey, above n 5, at 39.
[60] Dicey, *ibid*, at 73.

political restrictions faced by the House of Commons, whose members would, at least in theory, act in accordance with the wishes of their constituents, or through the ultimate threat that the House of Commons could be voted out at elections, allowing the electorate to enforce its will in a more direct manner. When analysed from the legal perspective, Parliament is sovereign. When analysed from a political perspective, it is the electorate and not Parliament which is sovereign.[61]

Dicey's distinction between political and legal sovereignty is not concerned with the nature of the limits placed on the power of Parliament, but with the perspective from which sovereignty is analysed. This can be illustrated by the way in which Dicey used the distinction between political and legal sovereignty to defend his conception of sovereignty from a potential criticism arising from Austin's account of sovereignty.

Austin's theory of jurisprudence defined law as a series of commands of the sovereign backed by a sufficient sanction to enforce these commands. The sovereign, by definition, was the body with ultimate power. It was answerable to no other body and no other body could overturn the commands of the sovereign. Despite these similarities, Austin vested sovereignty in the electorate as opposed to Parliament. It appeared, therefore, that Austin's interpretation of sovereignty challenged that of Dicey. Dicey responded to this challenge by explaining that Austin's theory provides a political conception of sovereignty, analysing the concept of sovereignty from a political as opposed to a legal perspective. Austin's theory relies on the identification of a politically sovereign body and it is only the commands of the politically sovereign body that form part of the legal system. Dicey, while recognising the political sovereignty of the electorate, described Parliament as the sovereign law-making power not merely because there were no legal limits on its powers, but because the law itself stated that there were no legal limits on the power of Parliament. Dicey was examining sovereignty from a legal perspective. Austin was analysing sovereignty from a political perspective.[62]

Loughlin challenges Dicey's distinction between legal and political sovereignty, arguing that it cannot be maintained.[63] Loughlin asserts that sovereignty is indivisible: it is impossible, therefore, for legal sovereignty to rest with Parliament and political sovereignty with the electorate. If the electorate is sovereign, then it must grant powers to Parliament to act on its behalf, transferring its sovereignty to Parliament. If this is the case, then parliamentary sovereignty is achieved and Parliament can enact legislation without this being challenged or questioned by the courts. However, the electorate is no longer sovereign as it can no longer control Parliament. Parliament could legislate contrary to the

---

[61] Dicey, *ibid*, at 72–4. The validity of this theory, both in terms of its theoretical justification and its accuracy as a description of Dicey's theory of sovereignty, will be analysed in more depth in ch 4, pp 96–103.
[62] Dicey, *ibid*, at 70–76.
[63] M Loughlin, *Public Law and Political Theory* (Oxford, Clarendon Press, 1992) 146–9.

wishes of the electorate. Alternatively, the electorate could only grant limited power to Parliament—the power to legislate but only according to the wishes of the electorate. If this is the case the electorate retains sovereignty. Parliament, however, is no longer sovereign.

Loughlin's analysis, however, misconstrues Dicey's theory. Loughlin's challenge rests on an analysis of sovereignty whereas, as we have discussed, Dicey's theory is best conceived as a theory of parliamentary legislative supremacy. It is a legal conception which ascribes legislative supremacy to Parliament, arguing that, as a legal fact, Parliament has no legal limits placed on its law-making power. Even if we were to argue that the political sovereign (the electorate) only grants Parliament the power to act according to its wishes, this does not challenge parliamentary legislative supremacy. Parliament still has the power legally to act contrary to the wishes of the electorate; the electorate can then elect a differently composed Parliament at the next general election, thereby asserting its sovereignty. Loughlin regards Dicey as drawing an analytical distinction between political and legal sovereignty, regarding the two as distinct components of a sovereign entity. However, Dicey's distinction between legal and political sovereignty is best understood as a distinction between different perspectives from which sovereignty can be analysed.[64]

The recognition that sovereignty can be analysed from different perspectives also helps to explain the relationship between political and legal sovereignty. This can be illustrated by the analyses of sovereignty provided by Neil McCormick and Trevor Allan. McCormick argues that politics and law are distinct concepts. Politics is about power; law is concerned with normativity. The two relate to each other as the exercise of power normally connects to issues of normativity, justifying the exercise of the power (for example, the electorate is urged to vote for a particular composition of Parliament because it is more likely to exercise its power in a normatively acceptable manner). Moreover, normativity depends on political factors. Legal decisions are not taken in a vacuum and depend on an assessment of politics. In the same way that law and politics overlap, so do our conceptions of legal and political sovereignty.[65]

Allan recognises that the existence of parliamentary legislative supremacy depends on whether it is an accurate description of a legal fact. However, this legal fact has political underpinnings and can be justified as a matter of political principle. Legislative supremacy is granted to Parliament because of its credentials as a democratically elected body. Dicey's theory of a self-correcting unitary democracy supports this interpretation.

Dicey argued that the internal and external limits placed on sovereign power were the same. Consequently, according parliamentary legislative power to Parliament was justified as a means by which to ensure that the electorate

---

[64] It is important to note here that this is an account of Dicey's analysis of sovereignty as found in his *Introduction to the Study of the Law of the Constitution*. As will be examined later, this is an over-simplification: see ch 4, pp 96–103.

[65] N McCormick, 'Beyond the Sovereign State' (1993) 56 *Modern Law Review* 1, 11–12.

retained political sovereignty: Parliament passes legislation that complies with the will of the electorate. Courts ensure that the will of the electorate prevails by according legal supremacy to the legislation passed by Parliament. Divergence between legislation and the will of the electorate may not challenge the legal fact of whether the courts accord sovereignty to the legislation passed by Parliament. However, it may challenge the political validity of maintaining parliamentary legislative supremacy.[66] This relationship between an analysis of sovereignty from the legal and the political perspective is also illustrated by Loughlin's relational conception of sovereignty.[67]

Discussions of sovereignty, therefore, need to distinguish between an analysis of sovereignty from the legal perspective and an analysis of sovereignty from a political perspective. However, a further confusion lies within Dicey's discussion of the distinction between legal and political sovereignty: he provides both a normative justification, and a factual analysis of parliamentary legislative supremacy. Continuing parliamentary legislative supremacy is justified by the functioning of a self-correcting unitary democracy. The self-correcting unitary democracy finds factual support through the recognition that the electorate does indeed possess the power to change the composition of Parliament. The arguments of Allan, Loughlin and McCormick, discussed above, focus on the normative justification of parliamentary sovereignty. These two analyses need to be separated.

Dicey's investigation of the legal principle of parliamentary legislative sovereignty is an investigation of the existence of a legal fact. He is investigating whether it is correct that Parliament cannot legally bind its successors. But a legal conception of parliamentary sovereignty could also be based on an investigation of other legal facts. It could, for example, investigate whether, legally, other institutions have the ability to restrict the law-making powers of Parliament. Theories of bipolar or dual sovereignty may be regarded in this light. They investigate the way in which courts interpret the will of Parliament through their interpretation of the wording of statutory provisions. These powers of interpretation may provide the courts with the power to restrict the law-making powers of Parliament.

We can obtain a better understanding of this perspective by analysing the way in which similar observations are made with regard to other aspects of constitutional law, in particular the role played by conventions. Conventions are non-legally binding rules and principles. Some conventions regulate or limit the manner in which legal powers are exercised. This is particularly pertinent with regard to the convention that the monarch assents to Bills presented for royal assent. Legally, the monarch is required to consent to legislation in order for it to be validly enacted. This means that the monarch has a legal power of veto over legislation. If assent is refused, then the Bill will not be legally recognised

---

[66] TRS Allan, 'The Limits of Parliamentary Sovereignty' [1985] *Public Law* 614, 621.
[67] M Loughlin, *The Idea of Public Law* (Oxford, Oxford University Press, 2003), 83–7.

as validly-enacted legislation. By convention, however, the monarch assents to all Bills presented to her, or to those Bills presented to her where her ministers have advised her to consent.[68] The assessment of the powers of the monarch is different when analysed from the perspective of her legal powers and the powers that she has as a question of constitutional reality.

There are further parallels between the example of the powers of the monarch to veto legislation, and an analysis of sovereignty. Although the monarch is restricted by convention, it is possible for her to breach this conventional restriction on the exercise of her legal powers. However, to do so would have consequences. Not only would the monarch face criticism for breaching convention, but it is also possible that this action would provoke a reaction from the legislature and the judiciary. The legislature may present the Bill as validly enacted legislation, which the courts could then accept. Parliament, with the consent of the monarch, could also modify the Act of Settlement (1700) legally recognising a different, more compliant individual as monarch.

This example illustrates two points. First the factual perspective aims to understand the constitutional reality of the distribution of legislative power by analysing the range of legal and conventional powers at the hands of the institutions of government. In a similar manner, the factual perspective analyses the way in which the electorate can exercise control over Parliament. Secondly, the real distribution of legislative power can be analysed at different times: it might operate differently on a day to day basis, and in exceptional circumstances (for example in a state of emergency or a situation of constitutional crisis).

Finally, each of these issues can be analysed from an internal and an external perspective. An analysis of internal sovereignty examines the powers of Parliament from the perspective of the state over which that Parliament exercises its powers. To examine whether the Westminster Parliament enjoys continuing parliamentary legislative supremacy from the internal perspective is to examine the powers of that Parliament vis-à-vis the powers of other bodies within the United Kingdom and the legal constraints placed on the Westminster Parliament by English constitutional law. If there is no other body capable of overturning law made by the Westminster Parliament, then we would argue that the Westminster Parliament enjoyed legislative supremacy from an internal perspective.

The external perspective assesses sovereignty from the viewpoint of other states. The Westminster Parliament would be supreme from an external perspective if it were the relevant actor for the purposes of international law; if the Westminster Parliament has the supreme power to act for the United Kingdom on the international stage.[69] The focus of sovereignty discussed in this book focuses on the internal perspective, discussing sovereignty from the perspective of constitutional principles.

[68] A Twomey, 'The Refusal or Deferral of Royal Assent' [2006] *Public Law* 580.
[69] See, P Oliver, above n 56, at 137; N McCormick, *Questioning Sovereignty: Law, State and Nation* (Oxford, Oxford University Press, 1999) 129–31.

Sovereignty is a complex concept. A better understanding of these complexities requires that we differentiate not only between different conceptions of sovereignty and supremacy, but between the different perspectives from which sovereignty can be analysed: as a question of legal principle, of normative political theory and of constitutional reality, assessing legal, conventional and political power. These assessments in turn can be analysed from an internal and an external perspective. Dicey's conception of sovereignty is best understood as one of continuing parliamentary legislative supremacy analysed from the internal, legal point of view: it determines whether Parliament does have the power legally in English law to enact legislation on any subject it likes, save that it is not able to bind its successors. However, he also examines constitutional reality from a political, if not a legal perspective, discussing the power of the electorate to constrain the powers of Parliament, as well as investigating normative political theory, with the aim of providing a justification for granting continuing parliamentary legislative supremacy to the Westminster Parliament due to its democratic composition.

IV. IN DEFENCE OF THE HUMAN RIGHTS ACT 1998

A. Could the United Kingdom Constitution provide for a Stronger Protection of Rights without Breaching Sovereignty?

There are two ways in which a stronger protection of human rights can be reconciled with Dicey's conception of parliamentary sovereignty. First, as will be argued in chapter two, it may be possible to provide for a stronger protection of human rights through the use of strong principles of interpretation.[70] This possibility arises due to the relationship between the continuing theory of parliamentary legislative supremacy and the doctrine of implied repeal. The doctrine of implied repeal applies when the court is faced with a conflict between two statutory provisions. It resolves conflicts by requiring that the later statute be applied. The later statute repeals the contradictory sections of the earlier statute, without the requirement of express words stating that the intention of the later legislation was to override the earlier legislation.

The application of the doctrine of implied repeal to provisions dictating the manner and form in which legislation is passed, as well as to substantive provisions of the law, upholds continuing parliamentary legislative supremacy. It is impossible for a future Parliament to bind an earlier Parliament, as the doctrine of implied repeal enables a future Parliament to relinquish the shackles placed on it by an earlier Parliament simply by passing ordinary legislation. If the Human Rights Act 1998 had included a section stating that its provisions could only be modified or overturned by legislation following a referendum, it would

---

[70] See the discussion in ch 2, pp 54–61.

be possible for a future Parliament in 2008 to overturn this section, merely by passing legislation that modified the Human Rights Act without holding a referendum. Failing to hold a referendum impliedly repeals the requirement to hold one.

The doctrine of implied repeal only applies to situations where the provisions of two different statutes contradict each other. Principles of interpretation can be used to avoid such conflicts, making it appear as if human rights provisions are entrenched. There is, however, a limit to the stronger protection of rights that can be achieved through interpretation. Interpretation can only achieve an 'entrenchment effect': it cannot 'entrench'. Entrenchment would occur if it were impossible to overturn human rights protections by ordinary legislation that did not require a special procedure. Strong principles of interpretation may limit the circumstances in which ordinary legislation can overturn human rights principles. However, they cannot remove the theoretical possibility that ordinary legislation can be used to overturn human rights provisions. Circumstances could still arise in which it is not possible to interpret legislation that challenges human rights principles in a manner to avoid conflict, thus enabling human rights provisions to be contradicted by future legislation.

Secondly, it will be argued in chapter three that entrenchment may be possible through modification of the rule that determines the identification of valid legislation. The theory of continuing parliamentary legislative supremacy requires a definition of the legitimate sovereign law-maker and the processes through which the sovereign law-maker enacts legally valid legislation. Without such a definition, it would be impossible to maintain a theory of parliamentary legislative supremacy. The theory requires that only the sovereign law-maker is able to enact valid legislation. To ensure that this is the case, a definition of the sovereign and of the way in which the sovereign enacts valid legislation is required. Courts can thereby guarantee that the legislation they apply is indeed legislation passed by the sovereign law-maker.

The theory of continuing parliamentary legislative supremacy also requires that any rule defining the sovereign and valid law-making processes cannot be altered by Parliament alone. If Parliament could modify this rule, then it would be possible for Parliament to bind its successors. Once it altered the provisions concerning the identification of legally valid legislation, courts would not recognise any measure as a valid statute unless it complied with the latest rule determining the identification of valid legislation, thus Parliament would have bound its successors.

This leaves open the possibility of entrenchment within the theory of continuing parliamentary legislative supremacy through the modification of the definition of legally valid legislation, provided that such modification cannot be made by Parliament acting alone. One way in which this may be achieved is through the classification of (i) the definition of the sovereign and (ii) of the processes the sovereign must use to enact legally valid legislation as part of the rule of recognition, as defined by HLA Hart. Hart's rule of recognition is enforced by the courts and determines the identification of valid legal rules. It is also a political fact, whose identification stems from analysing facts about the legal system. Modification of the rule of recognition occurs when the officials in the legal system accept a change in its content, accepting the new rule of recognition as a valid rule. It cannot be modified merely through the action of Parliament alone.

Entrenchment could occur if the rule of recognition were modified, such that legislative provisions that breached human rights were no longer regarded as legally valid rules. A modification of the rule of recognition achieves entrenchment as the courts will not recognise as legally valid any legislation that breaches human rights: they will have no legal effect, and will not be enforced. Such entrenchment does not breach continuing parliamentary legislative supremacy because Parliament cannot unilaterally modify the rule of recognition: the new rule must be accepted by the officials of the legal system, including the judiciary. It is this 'shift' in the rule of recognition that leads to entrenchment, not Parliament's actions in purporting to entrench those rights.

Although entrenchment in this manner is possible, it is hard to achieve, and difficult to distinguish from entrenchment that occurs through Parliament acting alone. In both instances there will exist a statute purporting to modify the definition of valid legal rules and an acceptance of this definition by the court. According to one interpretation of these facts, the statute and any supporting decision of the courts are simply evidence of a shift in the rule of recognition—they are not, in themselves, constitutive of that shift. According to a second interpretation, the same facts are evidence of a shift from continuing to self-embracing parliamentary legislative supremacy: the facts are regarded as evidence that Parliament was able to enact legislation changing the definition of valid legal rules that bound its successors.

This second interpretation is possible if the legislation purporting to modify the definition of valid legal rules is interpreted as including a 'manner and form' provision that binds future parliaments. A statute requiring that all legislation complies with human rights may be open to interpretation as a manner and form provision in two ways. First, the distinction between substantive and manner and form provisions is unstable: both entrench substantive legislative provisions. If it is acceptable for Parliament to bind its successors as to the manner and form in which legislation is passed, to ensure that human rights provisions can only be overturned by procedures that are harder to achieve than the passing of ordinary legislation, should it not also be acceptable to enable the entrenchment of human rights through a more direct route by entrenching substantive provisions of legislation? Both achieve the same effect, protecting human rights from restriction or contradiction by ordinary legislation.

Secondly, it could be argued that a statute requiring that all legislation complies with human rights can be classified as a manner and form provision because its effect is to alter the manner and form in which some legislative provisions can be passed, in turn modifying the definition of legally valid legislation. Following the enactment of this statute, it would no longer be possible to enact legislation that was contrary to human rights without also, perhaps only by express means, overturning the legislation requiring all statutes to comply with human rights. The difference between this provision and other manner and form provisions is only a matter of degree. Manner and form provisions purport to define the procedure that should be used to enact certain legislative measures. Legislation requiring that all statutes comply with human rights establishes a new component of all legislation—requiring that all legislation be passed in such a manner as to ensure its compliance with human rights.

If either of these methods are adopted to classify legislation requiring all statutes to comply with human rights provisions as providing a manner and form provision, then the subsequent striking down of legislation that failed to comply with human rights would be seen as evidence of the courts enforcing this earlier manner and form provision in favour of later legislation (which purported to impliedly repeal the earlier manner and form provision). Parliament alone would have succeeded in binding its successor, heralding a shift from continuing to self-embracing parliamentary legislative supremacy.

B. Should Convention Rights be Entrenched?

The possibility of entrenchment need not entail its desirability. Dicey's political theory of sovereignty is founded on the way in which continuing parliamentary legislative supremacy preserves democracy, upholding the will of the people as expressed through the legislation of Parliament. Similar arguments are made against the entrenchment of human rights. Entrenchment would enable courts to strike down legislation, overriding the will of the electorate as expressed through the will of the people. However, even Dicey recognised the need to reconcile the preservation of democracy with a protection of rights. For Dicey, this occurred through the way in which parliamentary sovereignty was balanced against the rule of law, enabling courts to protect rights. In addition, a growing unease with the extent to which the will of Parliament coincided with the will of the people led Dicey to proffer a political theory that rejected continuing parliamentary legislative supremacy, proposing instead a Referendum Act, requiring a referendum to change fundamental principles of the English constitution.[71]

Chapters five and six will argue that the Human Rights Act can be defended not because it seeks to preserve Dicey's conception of sovereignty while ensuring a stronger protection of human rights, but because it aims to balance the perceived competing needs of democracy and human rights. The Act facilitates a stronger protection of rights without undermining democracy. The Human Rights Act can be defended as a democratic dialogue model of human rights protections. Democratic dialogue models are defined as protections of human

[71] See ch 4, pp 98–101.

rights that do not grant to the courts the final ability to make authoritatively determinative accounts as to the compatibility of legislation with human rights. Rather, mechanisms are incorporated into the legal protection of rights that enable the legislature to respond to judicial determinations as to the compatibility of legislation with human rights.

Such models of rights protections facilitate inter-institutional dialogue between the judiciary and the legislature to determine the scope of human rights and the extent to which human rights provisions can be restricted or overridden to achieve other goals, rights and interests. They seek to provide a compromise between human rights and democracy, aiming to provide for a stronger protection of human rights than the common law alone, while also responding to the criticism that a stronger protection of human rights has an anti-democratic effect, enabling judicial determinations of the content of human rights to override the will of the legislature.

It will be argued that the Human Rights Act establishes two different forms of dialogue that give different relative powers to the legislature and to the courts. Section 3 tips the balance of power in favour of the courts. The court is able to read and give effect to legislation to ensure its compatibility with Convention rights. The legislature can respond to these judicial decisions by enacting alternative legislation that contradicts or modifies the conclusion of the courts. However, to do so requires carefully worded provisions. This may be difficult to achieve, particularly given that it will be clear to Parliament that such legislation contradicts the conclusions of the courts.

Section 4 of the Act tips the balance of power in favour of the legislature. The court is unable to provide a legal remedy that protects the rights of the individual in question, having the power only to make a declaration of incompatibility that does not affect the validity, continuing force or effect of the legislation in question. If human rights are to be protected, it requires intervention from the legislature or from the executive using the fast-track procedure to amend legislation found in section 10 of the Act.

The defence of this particular democratic dialogue model of rights protections will be made in three stages. First, it will be argued that the institutional characteristics of the legislature and the courts provide prima facie arguments for assuming that each of these institutions are more suited to resolving different issues concerning rights. These features are used either to argue that an institution is more likely to reach the right answer, or that they reach these answers through a more legitimate process. Courts are able to correct the legislature from passing broad legislative measures that inadvertently harm the rights of specific individuals and from enacting legislation that ignores long-standing legal or constitutional principles or that disadvantages minority groups whose rights may by insufficiently protected through the majoritarian focus of democratic law-making institutions. However, there are also limits to the way in which the judiciary can protect human rights. Judicial law-making is piecemeal and reactionary, capable of making only small incremental changes in response to particular legal actions litigated before the court. It may also be difficult, if not impossible, for the judiciary to create proper procedures for protecting human rights, particularly where the development of one particular protection of human rights can have consequences for other areas of the law that are not currently before the court, or require the creation of procedural mechanisms.

Secondly, it will be argued that although institutional arguments could be provided for preferring a rights protection that rests predominantly either on the legislature or the courts, these arguments are hard to sustain in the face of an assumption that at least some rights are contestable, this assumption being the foundation of democratic dialogue models of rights. It is not reasonable to assume that the court is more able to reach the right conclusion concerning the scope and application of a Convention right if this is contestable. In addition, a democratic means of determining the scope of a contestable right may be regarded as a better process than a judicial means for resolving contestable rights.

Thirdly, in order to enable the legislature to respond to a decision of the courts that provides a Convention-compatible reading of legislation under section 3 of the Human Rights Act, limits as to the use of section 3 stem from principles of interpretation themselves: for example, section 3 must not be used where to do so would be to undermine a fundamental feature of the legislation. This enables the legislature to modify or amend the court's determination as to the scope and application of a Convention right in this case.

These premises will be used to develop a theory of adjudication for the Human Rights Act, focusing on when the Act should be used to facilitate dialogue through the means of section 3, or through the means of section 4 of the Act. First, courts should use section 4 when faced with contestable rights, given that it is unreasonable to assume that the courts are performing a correcting function when faced with contestable rights. It is at least equally possible that the courts and the legislature, if they do disagree about rights issues, do so because they are adopting different, reasonable interpretations of a contestable right.

When faced with a non-contestable rights-issue, courts should use section 3, unless faced with one of the following scenarios: (i) a Convention-compatible interpretation would contradict a fundamental feature of the legislation in question; (ii) a Convention-compatible interpretation would require the court to radically rewrite legislative provisions, or to develop further procedural mechanisms that would have large practical ramifications for other areas of the law or (iii) a Convention-compatible interpretation would require the court to choose from a range of possible contestable Convention-compatible interpretations. The first restriction is necessary to preserve the dialogic model of rights protections, enabling the legislature to respond to a section 3 interpretation of the court. The second and third restrictions recognise limits placed on the remedial power of the court. Courts can make incremental changes, but are not able to make wide-ranging changes, particularly when it comes to establishing new procedural mechanisms that may have knock-on consequences for other areas of the law. Finally, courts should refrain from selecting from a range of possible Convention-compatible interpretations where this choice is best left to the legislature.

V. IN DEFENCE OF DICEY

The introduction has examined issues arising from tensions and complexities inherent to the theory of sovereignty. Assumptions surrounding the legal principle of sovereignty lead to the conclusion that the doctrine of implied repeal prevents the legislature from binding its successors. Yet, given the narrow scope of the doctrine of implied repeal and the range of principles of interpretation that can be used to restrict its application even further, it is possible to grant an entrenchment effect. This entrenchment effect questions the relationship between the legislature and the courts. Although Parliament remains supreme, courts can play a large role in protecting fundamental rights from accidental erosion by the legislature. This role is enhanced by sections 3 and 4 of the Human Rights Act. The extent to which courts protect fundamental rights also bolsters the justification of parliamentary sovereignty from a political perspective. Parliamentary sovereignty is designed to place political sovereignty in the electorate. A stronger judicial protection of rights helps to remedy flaws in the democratic process and ensure that democracy is balanced by an effective protection of human rights.

A further assumption regards the distinction between continuing and self-embracing theories of parliamentary sovereignty. Parliaments enjoying continuing sovereignty cannot bind their successors and are therefore unable to entrench human rights. Parliaments granted self-embracing sovereignty can bind their successors and be bound by their predecessors, enabling them to entrench human rights. This assumption misunderstands the nature of the distinction between continuing and self-embracing parliamentary sovereignty. It is possible for rights to be entrenched and for Parliament to retain continuing sovereignty. This is because the difference between continuing and self-embracing parliamentary sovereignty does not concern the *possibility*, but the *method* of entrenchment.

Parliaments enjoying self-embracing sovereignty can bind their successors merely by enacting legislation purporting to change the manner and form in which future legislation is enacted. A parliament granted continuing sovereignty cannot bind its successors if acting alone. However, enacting legislation that purports to change the manner and form in which future legislation is passed may trigger a change in the political facts which define legally valid legislation, where this change is accepted by other officials within the legal system, especially the judiciary.

This better understanding of the difference between continuing and self-embracing parliamentary sovereignty will be used in chapter seven to provide the foundation for a modest defence of continuing parliamentary sovereignty. Continuing parliamentary sovereignty facilitates comity between the legislature and the judiciary. It requires both the legislature and the judiciary to accept changes to political facts that modify the identity of the sovereign law-making institution and the process required to enact legally valid legislation. This inter-institutional comity has constitutional advantages. It provides a better balance between stability and flexibility, as well as providing checks and balances mechanisms that add to the legitimacy of our constitutional arrangements. This is not to argue that continuing parliamentary sovereignty is the best form of constitutional arrangement: rather, it is to argue that 'continuing', rather than 'self embracing' is the better form of parliamentary sovereignty.

2

Interpretation and Implied Repeal

THE HUMAN RIGHTS ACT 1998 treads a delicate line between providing a stronger protection of Convention rights and respecting parliamentary sovereignty. It does not entrench Convention rights because entrenchment is regarded as impossible to achieve without contravening continuing parliamentary legislative supremacy.[1] The Human Rights Act would have been entrenched if it were incapable of repeal by ordinary legislation. For example, if section 1 of the Human Rights Act 1998 were to have stated in section 1 that 'The provisions of the Human Rights Act, including this section, can only be amended or overturned by a statutory provision that obtains a two-thirds majority vote in both the House of Commons and the House of Lords and receives royal assent' then the Human Rights Act would be regarded as entrenched. Any statute purporting to overturn the Human Rights Act would fail, unless it was enacted by a two-thirds majority vote in the Commons and the Lords before receiving Royal Assent.

However, present constitutional orthodoxy prevents this form of entrenchment. This is because of the doctrine of implied repeal. The doctrine of implied repeal holds that, where there is a conflict between an earlier and a later statute, the provisions of the later statute prevail. The later statute impliedly repeals the earlier statute, as repeal occurs even if the later statute does not expressly state that it is intended to overturn the provisions of the earlier statute. Applying the doctrine of implied repeal to our imaginary Human Rights Act would prevent entrenchment in this manner. A statute could repeal the Human Rights Act even if this were enacted without a two-thirds majority vote. Enacting the statute to repeal the Human Rights Act without following the procedure set out in section 1 of the Act would impliedly repeal the requirements of section 1 of the Act. Consequently, section 1 is not entrenched and can be overturned by ordinary legislation.

This chapter aims to investigate this constitutional orthodoxy. It does so by investigating the scope of the doctrine of implied repeal. The doctrine of implied repeal only applies when two statutory provisions contradict one another. However, such contradiction does not occur if the later statute that appears to contradict an earlier statute can instead be interpreted so as to remove this apparent contradiction. The scope of the doctrine of implied repeal depends on

---

[1] For a discussion of the meaning of this term see ch 1, pp 15–17.

principles of statutory interpretation. The argument will be made that interpretation can be used to achieve an entrenchment effect. Interpretation alone cannot ensure that statutes are entrenched. However, it may remove so many possible contradictions as to make it appear to be impossible in practice to overturn certain statutory provisions through the doctrine of implied repeal—achieving an entrenchment effect. In order to make this argument, the chapter will first explore the legal principle of implied repeal, explaining how its application is narrower than at first thought. It will then explore the ways in which the Human Rights Act could have been worded, or reinterpreted, so as to provide for a stronger protection of rights than that found in the current Act.

I. CONTINUING PARLIAMENTARY LEGISLATIVE SUPREMACY AND THE DOCTRINE OF IMPLIED REPEAL: THE ORTHODOX ACCOUNT

Dicey's theory of continuing parliamentary legislative supremacy is, predominantly, a legal concept. For Dicey, the existence of continuing parliamentary legislative supremacy is a legal fact.[2] He supports the existence of this legal fact by referring to provisions of statutes that could have been interpreted as prohibiting future amendment, but which had been subsequently amended by the passing of ordinary statutes. His key example is the Act of Union with Scotland 1706, which he argued illustrated a clear intention on the part of the legislator to grant 'certain portions of them more than the ordinary effect of statutes.'[3] However, the Act of Union has been impliedly repealed by future legislation. For example, article 25, which required that professors of Scottish universities acknowledge, profess and subscribe to the Confession of Faith, was partially repealed by the Universities (Scotland) Act 1853.[4]

The common law doctrine of implied repeal also provides strong evidence for the existence of continuing parliamentary legislative supremacy as a legal principle. Continuing parliamentary legislative supremacy requires that Parliament can enact legislation on any subject matter it wishes. In turn, courts and other bodies cannot question or override this legislation. However, Parliament cannot enact legislation which legally binds its successors. The inability to bind successors occurs through the application of the doctrine of implied repeal. The doctrine, simply stated, requires courts to give precedence to later statutes, should two statutes be found to conflict. For example, if a statute of 1995 required the state to provide a grant of £500 a year to the parents of blue-eyed babies and a statute of 2005 required the state to provide a grant of £750 a year to the parents of blue-eyed babies, the court should apply the later statute. Parents would receive £750 as opposed to £500 a year.

---

[2] AV Dicey, *An Introduction to the Study of the Law of the Constitution*, 10th edn (London, Macmillan, 1959) 68.
[3] *Ibid*, at 65.
[4] *Ibid*.

The requirement that later statutes should be given precedence over earlier statutes upholds continuing parliamentary legislative supremacy. If, when faced with a conflict, courts were required to apply the provisions of the earlier statute, it would place a limit on the actions of future parliaments. To return to our example, if priority were given to the earlier statute, courts would have to apply the 1995 statute with its lower payment of £500. However, this would thwart the wishes of the later Parliament passing a statute in 2005 requiring a higher payment. In order to ensure that its wishes were applied, the later parliament would need to expressly repeal the provisions of the earlier statute. It would not be enough to merely pass legislation whose content repealed earlier provisions by implication—ie by containing provisions that contradicted earlier statutory enactments. The earlier parliament would have bound its future incarnations. It could not legislate to overturn prior legislative enactments unless it used a specific manner and form, that of express repeal.

However, it is not the existence of the doctrine of implied repeal per se that provides support for the theory of continuing parliamentary legislative supremacy. What is necessary is the application of the doctrine of implied repeal to manner and form as well as substantive statutory provisions. To modify the example given above, the 1995 Act may have required any modification to the amount paid to parents of blue-eyed children to be passed following a referendum. The 2005 Act is then passed increasing the amount paid, but without holding a referendum. If the doctrine of implied repeal applies to manner and form provisions as well as substantive provisions, then passing the 2005 Act without a referendum impliedly repeals the requirement for a referendum found in the 1995 Act. Hence, the 2005 Act would prevail. If the doctrine of implied repeal only applies to substantive provisions, then the 2005 Act would be declared invalid and the 1995 Act would prevail. Parliament would be able to increase payments made to the parents of blue-eyed children, but only after holding a referendum. Hence, Parliament would be able to bind its successors as to the manner and form in which subsequent legislation was passed—supporting self-embracing as opposed to continuing interpretations of parliamentary legislative supremacy.

The scope of the doctrine of implied repeal is, therefore, regarded as the key means by which to identify the content of the legal principle of parliamentary sovereignty. If the doctrine of implied repeal applies to manner and form provisions as well as to substantive provisions, then this supports continuing parliamentary legislative supremacy. If the doctrine of implied repeal only applies to substantive provisions, then this supports self-embracing parliamentary legislative supremacy. Support for the application of the doctrine of implied repeal to manner and form as well as substantive provisions is found in the seminal cases of *Vauxhall Estates Limited v Liverpool Corporation*[5] (*Vauxhall*) and *Ellen Street Estates Limited v Minister of Health* (*Ellen Street*).[6]

---

[5] [1932] 1 KB 733 (KB).
[6] [1934] 1 KB 590 (CA).

Both cases involved a conflict between the provisions of the Acquisition of Land (Compensation) Act 1919 and the Housing Act 1925. It was clear that the two provisions provided a different method of assessing compensation. However, the provisions of section 7(1) of the 1919 Act appeared to suggest that the provisions of the 1919 Act should override those of the 1925 Act, stating that:

> the provisions of the Act or order by which the land is authorised to be acquired, or of any Act incorporated therewith, shall, in relation to the matters dealt with in this Act, have effect subject to this Act, and so far as inconsistent with this Act those provisions shall cease to have or shall not have effect.

Both *Vauxhall* and *Ellen Street* concluded that the court should apply the provisions of the 1925 and not the 1919 Act. In *Vauxhall*, Avory J was of the opinion that the provisions of section 7(1) only applied to previous as opposed to future legislative provisions. To hold otherwise would be contrary to constitutional principles.[7] Humphreys J questioned the logic of the argument of counsel, which concluded that the 1919 Act could not be impliedly repealed, but that its provisions could be expressly repealed.[8] In *Ellen Street*, reliance was once again placed on constitutional principles, with Maugham LJ making the strongest statement that:

> The legislature cannot, according to our constitution, bind itself as to the form of subsequent legislation, and it is impossible for Parliament to enact that in a subsequent statute dealing with the same subject-matter there can be no implied repeal.[9]

However, recent cases have cast doubt on this constitutional orthodoxy. First, the *Factortame*[10] series of litigation questions whether the doctrine of implied repeal applies to section 2(4) of the European Communities Act 1972.[11] Secondly, judicial dicta in *Jackson v Attorney General*[12] provides support for the claim that the doctrine of implied repeal does not apply to manner and form provisions, thus suggesting that the United Kingdom constitution has moved from a theory of continuing to self-embracing parliamentary sovereignty.[13]

---

[7] *Vauxhall Estates Limited v Liverpool Corporation*, above n 5, at 743.

[8] *Ibid*, at 745–6.

[9] *Ellen Street Estates Limited v Minister of Health*, above n 6, at 597.

[10] *Factortame v Secretary of State for Transport* [1990] 2 AC 85 (HL); *R v Secretary of State for Transport ex parte Factortame Ltd and Others (No 2)* [1991] 1 AC 603 (HL).

[11] See, MB Akehurst, 'Parliamentary sovereignty and the supremacy of Community law' (1989) 60 *The British Yearbook of International Law* 351; TRS Allan, 'Parliamentary Sovereignty: Law, Politics and Revolution' (1997) 113 *Law Quarterly Review* 443; PP Craig, 'Sovereignty of the United Kingdom Parliament after *Factortame*' [1991] *Yearbook of European Law* 221; J Drexl, 'Was Sir Francis Drake a Dutchman? British Supremacy of Parliament after *Factortame*' (1993) 41 *The American Journal of Comparative Law* 551; D Nicol, *EC Membership and the Judicialisation of British Politics* (Oxford, Oxford University Press, 2001) ch 7; D Oliver, 'Fishing on the incoming tide' (1991) 54 *Modern Law Review* 442; HWR Wade, 'Sovereignty—Revolution or Evolution?' (1996) 112 *Law Quarterly Review* 568.

[12] *R (Jackson) v Attorney-General* [2005] UKHL 56, [2006] 1 AC 262.

[13] See, J Allan, 'The Paradox of Sovereignty: *Jackson* and the Hunt for a new Rule of Recognition?' (2007) 18 *King's College Law Journal* 1; R Ekins, 'Acts of Parliament and the

Although both of these are relevant to establishing whether continuing parliamentary legislative supremacy continues to exist as a legal principle of English law, their importance will not be discussed at this stage. Rather, the next section aims to place these cases in context, by examining the doctrine of implied repeal in more detail. It will be argued that, properly understood, the doctrine of implied repeal is more complex than a mere statement that, when faced with a conflict, courts are to apply the provisions of the later as opposed to the earlier statute. This complexity results in a much narrower scope of application, depending on the extent to which statutory provisions can be described as conflicting and, therefore, requiring the application of the doctrine.

The next section will investigate the doctrine to exemplify its narrow scope of application. Given the restrictions placed on its application, it may appear as if when faced with an apparent conflict between two statutory provisions, the court applies the provisions of the earlier rather than the later statute. Although this may appear to provide an example of statutory entrenchment, it is best understood as an example of a situation where an apparent conflict between two statutory provisions was resolved. The later statute was able to be interpreted so as not to contradict the provisions of the earlier statute. Consequently, there was no need to apply the doctrine of implied repeal.

II. THE NARROW SCOPE OF IMPLIED REPEAL

The doctrine of implied repeal has long been accepted as a principle of English law. Bennion cites the mention of the principle of *leges posteriores priores contrarias abrogant* in Coke.[14] Early examples of the doctrine can be found in decisions reported in 1685, where later statutory provisions regulating trade apprenticeships overturned the provisions found in 5 Eliz. cap 4.[15] It has become such an accepted principle of English law that it is rare to find judicial discussion concerning its precise scope or application. Most judicial references to the principle rely on the interpretation of Smith J:

Parliament Acts' (2007) 123 *Law Quarterly Review* 91; M Elliott, 'The Sovereignty of Parliament, the Hunting Ban and the Parliament Acts' (2006) 65 *Cambridge Law Journal* 1; C Graham, 'A Very British Affair—*Jackson v Attorney-General*' (2006) 12 *European Public Law* 501; J Jowell, 'Parliamentary Sovereignty under the New Hypothesis' [2006] *Public Law* 562; A McHarg, 'What is Delegated Legislation?' [2006] *Public Law* 539; T Mullen, 'Reflections on *Jackson v Attorney-General*: Questioning Sovereignty' (2007) 27 *Legal Studies* 1; M Plaxton, 'The Concept of Legislation: *Jackson v Her Majesty's Attorney-General*' (2006) 69 *Modern Law Review* 249; AL Young, 'Hunting Sovereignty: *Jackson v Her Majesty's Attorney-General*' [2006] *Public Law* 187.

[14] Coke, 1 Inst 25b, referred to in FAR Bennion, *Statutory Interpretation: a Code*, 4th edn (London, Butterworths, 2002) 255.
[15] *Nicholas v Cotterel* (1685) 3 Keb 448, 84 ER 815 and *Dominus Rex v Eeds* (1685) 3 Keb 618, 84 ER 913.

> The test of whether there has been a repeal by implication by subsequent legislation is this: Are the provisions of a later Act so inconsistent with, or repugnant to, the provisions of an earlier Act that the two cannot stand together?[16]

The most recent judicial discussions of the scope of the doctrine of implied repeal can be found in the Court of Appeal decision of *Smith International Inc v Specialised Petroleum Group Services Limited*,[17] considering the earlier dicta of the Court of Appeal in *Henry Boot Construction (UK) Ltd v Malmaison Hotel (Manchester) Ltd (Malmaison)*[18] and *Clark v Perks*.[19] Two main principles emerge. First, there is a general presumption against implied repeal. Secondly, an exception to the principle of implied repeal occurs when the principle *generalis specialibus non derogant* applies—ie earlier specific provisions of legislation are not impliedly repealed by later, general provisions of legislation.

These two principles in and of themselves already point to the conclusion that the scope of application of the doctrine of implied repeal is narrower than it first appeared. The doctrine is not the rule, but the exception. The aim of the court is not to ensure that later statutes overturn earlier statutes, but to strive to ensure that this only occurs when it is not possible to read later legislation so as not to contradict earlier legislation. In addition, the decision of Laws LJ in *Thoburn v Sunderland City Council (Thoburn)*[20] appears to have narrowed the scope of the doctrine of implied repeal even further. First, Laws LJ argues that the doctrine of implied repeal does not apply to constitutional statutes. Secondly, his opinion provides support for the argument of Adam Tomkins that the doctrine of implied repeal only applies to a conflict between two statutes on the same subject matter. These challenges will provide the springboard for a reformulation of the doctrine of implied repeal, which recognises that the doctrine is best understood as one of specific repeal. Later statutes only impliedly repeal earlier statues when the provisions of the later statute specifically contradict the provisions of the earlier statute. It is the requirement of specific contradiction that enables earlier statutes to appear entrenched. Statutes can be worded in such a way that it is difficult, if not practically impossible, for them to be specifically contradicted by words short of express repeal.

A. General Presumption against Implied Repeal

The general presumption against implied repeal requires that courts should strive to read the provisions of the later statute in a manner compatible with those found in the earlier statute. It is only when the two provisions are so

---

[16] *Church Wardens and Overseers of West Ham v Fourth City Mutual Building Society* [1892] 1 QB 654 (QB), 658. Cited in Bennion, above n 14, at 254.
[17] [2005] EWCA Civ 1357, [2006] 1 WLR 252.
[18] [2001] QB 388 (CA).
[19] [2001] 1 WLR 17 (CA).
[20] [2002] EWHC 195 (Admin), [2003] 1 QB 151.

incompatible that they cannot stand together that the doctrine of implied repeal applies. The presumption against implied repeal applies even more forcefully when courts interpret modern statutes.[21] Moreover, the burden of proof rests with the party claiming that a later provision has impliedly repealed an earlier provision.[22] All these factors indicate that the application of the doctrine of implied repeal should be a rare, not a frequent occurrence.

Malmaison provides an illustration of the extent to which courts will strive to find a compatible interpretation between two apparently contradictory statutory provisions, thus avoiding application of the doctrine of implied repeal. The case concerned a dispute over the terms of a building contract between Henry Boot (the contractor) and Malmaison (a chain of hotels). The dispute was referred to the arbitrator, who made an interim award in favour of Malmaison. Henry Boot appealed the decision before Dyson J, under the provisions of section 69 of the Arbitration Act 1996. Dyson J struck out the appeal from Henry Boot and, exercising his powers under section 69(8) of the 1996 Act, refused to grant permission for Henry Boot to appeal to the Court of Appeal. Henry Boot argued that the refusal of permission to appeal could be reviewed by the Court of Appeal. After concluding that section 69(8) did not permit an applicant to challenge a refusal of leave to appeal in the Court of Appeal, the attention of the court was drawn to section 55 of the Access to Justice Act 1999. The argument was made that section 55 of the 1999 Act impliedly repealed section 69(8) of the 1996 Act, thus enabling an applicant to challenge a refusal of leave to appeal. To understand the argument, we need to look at these statutory provisions in more detail.

Section 69(8) of the 1996 Act states that:

> The decision of the court on an appeal under this section shall be treated as a judgment of the court for the purposes of a further appeal. But no such appeal lies without the leave of the court which shall not be given unless the court considers that the question is one of general importance or is one which for some other special reason should be considered by the Court of Appeal.

Section 55(1) of the 1999 Act required that:

> Where an appeal is made to the county court of the High Court in relation to any matter, and on hearing the appeal the court makes a discussion in relation to that matter no appeal may be made to the Court of Appeal from that decision unless the Court of Appeal considers that (a) the appeal would raise an important point of principle or practice, or (b) there is some other compelling reason for the Court of Appeal to hear it.

It was argued that the decision of a court hearing an appeal from an arbitrator would amount to 'an appeal to the county court of the High Court in relation to

---

[21] *Government of the United States of America v Jennings* [1983] 1 AC 624 (HL) 3 WLR 450, 643–4, (Lord Roskill).
[22] *Lybbe v Hart* (1883) 29 Ch D 8, 15 (Chitty J).

any matter' and that, therefore, section 55(1) would require the Court of Appeal to determine whether to grant permission to appeal, whereas section 69(8) would require that the High Court should grant permission to appeal. The two provisions, therefore, appeared to be contradictory. The Court of Appeal, however, held that the 1999 Act did not impliedly repeal the 1996 Act. Waller and Swinton-Thomas LJJ held that the provisions of the 1996 Act were untouched, meaning that only the High Court needed to grant or refuse leave to Appeal. In essence the 1996 Act established a specific subset of appeals that was untouched by the more general powers of the Court of Appeal found in the 1999 Act.[23] Arden J concluded that the two Acts could be read together, with the 1996 Act requiring leave to appeal being granted by the High Court and the 1999 Act requiring additional permission to be granted by the Court of Appeal.[24]

The decision of *Malmaison* illustrates two ways in which courts strive to ensure that provisions of later legislation do not contradict the provisions of earlier legislation. First, when assessing whether two statutes are contradictory, the court pays particular attention to the legislative background and to the relationship between the statutory provision that appears to have impliedly repealed earlier legislation and other provisions found in both the earlier and the later legislation. In *Malmaison*, for example, Waller LJ concluded that the purpose of section 55 of the 1999 Act was to limit the right to a second appeal, but he also concluded that this did not require that the Court of Appeal had to grant leave to appeal for all these situations, noting other exceptions to this requirement found in the 1999 Act.[25]

Secondly, the court also has regard to whether the later Act expressly repeals other provisions of the earlier legislation. If provisions in the earlier legislation that are similar to the one that has arguably been impliedly repealed have been expressly repealed in the later legislation, then this strengthens the presumption against implied repeal. The 1999 Act had expressly repealed provisions of other statutes that had required leave for appeal to be granted by the High Court as opposed to the Court of Appeal. This was not the case for the 1996 Act. Therefore, there was a presumption against implied repeal. If Parliament had wished to repeal the 1996 Act it would have done so expressly, as it had done with similar statutory provisions.[26]

---

[23] This is an application of the principle of *generalia specialibus non derogant*, discussed in more detail in the following section.

[24] The Court of Appeal has subsequently approved the result of *Malmaison*, thereby confirming the lack of implied repeal: *Clark v Perks* [2001] 1 WLR 17 (CA); *North Page Shipping Ltd v Seatrams Shipping Corporation* [2002] EWCA Civ 405, [2002] 1 WLR 2397; *Athletics Union of Constantinople v National Basketball Association (2)* [2002] EWCA Civ 830, [2002] 1 WLR 2863. However, no decision has been reached as to whether the two Acts should be read as requiring additional permissions, or whether the general provisions of the 1999 Act do not impede the specific provisions of the 1996 Act.

[25] [2001] QB 388, 401–3.

[26] *Ibid*, at 403. See also *Re Chance* [1936] Ch 266 (Ch); *Critchell v Lambeth Borough Council* [1957] 2 QB 535 (CA).

B. *Generalia Specialibus Non Derogant*

The principle that general provisions do not override earlier specific provisions is a long-established principle of statutory interpretation, finding its most authoritative statement in the judgment of Lord Selbourne LC in *Seward v The Vera Cruz*:

> Now if anything be certain it is this, that where there are general words in a later Act capable of reasonable and sensible application without extending them to subjects specially dealt with by earlier legislation, you are not to hold that earlier and special legislation indirectly repealed, altered, or derogated from merely by force of such general words, without any indication of a particular intention to do so.[27]

In *Seward v The Vera Cruz* a dispute arose over the jurisdiction of the Admiralty Court to hear an action for damages brought by a widow on behalf of her son and her husband who were killed in a collision between their vessel and the *Vera Cruz*. An earlier statutory provision granted jurisdiction to the common law courts to hear claims for damages brought by individuals on behalf of those killed by a wrongful act, neglect or default. A later statute granted jurisdiction to the High Court of Admiralty over 'any claim for damage done by a ship'. It was held that the later statute did not impliedly repeal the earlier statute. The earlier statute established jurisdiction of the common law courts to hear specific actions for damages in lieu of death caused by a wrongful act or neglect or default. The later statute established a general provision for the High Court of Admiralty to hear actions for damages caused by ships. This general provision did not repeal the earlier specific provision. Consequently, the Court of Admiralty had no power to hear the action for damages.

The same principle was applied in the more recent decision of *Smith International Inc v Specialised Petroleum Services Group Limited*.[28] The case concerned the ability to appeal a decision from the Patents Court to the Court of Appeal. Section 97(3) of the Patents Act 1997 provided for a general prohibition of appeals from decisions of the Patent Court, subject to two exceptions, where leave to appeal had been granted either by the Patent Court or the Court of Appeal. The issue arose as to whether this provision had been impliedly repealed by section 55 of the Access to Justice Act 1999, which required all appeals from decisions of the High Court to be granted leave of appeal from the Court of Appeal. The Patent Court is part of the High Court. The Court of Appeal held that the earlier provisions of the 1977 Act established a specific procedure for appeal from a section of the High Court, the Patent Court, that was not contradicted by the later, more general form of appeal found in the 1999 Act governing appeals in general from the High Court to the Court of Appeal.[29]

---

[27] (1884) 10 App Cas 59 (HL), 68.
[28] [2005] EWCA Civ 1357, [2006] 1 WLR 252.
[29] *Ibid*, at [14]–[15].

A similar principle operates when there is a conflict between an earlier general statute and a later specific statute. In *Mount v Taylor*,[30] for example, a dispute arose over an earlier statutory provision which granted a general right to costs and a later statutory provision granting the right to costs only following a court order. The later specific statute did not impliedly repeal the earlier statute. Instead, the general provisions remained in force, with the later specific provisions providing for specific exceptions to the general rule.

C. Constitutional Statutes

In *Thoburn*, Laws LJ drew a distinction between constitutional and other statutes. He classified as constitutional those statutes that condition the legal relationship between the citizen and the state or which diminish or enlarge fundamental constitutional rights. He included the Magna Carta 1215, the Bill of Rights 1689, the Reform Acts of 1832, 1867 and 1884, the European Communities Act 1972, the Human Rights Act 1998, Scotland Act 1998 and the Government of Wales Act 1998 in his list of constitutional statutes. However, Laws LJ did not merely provide a list of statutes that regulated matters deemed 'constitutional' according to their subject matter. He argued further that constitutional statutes, unlike ordinary statutes, could not be impliedly repealed.[31] If Laws LJ is correct, then the scope of application of the doctrine of implied repeal narrows even further. It does not apply to constitutional statutes.

Laws LJ justified his conclusion by relying on the *Factortame* litigation, particularly on *Factortame (1)*.[32] *Factortame (1)* does not discuss implied repeal specifically. However, Laws LJ relies on an argument that could have been, but was not made, when deciding *Factortame (1)*. The *Factortame* litigation concerned an apparent conflict between the provisions of the Merchant Shipping Act 1988 and section 2(4) of the European Communities Act 1972. The Merchant Shipping Act restricted the registration of fishing vessels as British (and therefore able to fish in British waters) to those with a sufficiently British ownership and crew. Such a requirement appeared to contradict directly effective provisions of the EC Treaty, which would have enabled all those of European Union nationality to fish in British waters.[33]

It would have been open to the court to conclude in *Factortame (1)* that this apparent conflict should be resolved in favour of the later statute. Future legislation that contradicted directly effective European Community law could not be construed and given effect subject to the provisions of directly effective European Community law. Consequently, such legislation, including the Merchant Shipping Act 1988, would impliedly repeal section 2(4) of the European

[30] (1868) LR 3 CP 645 (CP).
[31] [2002] EWHC 195, [2003] QB 151, [63].
[32] *Factortame v Secretary of State for Transport* [1990] 2 AC 85 (HL).
[33] Art 52, now Art 43 EC.

Communities Act 1972. Lord Bridge, however, argued that section 2(4) applied so as to effectively incorporate a section into the Merchant Shipping Act 1988 which,

> enacted that the provisions with respect to registration of British fishing vessels were to be without prejudice to the directly enforceable Community rights of nationals of any member state of the EEC.[34]

Laws LJ regards Lord Bridge's statement as evidence that the doctrine of implied repeal did not apply to the European Communities Act. By accepting that section 2(4) operated in this manner, the House of Lords 'effectively accepted that section 2(4) could not be impliedly repealed, albeit the point was not argued'.[35]

Laws LJ's statement is open to two possible interpretations. First, he could be making a theoretical claim about the scope of the doctrine of implied repeal. Secondly, Laws LJ could be making a more pragmatic claim. Although the doctrine of implied repeal applies in theory to constitutional statutes, it is rare for the doctrine to apply to constitutional statutes in practice. This is because it would be rare for the courts to find that a later statute had repealed a constitutional statute by implication. The first interpretation would not only provide for a much narrower scope of application of the doctrine of implied repeal than the second interpretation, but it would also pose a greater challenge to continuing parliamentary legislative supremacy. Constitutional statutes would be entrenched and would require express and not implied repeal. It will be argued, however, that support for this first interpretation is weak. Laws LJ is best understood as making a pragmatic claim. Although it is theoretically possible for constitutional statutes to be impliedly repealed, this is hard to achieve in practice given that the courts will strive to read later statutes in order not to contradict the provisions of earlier constitutional statutes.

The strongest argument in favour of regarding Laws LJ as making the strong claim that constitutional statutes are immune from implied repeal stems from the words that Laws LJ uses in his judgment. He states that:

> The common law has in recent years allowed, or rather created, exceptions to the doctrine of implied repeal, a doctrine which was always the common law's own creature. There are now classes or types of legislative provision which cannot be repealed by mere implication. These instances are given, and can only be given, by our own courts, to which the scope and nature of parliamentary sovereignty are ultimately confided.[36]

Later in his judgment, Laws LJ states clearly that '[o]rdinary statutes may be impliedly repealed. Constitutional statutes may not'.[37] Laws LJ clearly appears to imply that the doctrine of implied repeal does not apply to constitutional statutes and it is this fact that distinguishes them from ordinary statutes.

---

[34] [1990] 2 AC 85 (HL), 140.
[35] [2002] EWHC 195, [2003] QB 151, [61].
[36] *Ibid*, at [60]
[37] *Ibid*, at [63].

Further support for the strong interpretation that the doctrine of implied repeal does not apply in principle to constitutional statutes is gleaned from Laws LJ's remarks that directly effective European Community law prevails over inconsistent later statutory provisions.[38] This appears to suggest that the doctrine of implied repeal does not apply to the European Communities Act 1972, an example of a constitutional statute. It was not the case that interpretation was used to remove a conflict between two statutory provisions. Rather, there is a conflict, but instead of the later statute overriding the earlier statute, the earlier prevailed over the later statute in contradiction to the doctrine of implied repeal.

Despite these arguments, the better interpretation of Laws LJ's statement is that he is merely explaining that it is difficult in practice for constitutional statutes to be overturned by implication. First, even though Laws LJ refers to constitutional statutes as an 'exception' to the doctrine of implied repeal, the mere classification of this phenomenon as an 'exception' does not provide conclusive proof that the doctrine of implied repeal can never apply to constitutional statutes. The principle of *generalia specialibus non derogant* is also described by Bennion as an exception to the doctrine of implied repeal.[39] However, this 'exception' is not viewed as providing a challenge to the operation of the doctrine of implied repeal or to the principle of continuing parliamentary legislative supremacy. It is explained through principles of interpretation. Later statutes are interpreted in a manner to ensure that their general provisions do not contradict earlier specific provisions. The same may be true of Laws LJ's 'exception' that the doctrine of implied repeal does not apply to constitutional statutes.

Secondly, Laws LJ explains that constitutional statutes are immune from the doctrine of implied repeal by referring to the way in which principles of interpretation will be used by the court to remove potential conflicts between constitutional statutes and future legislation:

> For the repeal of a constitutional Act or the abrogation of a fundamental right to be effected by statute, the court will apply this test: is it shown that the legislature's *actual*—not imputed, constructive or presumed—intention was to effect the repeal or abrogation? I think the test could only be met by express words in the later statute, or by words so specific that the inference of an actual determination to effect the result contended for was irresistible. The ordinary rule of implied repeal does not satisfy this test. Accordingly it has no application to constitutional statutes.[40]

When analysing conflicts between constitutional and ordinary statutes, the presumption that Parliament would not have intended to impliedly repeal earlier provisions of legislation is even stronger than that which applies to conflicts between two ordinary statutes. Only express words, or words so specific that

---

[38] [2002] EWHC 195, [2003] QB 151, at [61].
[39] Bennion, *Statutory Interpretation: a Code*, above n 14.
[40] [2002] EWHC 195 (Admin), [2003] QB 151, [63].

they cannot be interpreted in any other way than as an intention to repeal the earlier constitutional statute by implication, will require the courts to apply the later statute over and above the provisions of the earlier statute. If we regard the 'ordinary rule of implied repeal' as merely requiring a potential conflict between two statutes, then it is clear that it will not satisfy the test required by Laws LJ to demonstrate a clear intention to overturn the provisions of a constitutional statute. If there is a misunderstanding here of the scope of the doctrine of implied repeal, it is not that of believing that the doctrine of implied repeal does not apply to constitutional statutes. Rather, it is to fail to recognise that the doctrine of implied repeal is the exception as opposed to the rule. Courts strive to avoid conflicts between statutory provisions and will strive even further to ensure that Parliament really did intend to overturn the provisions of earlier, constitutional legislation.

Thirdly, to interpret Laws LJ as making a practical claim as to the difficulty of finding that later statutory provisions contradict earlier, constitutional legislation provides a better explanation of Laws LJ's reference to *Factortame (1)*. Laws LJ states that it was not the case that the Merchant Shipping Act 1988 operated to provide a *pro tanto* repeal of the European Communities Act 1972. Rather, it was the case that the 1988 Act took effect subject to the provisions of the 1972 Act.[41] The 1988 Act was interpreted in a manner that ensured that there was no conflict between its provisions and those of the 1972 Act. Hence, the doctrine of implied repeal could not apply in practice. There was no conflict between the two statutes as the 1988 statute could be given effect subject to the provisions of the 1972 statute.

Fourthly, Laws LJ's example stemming from the European Communities Act 1972 does not provide evidence of an exception to the doctrine of implied repeal. Laws LJ argued that the 1972 Act is an example of a constitutional statute and explained that later legislation that contradicted directly effective Community law would not prevail over directly effective European Community law, which obtains its force in English law from the 1972 Act. However, Laws LJ's argument confuses two possible types of conflict: between national law and directly effective European Community law, and between two provisions of national law. The Merchant Shipping Act 1988 provides an example of a conflict between national law and directly effective European Community law. The Act would not permit Spanish-owned fishing vessels to fish in British waters. Directly effective provisions of European Community law would allow fishing by Spanish ships. However, it is at least arguable that there was no conflict between the provisions of the 1972 Act and the 1988 Act. The 1972 Act required the provisions of the 1988 Act to be read and take effect subject to the provisions of directly effective European Community law. The 1988 Act would only challenge the requirement to read and give effect to its provisions subject to directly effective European Community law if it were not possible to read and give

---

[41] *Ibid*, at [61].

effect to its provisions in this manner. However, it is at least arguable that this could be achieved by reading a section into the 1988 Act requiring its provisions to take effect subject to directly effective European Community law, as argued by Lord Bridge in *Factortame (1)*. To argue that directly effective provisions of EC law prevail over contradictory provisions of national law, therefore, need not entail the conclusion that section 2(4) of the European Communities Act 1972 prevails over the provisions of later statutes that contradict directly effective European Community law.

Fifthly, to interpret Laws LJ as arguing that the doctrine of implied repeal has no practical application to constitutional statutes provides a better explanation of his reference to *Factortame (1)*. He refers to the leading judgment of Lord Bridge, who concluded that section 2(4) of the European Communities Act 1972 had the effect of reading words into the 1988 Act, namely a requirement that its provisions were to be read without prejudice to directly effective European Community rights.[42] The need for the later 1988 Act to be read subject to the provisions of directly effective European Community law was accepted by counsel for *Factortame*[43] and for the government.[44] No argument was made regarding the doctrine of implied repeal in *Factortame (1)* because counsel for both parties had accepted that it was possible to construe the provisions of the 1988 Act in a manner compatible with the 1972 Act. The later statute was given its proper meaning in the context of the earlier statute, taking effect subject to the provisions of directly effective European Community law. This interpretation removed the conflict between the two statutes, meaning in turn that the doctrine of implied repeal did not apply. There were no contradictory provisions of statutes and hence there was no need for a later statute to overturn the contradictory provisions of an earlier statute. The case involved an application of principles of interpretation and not the doctrine of implied repeal.

Finally, the weaker explanation fits better with previous judicial statements suggesting that it would be extremely difficult, if not impossible, to impliedly repeal provisions of certain fundamental statutes. For example, in a petition before the House of Lords' Committee of Privileges, regarding the position of elected Irish peers to the United Kingdom Parliament found in the Union with Ireland Act 1800, Lord Wilberforce stated that:

> In strict law there may be no difference in status, or as regards the liability to be repealed, as between one Act of Parliament and another, but I confess to some reluctance to holding that an Act of such constitutional significance as the Union with Ireland Act is subject to the doctrine of implied repeal or of obsolescence—all the more when these effects are claimed to result from later legislation which could have brought them about by specific enactment.[45]

---

[42] [1990] 2 AC 85, 140.
[43] *Ibid*, at 89.
[44] *Ibid*, at 114.
[45] *Earl of Antrim's Petition (House of Lords)* [1967] 1 AC 691 (Committee of Privileges) 724.

Lord Wilberforce is not arguing that the doctrine of implied repeal does not apply to constitutional statutes. Rather, he is explaining how, with regard to constitutional statutes, it may be difficult to find an instance in which there is a clear intention on the part of Parliament to impliedly repeal the provisions of a constitutional statute. It has already been established that there is a presumption against implied repeal and that this presumption operates even more strongly when the later statute includes reference to provisions that have been expressly repealed. This presumption applies with even greater force when applied to statutes with constitutional importance: there is a strong argument that Parliament would not have intended to impliedly repeal a statute of such constitutional significance.

The existence of constitutional statutes, therefore, points to a further narrowing of the doctrine of implied repeal. It is not the case that the doctrine of implied repeal does not apply to constitutional statutes. Rather, principles of interpretation that are used to ensure that the doctrine applies only where there is a contradiction between two statutory provisions apply even more forcefully when applied to constitutional statutes. Courts will strive to ensure that later statutes are read so as not to contradict the provisions of earlier, constitutional statutes. Our analysis of Laws LJ's judgment has already provided a suggestion of how this may be achieved—through the wording of section 2(4) of the European Communities Act 1972. This possibility will be investigated further. However, one further possible restriction of the scope of application of the doctrine of implied repeal needs to be investigated before conclusions can be drawn as to the way in which the doctrine is best understood as requiring specific repeal.

D. Conflict between two Statutes on the same Subject?

Adam Tomkins argues for a further additional rule governing the application of the doctrine of implied repeal: that implied repeal only applies when there is a conflict between two statutes on the same subject matter.[46] The doctrine of implied repeal does not apply where statutory provisions would dictate different outcomes, but the statutes themselves govern different subjects. He develops his arguments specifically with regard to conflicts between the European Communities Act 1972 and subsequent legislation that contradicts directly effective European Community law. He argues that the doctrine of implied repeal did not apply to the conflict arising in *Factortame*, because it was a conflict between two statutes on different subjects: one incorporating directly effective European Community law into English law and the other regulating the registration of fishing vessels.[47] The European Communities Act 1972 could

---

[46] A Tomkins, *Public Law* (Oxford, Oxford University Press, 2003) 107.
[47] *Ibid*, at 119.

only be impliedly repealed by future legislation whose subject matter also concerned the incorporation of European Community law into English law, or the relationship between European Community law and English law.

Tomkins finds support for his interpretation of the scope of the doctrine of implied repeal in a statement of Maugham LJ in *Ellen Street* that it is,

> impossible for Parliament to enact that in a subsequent statute dealing with the same subject matter there can be no implied repeal.[48]

Maugham LJ appears to restrict the application of the doctrine of implied repeal to conflicts between two statutes on the same subject matter. It is impossible for implied repeal to be removed in these circumstances. However, it may be possible for Parliament to enact legislation that is not impliedly repealed by subsequent statutes that appear to contradict the earlier statute, but which do not concern the same subject matter. A similar statement is made by Lord Sterndale MR in *Wallwork v Fielding* that:

> it is obvious on any principles that where the subsequent Act does not deal with the subject matter of the previous Act at all, and contains nothing whatever that affects it, there can be no implied repeal of the earlier by the later Act.[49]

The strongest support for Tomkins's interpretation of the scope of the doctrine of implied repeal is found in *Thoburn*.[50] The case involved a conflict between sections 2(2) and 2(4) of the European Communities Act 1972 and the Weights and Measures Act 1985. Sections 2(2) and 2(4) of the 1972 Act create a prospective Henry VIII clause. The executive is empowered to use delegated legislation to amend primary legislation in order to incorporate provisions of European Community law into English law. A prospective Henry VIII clause is created as the executive has the power to amend legislation enacted after the 1972 Act. The Weights and Measures Act 1985 stipulated that both metric and imperial measurements were to be regarded as legally valid weights and measures. Following its enactment, an EC directive was passed stipulating that only metric measurements would be legally valid for certain types of goods sold in bulk. The Units of Measurements Regulations 1994 were enacted to incorporate the provisions of the directive into English law. Thoburn, and others—the 'Metric Martyrs'—were prosecuted for selling goods in imperial measurements alone in contravention of the 1994 regulations.

Counsel for Thoburn argued that the 1985 Act had partially impliedly repealed the 1972 Act, restricting the scope of its application. The executive no longer enjoyed a broad power to enact delegated legislation to incorporate any provision of European Community law into English law. It no longer had the power to pass regulations which removed the legality of imperial measurements found in the later 1985 Act. Laws LJ rejected this argument. Following a

---

[48] [1934] 1 KB 590 (CA), 597.
[49] [1922] 2 KB 66, 71.
[50] [2002] EWHC 195 (Admin), [2003] QB 151.

reference to Maugham LJ's judgment in *Ellen Street*,[51] he held that there was no conflict between the 1972 Act and the 1985 Act. Consequently, the doctrine of implied repeal did not apply.[52] One justification for why the doctrine of implied repeal did not apply in these circumstances is the argument that the doctrine of implied repeal only applies to conflicts arising between two statutes on the same subject matter. The 1972 Act related to the incorporation of provisions of directly effective European Community law into English law. The 1985 Act concerned the classification of legally valid weights and measures. There could be no conflict between these two statutes as they regulated different subject matters.[53]

However, these judicial statements are best understood not as a requirement that the doctrine of implied repeal only applies to conflicts arising between statutes governing the same subject matter, but as further evidence of the need to ensure that a later statute really does contradict the provisions of an earlier statute in order for the doctrine of implied repeal to apply. Normally, contradictions only occur between statutes governing the same general subject matter. However, it is possible that a contradiction could occur between statutes that, in general terms, are concerned with different subject matter, but which nevertheless contain statutory provisions on the same subject matter that do contradict one another. It is not the case that the doctrine of implied repeal only applies to contradictions between statutes that regulate the *same general subject matter*, but it is the case that the doctrine of implied repeal only applies when there is a specific contradiction between *two statutory provisions on the same subject matter*.

This second interpretation provides a better explanation of the judicial pronouncements made in both *Ellen Street* and *Wallwark v Fielding*. In *Ellen Street* section 7(1) of the 1919 Act required that statutes regulating the matters dealt with by the 1919 Act should 'have effect subject to' the provisions of the 1919 Act and also that any Act 'inconsistent' with the provisions of the 1919 Act 'shall cease to have or not have effect'. Counsel argued that section 7(1) meant that the 1919 Act could only be repealed expressly and not by implication. Hence, the 1919 Act established a specific manner and form requirement. If we read Maugham LJ's statement in this context, it provides a clearer explanation of the meaning of section 7(1) and why it was not capable of being interpreted in the manner suggested by counsel. Section 7(1) had tried to entrench the provisions of the 1919 Act by suggesting that all statutes on the same subject matter as the 1919 Act should take effect subject to its provisions and, where inconsistent, that the provision inconsistent with the 1919 Act should not have effect. Parliament could not legislate effectively in this manner as to do so would be contrary to the doctrine of implied repeal. Although section 7(1) required

---

[51] *Ibid*, at [42].
[52] *Ibid*, at [50].
[53] See, NW Barber and AL Young, 'The Rise of Prospective Henry VIII Clauses and their Implications for Sovereignty' [2003] *Public Law* 112.

provisions inconsistent with it to be invalid, the doctrine of implied repeal would instead hold that future provisions inconsistent with the 1919 Act would impliedly repeal the 1919 Act, including the provision in section 7(1) that the provisions would be invalid. It is in this sense that it is 'impossible for Parliament to enact that in a subsequent statute dealing with the same subject matter there can be no implied repeal.'[54]

Although Lord Sterndale in *Wallwark v Fielding* states that the doctrine of implied repeal does not apply to a conflict between two statutes dealing with different subject matter, he makes it clear that the doctrine of implied repeal does not apply when the 'subsequent Act does not deal with the subject matter of the previous Act at all'.[55] His concern is not whether the two statutes that appear to contradict each other concern the same subject matter in general. Rather, he is concerned to establish whether there is a purported conflict between statutory provisions found in two statutes. This could only occur where two statutory provisions regulated the same subject matter in a contradictory manner. Where this is the case, the later statutory provision impliedly repeals the earlier statutory provision.

This interpretation is reinforced when Lord Sterndale's comments are placed in context. *Wallwark v Fielding* concerned a conflict between a general and a specific statute. A statute of 1882 granted the power to the Watch Committee to suspend a borough policeman. A later statute of 1919 granted the power to the Secretary of State to make regulations for the governance of the police force, requiring police authorities to comply with these regulations. The Secretary of State passed a regulation setting out the procedure to be followed by police authorities when faced with a charge against a police officer. Nothing in the 1919 Act, or in the procedures established by regulations made under that Act, referred to the power to suspend a police officer. There was no conflict between the two provisions because the specific provisions of the earlier Act were not overturned by the general provisions of the later Act. The earlier statute created a power to suspend a police officer and the later statute created a power to make regulations to govern the police force in general. Although both concerned the regulation of the police, the provisions of the later statute did not contradict the provisions of the earlier statute. Hence, the doctrine of implied repeal did not apply.

Thoburn is also better understood as a case restricting the application of the doctrine of implied repeal to a conflict between two statutory provisions governing the same subject matter, as opposed to requiring that two statutes must regulate the same area in general. When explaining the doctrine of implied repeal, Laws LJ does not expressly refer to the need for statutes to be on the same subject matter for the doctrine of implied repeal to apply. Instead, he states that:

---

[54] [1934] 1 KB 590 (CA), 597.
[55] *Wallwork v Fielding* [1922] 2 KB 66, 71.

if Parliament has created successive statutes which on the true construction of each of them make them irreducibly inconsistent provisions, the earlier statute is impliedly repealed by the later.[56]

There is no inconsistency between the provisions of the European Communities Act 1972 and the Weights and Measures Act 1985 because there are no irreducibly inconsistent provisions to be found in the two statutes. Sections 2(2) and 2(4) confer a power to enact delegated legislation that can modify or overturn primary legislation, even legislation passed after 1972, in order to facilitate the incorporation of European Community law into English law. Section 1 of the 1985 Act did nothing to remove or modify the power granted to the executive. It was a measure listing legally valid weights and measures, which included imperial measurements. Its provisions were not inconsistent with those of the 1972 Act. Rather, it provided an example of a future statute whose provisions could be modified by exercising the power granted under the 1972 Act.

Statements to the effect that the doctrine of implied repeal only applies to conflicts between two statutes on the same subject matter do not provide a further restriction of the doctrine of implied repeal. Rather, they are best understood as a recognition that the doctrine only applies when a court is faced with two statutory provisions in different statutes that cannot stand together. It is not possible for the court to interpret the later statute in the light of the earlier statute. Consequently, the provisions of the later statute impliedly repeal the provisions of the earlier statute.

E. Specific Repeal

The doctrine of implied repeal is narrower in scope than it first appears. There is a general presumption against implied repeal. The doctrine is best understood not as a rule, but as an exception. In most cases of apparent conflict, courts will interpret a later statute so as not to contradict an earlier statute, thus occasionally it may appear as if the will of an earlier Parliament prevailed over than of a later Parliament. The principle of *generalia specialibus non derogant* ensures that later, general, provisions of legislation do not impliedly repeal earlier, more specific, legislation. Later specific legislation is not interpreted as impliedly repealing more general, earlier provisions of legislation. Instead, the later legislation will be interpreted as a new exception to the earlier more general provision. The presumption against implied repeal operates most strongly when applied to constitutional statutes. Only specific or express words of Parliament will suffice to overturn the presumption that the later statute can be read so as not to contradict an earlier constitutional statute. Our examination of the scope of the doctrine of implied repeal has also revealed the close connection between interpretation and implied repeal. Implied repeal only applies when it is not

---

[56] [2002] EWHC 195 (Admin), [2003] QB 151, [37].

possible for later statutory provisions to be interpreted so as not to specifically contradict earlier statutory provisions. To understand this further, we need to investigate broad classifications of statutory provisions, in order to determine when specific contradictions between statutory provisions occur.

We have already drawn a distinction between substantive and manner and form provisions. Continuing parliamentary legislative supremacy is only supported if the doctrine of implied repeal applies to manner and form as well as substantive provisions. This distinction also serves to illustrate the way in which later statutes do or do not contradict earlier statutory provisions. A conflict occurs between substantive provisions when it is clear that the earlier and the later substantive provision contradict each other. For example, if Statute A contained a provision prohibiting parking on double yellow lines and Statute B, a later statute, permitted parking on double yellow lines, then the two provisions would clearly contradict each other. The doctrine of implied repeal would apply and Statute B, as the later statute, would impliedly repeal the provisions of Statute A. A conflict would not occur, however, if Statute A prohibited the parking on double yellow lines and Statute B prohibited parking on double blue lines. There is no contradiction here. Statute B merely adds a further parking prohibition. Nor would a conflict occur if Statute B allowed ambulances to park on double yellow lines. This would be interpreted as providing a specific exception to the earlier general provision. Nor would conflict arise if a later statute governing parking in general allowed cars to park on all roads in Oxford town centre. This later general provision would not impliedly repeal the earlier, specific provision prohibiting parking on double yellow lines, including those found painted on roads in Oxford town centre.

Conflicts between manner and form provisions occur in two distinct ways. First, a conflict would arise if two statutes were to enact contradictory manner and form provisions. It may be the case, for example, that Statute A enacts that the law relating to parking offences can only be modified if Parliament passes legislation with a two-thirds majority in both the House of Commons and the House of Lords. Statute B could then be passed requiring a four-fifths majority in both the House of Commons and the House of Lords to enact legislation modifying parking offences. This conflict occurs in the same way as the conflict between substantive provisions discussed above. The two statutory provisions specifically contradict each other, replacing the earlier requirement for a two-thirds majority with the requirement to obtain a four-fifths majority. Secondly, a conflict could occur if statute C were passed modifying parking offences, which was not enacted with a two-thirds majority vote in the House of Commons and the House of Lords. Enacting legislation without obtaining a two-thirds majority vote in the House of Commons and the House of Lords impliedly repeals the manner and form requirement. This does not concern a specific contradiction between two statutory provisions. Instead, the contradiction occurs as the legislation was enacted in contravention of the provisions of the earlier statute.

Further complexities arise when we analyse the way in which the doctrine of implied repeal applies to power-conferring as opposed to duty-imposing rules. Both of the examples discussed above concern duty-imposing rules. The conflict between substantive provisions concerned duty-imposing rules regulating parking offences. The statutes imposed a duty not to park on double yellow or double blue lines. The conflict between manner and form provisions concerned duties imposed on the legislature to enact valid legislation. The statutes imposed a duty on the legislature to obtain a two-thirds or a four-fifths majority in both the House of Commons and the House of Lords if they were to enact legislation regulating parking offences.

Power-conferring rules do not impose duties, but rather empower individuals to take certain actions. Section 10 of the Human Rights Act 1998 and section 2(2) of the European Communities Act 1972 are both examples of power-conferring rules. They grant a power to the executive to use delegated legislation to amend provisions of primary legislation, either to ensure their compatibility with Convention rights or in order to incorporate provisions of European Community law into English law. There is no duty placed on the minister to act in this manner, though there are duties that dictate the way in which a minister should enact such delegated legislation. Schedule 2 of the Human Rights Act, for example, requires that delegated legislation enacted under the provisions of section 10 should be laid before and approved by each House of Parliament before it is enacted, unless it is necessary to make this order without the approval of both Houses given the urgency of the matter in question.

A conflict between two duty-imposing provisions arises when two statutory provisions impose contradictory duties on the same individual. This may provide a possible explanation for why the doctrine of implied repeal appeared not to apply to the conflict between the Merchant Shipping Act 1988 and the European Communities Act 1972 in *Factortame (2)*.[57] The European Communities Act imposes a duty on the courts to construe and give effect to all legislation, including that passed after the 1972 Act, subject to the provisions of directly effective European Community law. The Merchant Shipping Act 1988 contained provisions that contradicted directly effective European Community law. Although both are duty-imposing provisions, the 1972 Act imposed a duty on the courts and the 1988 Act imposed a duty on those wishing to fish in UK waters. There is no conflict between the two provisions unless the provisions of the 1988 Act make it impossible for the courts to fulfil their duty to give effect to the 1988 Act subject to the provisions of directly effective European Community law. It is at least arguable that the courts could continue to fulfil their duty to give effect to the 1988 Act subject to the directly effective provisions of European Community law by reading an exception into the Act such that it only applied to non-European Union nationals.

---

[57] *R v Secretary of State for Transport ex parte Factortame Ltd and Others (No 2)* [1991] 1 AC 603 (HL).

The complexities surrounding the application of the doctrine of implied repeal to section 3(1) of the Human Rights Act arise because section 3(1) is a limited duty-conferring rule, which provides the court with a duty and a correlative power when it is impossible for it to fulfil its duty. This classification helps to explain why section 3(1) does not impliedly repeal earlier legislation whose provisions contradict Convention rights. Lord Irvine explained this conclusion by stating that the Human Rights Act 1998 established a different mechanism to the doctrine of implied repeal, its provisions relying on interpretation as opposed to repeal to protect Convention rights.[58] He further argued that there was no application of the doctrine of implied repeal, as the Human Rights Act did not incorporate Convention rights into English law. Therefore, there was no conflict between the Human Rights Act and earlier statutory provisions that contravened Convention rights.[59]

Nicholas Bamforth, while agreeing with the conclusion, provides a different and better explanation based on the wording of section 3(1). Section 3(1) requires statutes to be construed and given effect in a manner compatible with Convention rights, so far as it is possible to do so. Consequently, either the court will find it possible to construe and give effect to the earlier statute to remove its apparent conflict with Convention rights, or it will find it impossible to interpret the statute in this manner. In the first instance, Convention rights are protected. In the second, the court may only make a declaration of incompatibility. In both instances, there is no conflict between the statute and the Human Rights Act itself: both are applications of section 3(1). There is no implied repeal of the earlier statute by the later statute as there is nothing in the Human Rights Act that requires earlier statutes to be Convention-compatible. Statutes are only required to be read and given effect in a Convention-compatible manner where possible to do so.[60] In the same way, a later statute whose provisions were incompatible with Convention rights would not impliedly repeal the Human Rights Act. If the provisions of the statute could be read in a manner compatible with Convention rights, then the court would read and give effect to the later statute to remove the incompatibility, applying section 3(1). If this were not the case, the later statute would not contradict section 3(1). Rather, section 3(1) would apply and the statute would be an example of a situation where it is not possible to interpret the later statute to remove its incompatibility with Convention rights.[61]

Bamforth's explanation relies on the features of section 3(1) as a limited duty-imposing rule. Section 3(1) confers a duty on the court to read and give effect to legislation in a manner compatible with Convention rights, so far as it is possible to do so. Section 4 grants a further power to the court to issue a declaration of incompatibility where it is not possible to read and give effect to legislation

---

[58]   Hansard HL vol 584, col 1261 (19 January 1998).

[59]   *Ibid*.

[60]   N Bamforth, 'Parliamentary Sovereignty and the Human Rights Act 1998' [1998] *Public Law* 572, 575.

[61]   *Ibid*.

so as to ensure its compatibility with Convention rights. Legislation that contradicts Convention rights does not impose a contradictory duty on the judiciary. It merely provides an example of legislation that cannot be read to ensure its Convention-compatibility. It does not contradict section 3(1) as section 3(1) imposes a restricted as opposed to an absolute duty on the court.

This classification of the nature of section 3(1) also casts light on the debate as to whether section 3(1) itself can be impliedly repealed. Lord Lester[62] and Anthony Bradley[63] both appear to argue that section 3(1) can only be expressly as opposed to impliedly repealed. However, a better interpretation is that section 3(1) can be impliedly repealed, but that this would only be the case where a future legislative provision imposed a contradictory duty of interpretation on the judiciary. For example, a 2008 statute that required all legislation to be interpreted in a manner compatible with the EU Charter of Fundamental Rights and Freedoms would partially repeal section 3(1). If Convention rights conflicted with provisions of the EU Charter, the courts would face contradictory duties.[64]

Conflicts between power-conferring rules only occur when there is a specific contradiction between two different power-conferring statutory provisions, such that the later power contradicts the earlier power. For example, section 1 of a fictional Human Rights Amendment Act 2008 would impliedly repeal section 10 of the Human Rights Act 1998 if it restricted the power to enact legislation to modify primary legislation to statutes enacted prior to the Human Rights Act 1998. This would contradict the prospective Henry VIII clause found in section 10, which empowers the executive to pass delegated legislation to modify statutes enacted after the Human Rights Act 1998. A later substantive provision does not contradict the earlier power-conferring provision. This explains why the Weights and Measures Act 1985 did not impliedly repeal section 2(2) of the European Communities Act 1972. The 1985 Act did not contradict the power conferred on the executive to modify legislation enacted after 1972 in order to implement European Community law in to English law.

This clarification of the scope of the doctrine of implied repeal, and its relationship to interpretation, provides a springboard for our analysis of the ways in which Convention rights could have been provided with a stronger protection than is currently found in the Human Rights Act without contradicting continuing parliamentary legislative supremacy. Section 3(1) already provides a duty on the court to read legislation to ensure its compatibility with Convention rights so far as it is possible to do so. It also may appear to be immune from the

---

[62] Lord Lester, 'Opinion: The Art of the Possible—Interpreting Statutes under the Human Rights Act' [1998] *European Human Rights Law Review* 665, 670 and 'Interpreting Statutes under the Human Rights Act' (1999) 20 *Statute Law Review* 218, 221.

[63] A Bradley, 'Conflicting statutory provisions—the impact of fundamental rights' (2001) 151 *New Law Journal* 311. But see M Shrimpton, who argues that Bradley's interpretation contradicts parliamentary legislative supremacy in 'Implied and Express Repeal' (2001) 151 *New Law Journal* 450.

[64] This is the case even though, in substance, the outcome may be the same as if s 3(1) still applied, given that the Charter incorporates rights similar to those found in the ECHR.

doctrine of implied repeal, although as we have explained here this occurs because of the precise wording of section 3(1) and the complex application of the doctrine of implied repeal. The following section investigates other ways in which human rights could be given an entrenchment effect—where principles of interpretation and the narrow scope of the doctrine of implied repeal may make it appear as if human rights are entrenched.

III. HOW TO GIVE HUMAN RIGHTS AN 'ENTRENCHMENT EFFECT'

It is clear that the Human Rights Act does not entrench Convention rights. However, the scope of the doctrine of implied repeal and its application to section 3(1) may already give the Act a form of entrenchment effect. Later legislation that contravenes Convention rights does not impliedly repeal section 3(1). This is not because section 3(1) is entrenched, being only capable of being overturned by express as opposed to implied repeal, but because later legislation that contravenes Convention rights does not contradict the partial duty-imposing provision found in section 3(1). This entrenchment effect, however, only provides a weak protection of human rights. It is possible for future legislation to override human rights, given that the Human Rights Act only requires such legislation to be read and given effect to in a manner that ensures its compatibility with Convention rights, so far as this is possible to achieve. This section will discuss three possible ways in which the Human Rights Act could achieve an entrenchment effect that provides for a stronger protection of human rights, while still preserving continuing parliamentary legislative supremacy.

A. Construe and Give Effect

One possible model for providing a stronger protection of Convention rights is section 2(4) of the European Communities Act 1972, which requires that 'any enactment passed or to be passed . . . shall be construed and have effect subject to the foregoing provisions of this section'. Section 2(1) of the 1972 Act incorporates 'rights, powers, liabilities, obligations and restrictions' arising from European Community law. Consequently, section 2(4) is interpreted as requiring that all statutes, including those passed after the 1972 Act came in to force, are to be construed and given effect subject to the provisions of directly effective European Community law.

Three differences between the European Communities Act 1972 and the Human Rights Act 1988 explain why modifying the Human Rights Act so as to mirror section 2(4) of the 1972 Act would provide a stronger protection of Convention rights. First, section 2(4) does not restrict the duty imposed on the courts to construe and give effect to legislation to ensure that it takes effect subject to directly effective Community law. There is no requirement, for example, that courts should only strive to construe statutes so far as possible to ensure that they take effect subject to directly effective European Community law. Nor is an alternative power granted to the courts, should they not find it possible to construe legislation to take effect subject to directly effective European Community law. Secondly, courts are not required to *read*, but to *construe* statutory provisions. 'Read' appears to suggest that courts are still required to pay attention to the wording of the statute, providing a possible interpretation of its provisions. A 'reading' of a statute is more likely to be limited by semantics and principles of interpretation which focus on discerning the meaning of the statute's provisions. 'Construe' appears to suggest that courts can go further, moving away from the limits imposed by ensuring that their *reading* of a statute is a linguistically valid interpretation of its provisions. Thirdly, and perhaps most importantly, section 2(4) does not require statutes to take effect *in a manner compatible with* Community law, but to take effect *subject to* directly effective provisions of European Community law. This suggests that courts are required to give priority to provisions of directly effective European Community law, even in the face of possible contradictions by future legislation.

As explained above, the European Communities Act 1972 imposes a duty on courts with regard to the way in which it construes future legislation. The Merchant Shipping Act 1988 would only impliedly repeal section 2(4) of the 1972 Act if courts were unable to construe and give effect to its provisions subject to directly effective European Community law. One possible way in which it might have been possible for the court to have construed and given effect to the 1988 Act subject to directly effective European Community law would have been to construe 'British' to mean 'European'. This would have removed the conflict as it would have enabled European individuals to register their vessels and fish in British waters, as required by the principles of article 43, later article 52, of the EC Treaty.

The reasoning in *Factortame (1)* provides a further means by which conflict between the 1988 Act and the 1972 Act could have been avoided. If we interpret section 2(4) of the 1972 Act as requiring all legislation to include a section stating that its provisions take effect subject to directly effective European Community law, then even legislation that contradicts directly effective EC law can be construed and given effect subject to directly effective European Community law.[65] In effect, the court interprets section 2(4) in a disjunctive manner. Courts first strive to read statutes to ensure that they take effect subject to directly effective European Community law. Where this is not possible, courts nevertheless are required to ensure that statutes take effect subject to directly effective European Community law. Although this may appear to be a

---

[65] This is often referred to as the 'constructivist' interpretation of *Factortame*. See, PP Craig, 'Sovereignty of the United Kingdom Parliament after *Factortame*' [1991] 11 *Yearbook of European Law* 221, 251. A similar argument was made by Denning MR in *McCarthy's Limited v Smith* [1981] QB 180. See, TRS Allan, 'Parliamentary Sovereignty: Lord Denning's Dextrous Revolution' (1983) 3 *Oxford Journal of Legal Studies* 22.

strained interpretation of section 2(4) it can be justified as one that fulfils the purposes of the 1972 Act. The European Communities Act 1972 aimed to ensure that the United Kingdom adhered to the requirements imposed on it by membership of the European Communities, now the European Union. This includes the obligation to uphold the supremacy of directly effective European Community law.[66]

The above argument is not presented as a conclusive explanation of the *Factortame* litigation. Although it may explain the outcome in *Factortame (1)*, it is important to note that this argument was not repeated in *Factortame (2)*. Nevertheless, it does provide an illustration of a way in which the Human Rights Act could be reworded to provide a stronger protection of Convention rights without contradicting continuing parliamentary legislative supremacy. However, it is important to note two weaknesses of this method of providing for a stronger protection of human rights. First, this only achieves an entrenchment effect. Although it may make it difficult for Parliament to legislate contrary to Convention rights, it would not make it impossible. If section 3(1) were reworded to require courts to construe and give effect to legislation subject to the provisions of Convention rights, this section could still be impliedly repealed by future legislation that imposed a contradictory interpretative duty on the courts. This could be achieved, for example, by enacting legislation which included a section requiring that the statute or certain of its provisions were to take effect 'notwithstanding', or 'regardless' of Convention rights or of the newly worded section 3(1). It would also be possible for Parliament to pass legislation which expressly repealed the reworded section 3(1).

Secondly, the apparent lack of application of the doctrine of implied repeal to section 2(4) of the European Communities Act is justified through reading the duty of the court to 'construe' and to 'give effect' to legislation subject to directly effective European Community law disjunctively. This requires the court to give effect to legislation subject to directly effective European Community law, even if it cannot be construed to take effect subject to directly effective European Community law. This disjunctive interpretation was justified to achieve the purposes of the European Communities Act 1972. This interpretation of 'construe and give effect' may not be possible for a newly reworded Human Rights Act. It would depend on whether there was sufficient evidence to support the claim that Parliament intended all legislation to take effect subject to Convention rights, effectively legislating to ensure that Convention rights overrode contradictory legislative provisions. It may be harder to provide evidence of this intention, given that the European Convention on Human Rights does not include a principle equivalent to that of the supremacy of directly effective European Community law.

---

[66] For further discussion see TRS Allan, *Law Liberty and Justice: the Legal Foundations of British Constitutionalism* (Oxford, Clarendon Press, 1993) 274–80 and TRS Allan, *Constitutional Justice: a Liberal Theory of the Rule of Law* (Oxford, Oxford University Press, 2001) 228–9.

B. Dominant and Subordinate Statutory Provisions and the Principle of Legality

The second method by which Convention rights could be given a stronger protection than that found in section 3(1) of the Human Rights Act requires a longer explanation. First, we need to explain the distinction between dominant and subordinate statutory provisions. This distinction is made when resolving conflicts that occur between provisions arising in the same statute. When this occurs, the dominant provision prevails over the subordinate provision. For example, if section 1 of the imaginary 'Criminal Offences Act 2008' states that 'no person may be punished retrospectively for a criminal offence' and section 15 creates a new offence of conspiracy to incite terrorist activities that has retrospective effect, then these two sections in the same statute would contradict each other. The court would resolve this conflict by determining whether section 1 or section 15 was the dominant provision of the statute. If it were concluded that section 1 was the dominant provision, as it refers to a long-established principle of the criminal law that was meant to apply to all offences, then it would prevail over section 15. Section 15 would be interpreted so that the new offence would not take effect retrospectively.

The principle that dominant provisions override subordinate provisions could be used to achieve an entrenchment effect if it were expanded to apply to conflicts between statutory provisions in different statutes in addition to conflicts between provisions found within the same statute. In addition the Human Rights Act 1998 would have to be reworded to require the protection of Convention rights in English law. This new provision would also need to be classified as a dominant statutory provision, such that it would override any other statutory provision that contradicted Convention rights. Even though this would entail that the earlier provision protecting Convention rights would override the later statutory provisions contradicting Convention rights, this would not contravene the doctrine of implied repeal. The potential conflict between these contradictory provisions would be resolved by interpretation, requiring the dominant provision to override the subordinate provision, in a manner similar to the principle of *generalia specialibus non derogant*.

One possible example of how this might be achieved is found in the minority opinion of the New Zealand Court of Appeal case of *R v Pora (Pora)*.[67] *Pora* involved a conflict between two provisions in the same statute: the Criminal Justice Act 1985. However, although the provisions were included in the same statute, they were not enacted at the same time. The second, contradictory provision had been incorporated into the 1985 Act by a later statutory amendment. Section 4(2), which was included in the original version of the 1985 Act, prohibited retrospective punishment, forbidding the making of any order in the nature of a penalty that could not have been made at the time the offence was

---

[67] [2001] 2 NZLR 37 (Court of Appeal of New Zealand).

committed. Section 80 of the Act, inserted later by section 2(4) of the Criminal Justice Amendment Act 1999, expressly provided that those guilty of murder, where the murder also involved an invasion of the home of the victim, should be sentenced to life imprisonment subject to a minimum 13-year mandatory component. This sentence was to apply even if the offence was committed before the legislation came into force. This section of the Act had been introduced in tandem with the Crime (Home Invasion) Act 1999, which came into force 13 days prior to the Criminal Justice Amendment Act 1999.

Pora was convicted of murder involving a home invasion that occurred prior to the Act coming into force. The New Zealand Court of Appeal concluded that Pora was not subject to the provisions of section 80 and, therefore, his sentence was not subject to the requirement of a minimum 13-year mandatory term. The majority reached this conclusion by holding that section 80, as a later and more specific statutory provision, would override section 4(2). However, its provisions were limited. They only applied retrospectively to the 13-day difference between the coming into force of the Criminal Justice Amendment Act and the Crime (Home Invasion) Act 1999. Pora had not committed his crime during that period. The minority refused to apply these principles, arguing instead that section 4(2), as a dominant statutory provision, should be applied over and above section 80. Consequently, section 80 did not have retrospective effect.

Of particular interest is the manner in which the minority reached their conclusion that simultaneously appeared to refuse to apply the doctrine of implied repeal while also asserting that this would not challenge continuing parliamentary legislative supremacy. Their justification stemmed from section 6 of the New Zealand Bill of Rights Act 1990 and the principle of legality, established in *R v Secretary of State for the Home Department ex parte Pierson*[68] and *R v Secretary of State for the Home Department ex parte Simms*.[69] When combined, this meant that statutory provisions protecting fundamental rights could only be overturned by express repeal, or where later specific words demonstrated a clear intention on the part of the legislature to overturn fundamental rights. Section 6 of the New Zealand Bill of Rights Act states that:

> Whenever an enactment can be given a meaning that is consistent with the rights and freedoms contained in this Bill of Rights, that meaning shall be preferred to any other meaning.

The minority interpreted this provision as requiring courts to adopt a meaning of the Criminal Justice Act 1985 that protected the right against retrospective punishments. This could be achieved by using the principle of legality which requires that 'fundamental rights cannot be overridden by general or ambiguous words'.[70] Consequently, when analysing a potential conflict between a statutory

---

[68] [1998] 1 AC 539 (HL).
[69] [2000] 2 AC 115 (HL).
[70] *Ibid*, at 131 (Lord Hoffmann) cited in *Pora* [2001] 2 NZLR 37 (Court of Appeal of New Zealand), [53] (Elias CJ and Tipping J) and [157] (Thomas J).

provision protecting fundamental rights and one purporting to limit fundamental rights, the latter would be interpreted to be consistent with fundamental rights, unless it expressly or specifically purported to override the fundamental right. Section 80 of the 1985 Act did not specifically or expressly override the provision against the imposition of retrospective punishments found in section 4(2) of the Act. Hence section 4(2) was to be applied in preference to section 80. As the dominant statutory provision, section 4(2) overrode section 80, the subordinate provision. The classification of section 4(2) as the dominant statutory provision derived from a combination of the New Zealand Bill of Rights Act 1990 and the principle of legality.[71] Thus the principle that dominant statutory provisions override subordinate statutory provisions was extended to conflicts between provisions found in the same statute, where one provision was enacted after the other by a later statutory amendment.

The opinion of the minority in *Pora* does concern a conflict between two statutory provisions found in the same statute. However, given that the subordinate provision was enacted after the dominant provision, it may be argued by analogy that this principle can be applied to conflicts occurring between statutory provisions found in two different statutes. The doctrine of implied repeal would appear to require that section 80 should override section 4(2), as section 80 was enacted after section 4(2). Consequently, if the doctrine of implied repeal does not apply when an earlier dominant statutory provision overrides a later subordinate statutory provision arising in the same statute, it can also be argued that it would not apply to conflicts between earlier and later dominant and subordinate statutory provisions found in different statutes. The principle that a dominant statutory provision overrides a subordinate statutory provision is used to avoid the conflict between two statutory provisions. The later statutory provision does not contradict the earlier statutory provision as it is interpreted as subordinate to, and hence to take effect subject to, the earlier dominant statutory provision.

An entrenchment effect could be achieved, therefore, if the Human Rights Act were reworded to provide for the protection of Convention rights and this was regarded as a dominant statutory provision. The classification of this new provision of the Human Rights Act as a dominant statutory provision could be supported by the principle of legality. As a result, later legislation that contradicted Convention rights would be read so as to take effect subject to the dominant provision requiring the protecting of Convention rights. Again, this would not completely entrench Convention rights. It would still be possible for Parliament to legislate contrary to Convention rights. This could be achieved through implied repeal if Parliament were to enact a later statutory provision requiring that legislation take effect to comply with a different set of human rights provisions, or not comply with Convention rights, which was interpreted by the courts as a dominant statutory provision. Implied repeal would also occur if

---

[71] *Pora, ibid,* at [36]–[40] (Elias CJ and Tipping J) and [149] (Thomas J).

Parliament were to enact legislation expressly stating that it was to take effect notwithstanding Convention rights.

C. Misfired Statutes

We have already discussed how principles of interpretation can be used to avoid conflicts between constitutional statutes and later statutory provisions. In particular, we concluded that the best interpretation of Laws LJ's statement in *Thoburn* was to recognise that it would be rare for the doctrine of implied repeal to apply to constitutional statutes in practice, given that courts would strive to ensure that later statutory provisions would be read to comply with the provisions of earlier, constitutional statutes. The doctrine of misfired statutes is similar to our interpretation of *Thoburn*. It applies to a conflict between a fundamental right and a later statute that appears to negate the fundamental right. If the court is of the opinion that the statute has 'misfired'—ie that it has accidentally overturned fundamental rights—then the court gives effect to the later statutory provision so as to correspond to Convention rights. The legislature is deemed to have accidentally overturned fundamental rights when it enacts legislation that contradicts fundamental rights, but where it is not clear that Parliament specifically and expressly intended to legislate contrary to Convention rights.

An example of the application of this doctrine is found, once more, in the minority judgment in *Pora*. A further justification for the conclusion that section 80 did not impliedly repeal section 4(2) stemmed from regarding section 80 as having 'misfired'. It was argued that the New Zealand Parliament had not really appreciated that section 80 would transgress the principle against retrospective punishment, being under the apprehension that setting mandatory components of life sentences would only affect parole decisions and therefore was not an example of a punishment. The fact that the statute had 'misfired' could then be taken into account when determining the solution to this apparent conflict between two statutory provisions. Section 4(2) was to be preferred as it was not clear that Parliament intended to specifically and expressly legislate contrary to the right against retrospective punishment.[72]

Although the doctrine of misfired statutes may be similar in outcome to the dicta of Laws LJ in *Thoburn* it has a broader potential scope of application. The statute was deemed to have misfired not merely because it contradicted fundamental human rights, but because the minority in *Pora* concluded that it was not Parliament's true intention to legislate to create an offence that applied retrospectively. Parliament had not realised that the setting of the mandatory component of a life sentence could be categorised as a 'punishment' for the purposes of the application of the principle against retrospective punishments. A divergence between the meaning of the express words and the intention of

---

[72] *Ibid*, at [45]–[47] (Elias CJ and Tipping J) and [153] (Thomas J).

Parliament, gathered for example from ministerial statements in Hansard, may provide evidence of a statute having misfired. In particular, section 19 of the Human Rights Act 1998 may furnish evidence of a divergence between statutory words and the intention of Parliament, where a section 19 statement is made to the effect that legislation is intended to comply with Convention rights, but where it is found later that the statute in question does not comply with Convention rights. However, the principle of parliamentary privilege means that, in practice, the doctrine of misfired statutes would add little to the ways in which courts can currently read a statute to ensure that it complies with Convention rights.

In common with the other means by which a stronger protection could be provided to Convention rights, Parliament would still retain the ability to legislate contrary to Convention rights. This could be achieved through implied repeal. It would merely require Parliament to make it clear that its intention was to legislate contrary to Convention rights. If it were clear from ministerial statements, the legislative history of the statute in question and statements made in Parliament that the legislature did intend to legislate contrary to Convention rights, then it would be hard for the courts to construe this legislation as a misfired statute. The doctrine of implied repeal would apply and this later legislation would override the statutory provision protecting Convention rights.

IV. CONCLUSION

It is possible to provide a stronger protection of Convention rights than that provided in the Human Rights Act without breaching continuing parliamentary legislative supremacy. The strongest protection would be provided by modifying section 3(1), so that it required courts to construe and give effect to legislation such that its provisions took effect subject to Convention rights. This could be combined with the recognition by the courts that section 3(1) was a dominant statutory provision that was to prevail were it to be contradicted by a later, subordinate statutory provision, and careful scrutiny of all legislation that restricted Convention rights, to ensure that the legislation had not misfired. To provide this stronger protection of Convention rights achieves an entrenchment effect, making it difficult for the legislature to legislate contrary to Convention rights. It may also make it appear as if the Human Rights Act 1998 applies over and above later legislation that restricts Convention rights. However, as argued above, it is still possible for Parliament to legislate contrary to Convention rights and for this to be achieved by enacting legislation that impliedly repeals the stronger protection of Convention rights.

Our argument has focused on the scope of the doctrine of implied repeal, which we regarded as providing the strongest evidence for the existence of continuing parliamentary legislative supremacy as a legal fact. However, it still remains to illustrate conclusively that these stronger protections of Convention rights would not contradict continuing parliamentary legislative supremacy. To demonstrate this conclusively, we need to return to the way in which the doctrine of implied repeal supports continuing parliamentary legislative supremacy. Continuing parliamentary legislative supremacy requires that the doctrine of implied repeal applies to both substantive and manner and form provisions. This in turn ensures that Parliament cannot bind its successors and, in particular, that it cannot entrench legislative measures. Should it attempt to do so, later contradictory legislation impliedly repeals the earlier legislation.

The entrenchment effects discussed above do not challenge the constitutional orthodoxy that Parliament cannot bind its successors. These entrenchment effects occur either due to the creation of new exceptions to the doctrine of implied repeal, or through the use of principles of interpretation to resolve apparent conflicts between statutes. The modification of section 3(1) of the Human Rights Act, such that courts are required to give effect to legislation subject to directly effective Convention rights and the entrenchment effect created through an analysis of 'misfired' statutes both rely on interpretation to remove perceived conflicts. The principle that dominant statutory provisions override subordinate statutory provisions is an exception to the doctrine of implied repeal. However, it is an exception that is similar in effect to the principle *generalia specialibus non derogant*. In the same way that general provisions do not override earlier specific provisions, despite an apparent contradiction, subordinate legislative provisions do not override earlier dominant legislative provisions. Both may also be understood as an example of how courts read general provisions down, or read words into legislation in order to achieve compatibility between two apparently contradictory statutory provisions.[73] In *Seward v The Vera Cruz*[74] the later general statute, which granted jurisdiction to the High Court of Admiralty to hear all actions concerning damage caused by ships, was read down so as not to contradict the earlier statutory provision granting jurisdiction to the common law courts to hear actions for damages in lieu of death caused by a wrongful or negligent action or omission. In *Pora*, section 80, which applied a retrospective minimum component of a mandatory life sentence for those committing the offence of murder involving home invasion, could have been read to ensure that it did not contradict section 4(2) prohibiting retrospective criminal penalties by reading words into section 80, requiring that it took effect subject to section 4(2). Each of the entrenchment effects discussed above does enable Parliament to overturn the stronger protection provided for Convention rights through implied repeal as well as express repeal.

Nor is it the case that these entrenchment effects challenge the position that the doctrine of implied repeal applies to manner and form as well as substantive

[73] Although it is accepted that support for this expanded application of the doctrine that dominant statutory provisions override subordinate statutory provision is weak, stemming only from the assessment of the minority.
[74] (1884) 10 App Cas 59 (HL).

provisions of legislation. The only form of entrenchment effect requiring a modification of the current provisions of the Human Rights Act is that which would occur if section 3(1) were to be modified to require that all legislation be construed and take effect subject to the provisions of Convention rights. However, this legislation does not propose a specific manner and form requirement that must be adhered to by future parliaments. Rather, it imposes a duty on the courts as to how they are to construe and give effect to legislation. Future legislation that contradicts Convention rights does not impliedly repeal the modified section 3(1) as it does not contradict the duty of the courts to construe and give effect to this legislation subject to Convention rights. It could be impliedly repealed were Parliament to enact that legislation took effect notwithstanding Convention rights, or if Parliament enacted legislation which placed courts under a contradictory duty which made it impossible for the courts to construe and give effect to legislation in a manner compatible with Convention rights.

Although it may appear as if Parliament needs to adopt a specific manner and form to overturn the modified section 3(1), this is not the case. This apparent manner and form requirement is not found in prior legislation that a future parliament need adhere to. It stems merely from the scope of the doctrine of implied repeal. In this sense, the modified section 3(1) is no different from other statutory provisions. Convention rights may appear to be entrenched and earlier legislation may appear to override later legislation, but this is not the case. Rather, the later legislation does not contradict the earlier legislation. There is no need for the doctrine of implied repeal to apply.

3

Redefinition and the Rule of Recognition

THE PREVIOUS CHAPTER argued that it was possible to provide a stronger protection of Convention rights than that found within the current Human Rights Act without breaching continuing parliamentary legislative supremacy. The narrow scope of the doctrine of implied repeal, and the way in which interpretation can be used to remove apparent conflicts between statutory provisions, combine to provide for an 'entrenchment effect'. However, this does not achieve entrenchment of Convention rights. Although an 'entrenchment effect' may make it difficult in practice to impliedly repeal human rights, it is still possible in theory. The legislature can overturn the statutory provision used to create an 'entrenchment effect' by both express and implied repeal. This chapter will investigate whether an even stronger protection can be granted to Convention rights.

Constitutional orthodoxy would argue that it is not possible to entrench Convention rights without contravening continuing parliamentary legislative supremacy. The very distinction between continuing and self-embracing parliamentary legislative supremacy turns on this assessment. Legislatures enjoying self-embracing parliamentary legislative supremacy can bind their successors. Those enjoying continuing parliamentary legislative supremacy cannot. Entrenchment would either require the adoption of a self-embracing model of parliamentary legislative supremacy, or the abrogation of sovereignty from the Westminster Parliament and its transfer to another institution enjoying limited sovereignty.[1]

This chapter will argue against this constitutional orthodoxy. To do so, it will reinvestigate the distinction between continuing and self-embracing parliamentary legislative supremacy. It will be argued that the distinction between the two does not depend on the *possibility* of entrenchment, but on the *method* through which this entrenchment is achieved. Legislatures enjoying self-embracing parliamentary legislative supremacy can entrench legislation merely by enacting a statute modifying the manner and form required to enact legally valid legislation. If Parliament were to enact legislation requiring that Convention rights

---

[1] AV Dicey, *An Introduction to the Study of the Law of the Constitution*, 10th edn (London, Macmillan, 1959) 69, fn 1.

could not be overturned or contravened unless it was by a legislative measure that had been passed by a two-thirds majority in both the House of Commons and the House of Lords, then this action alone would entrench Convention rights. Future parliaments would be bound by this manner and form provision. Courts would fail to recognise legislation that contravened Convention rights that had not obtained the requisite two-thirds majority as legally valid legislation. A legislature enjoying continuing parliamentary legislative supremacy would not bind its successors were it to merely enact legislation entrenching Convention rights in this manner. The doctrine of implied repeal would operate such that future parliaments could overturn this manner and form requirement by implied repeal. However, as will be argued below, Parliament acting in combination with other institutions could successfully entrench legislation if its actions in combination with those of other institutions modified the definition of legally valid legislation. Continuing parliamentary legislative supremacy does not prohibit entrenchment. It merely prevents entrenchment that could occur through Parliament acting alone.

I. CONTINUING AND SELF-EMBRACING PARLIAMENTARY LEGISLATIVE SUPREMACY

The assertion that the distinction between continuing and self-embracing parliamentary legislative supremacy depends on whether Parliament can entrench legislation, thereby binding its successors, is clearly illuminated by contrasting Dicey's theory of parliamentary legislative supremacy with the alternative conceptions of parliamentary sovereignty provided by Jennings[2] and Heuston.[3] Dicey states that Parliament cannot bind its successors. Both Jennings and Heuston conclude that Parliament can bind its successors. This is clear both from their accounts of parliamentary sovereignty and the case law used to support their accounts. Both Jennings and Heuston relied on two cases from the Commonwealth to support their views—*Harris v Minister for the Interior (Harris)*,[4] a decision of the Supreme Court of South Africa and *Attorney-General for New South Wales v Trethowan (Trethowan)*,[5] a decision of the Privy Council on appeal from the High Court of Australia. Both concerned legislation which included requirements as to the manner and form in which its provisions could be repealed. In both cases, these manner and form requirements bound future Parliaments, such that legislation enacted in contravention of these requirements was held to be invalid.

---

[2] Sir WI Jennings, *The Law and the Constitution*, 5th edn (London, University of London Press, 1959).

[3] RFV Heuston, *Essays in Constitutional Law*, 2nd edn (London, Stevens and Sons, 1964).

[4] [1952] (2) SA 428 (Appellate Division of the Supreme Court of South Africa).

[5] [1931] HCA 3, (1931) 44 CLR 394 (High Court of Australia). See also [1932] AC 526 (PC).

Harris concerned an interpretation of the provisions of the South Africa Act 1909, which established the Parliament of the Union of South Africa. Prior to the enactment of the 1909 Act, the Parliament of South Africa was governed by the provisions of the Colonial Laws Validity Act 1865 which granted Parliament the power to enact legislation, but did not grant the power to legislate in a manner that would be inconsistent with provisions of legislation passed by the United Kingdom Parliament which extended to South Africa. The 1909 Act removed this restriction, allowing the Parliament of the Union of South Africa to 'repeal or alter any of the provisions of this Act'.[6] Section 35(1) of the 1909 Act provided that legislation could not be passed by the Parliament of the Union of South Africa which would disqualify persons from voting in the Cape Province by reason of race or colour, unless the legislation was 'passed by both Houses of Parliament sitting together, and at the third reading be agreed to by not less than two-thirds of the total number of members of both Houses'. In addition, section 152 provided that section 35(1) of the Act, as well as section 152, could only be repealed or amended by measures passed by two-thirds of the members of both Houses in a joint sitting. In 1951, after South Africa had achieved recognition as an independent state, the Separate Representation of the Voters Act 1951 was passed by the Union Parliament, which deprived the 'Cape Coloured' voters of their voting rights in the Cape Province. The 1951 Act was passed by a simple majority vote of both Houses sitting separately. According to the doctrine of continuing parliamentary legislative supremacy, passing the 1951 Act with a simple majority of both Houses would have impliedly repealed the 1909 Act requiring a two-thirds majority of both Houses sitting together. The unanimous decision of the Appellate division of the Supreme Court of South Africa, however, held that the 1951 Act was invalid. It was not valid law as it had not been passed according to the manner and form prescribed by the 1909 Act. In reaching this conclusion, the court recognised that this meant that the legal sovereignty of the Union Parliament was divided between Parliament as normally constituted and Parliament as constituted by the requirements of section 152.

Trethowan concerned similar manner and form requirements regarding the powers of the legislature in New South Wales. The legislature of New South Wales derived its authority from section 5 of the Colonial Laws Validity Act 1865 which granted it the full power to make laws, provided that they were made 'in such manner and form as may from time to time be required by any Act of Parliament, letters patent, Order in Council or colonial law, for the time being in force of the said colony'. The New South Wales legislature passed the Constitution Act 1902 establishing, inter alia, the Legislative Council. In 1929, the New South Wales legislature enacted the Constitution (Legislative Council) Amendment Act 1929 which inserted a new section, 7A, into the Constitution Act 1902. Section 7A provided that the Legislative Council could not be

---

[6] South Africa Act 1909 s 152.

abolished, nor could its powers be altered, unless the Bill proposing such measures were passed by both houses of the legislature and had been approved by a majority of the electorate and by the Governor-General. The same procedure was required to amend section 7A.

In 1930, a Bill was passed proposing the abolishment of the Legislative Council. The Governor-General had been requested to sign the Bill, even though it had not been presented to the electorate. An application was made for an injunction to prevent the presentation of the Bill to the Governor-General until it had been approved by the electorate. After concluding that the enactment of section 7A was within the powers of the New South Wales legislature, being a measure concerning the manner and form in which legislation is to be passed, the Privy Council concluded that the Bill could not be presented to the Governor-General without having first received the assent of the electorate.

Given this evidence, it is hard to see how the distinction between continuing and self-embracing parliamentary legislative supremacy could be understood in terms other than of the ability, or otherwise, of Parliament to bind its successors. However, this shorthand understanding of the distinction between the two theories confuses a distinction as to the *method* of entrenchment with the *possibility* of entrenchment. To understand this we need to examine how self-embracing parliamentary legislative supremacy provides for the entrenchment of manner and form provisions.

II. MANNER AND FORM AND REDEFINITION

This section will argue that self-embracing theories of parliamentary legislative supremacy enable the legislature to bind its successors as to the manner and form of future legislation because of the role such provisions play in the definition of valid legislation. It will then examine the different ways in which continuing and self-embracing theories of parliamentary legislative supremacy determine the definition of valid legislation. This will not only provide a better explanation of the distinction between these two conceptions of parliamentary legislative supremacy, but will serve as a springboard to our examination of the way in which Convention rights could be entrenched without contravening continuing parliamentary legislative supremacy.

A. Why can Manner and Form Provisions be Entrenched?

It is clear from an examination of the theories of both Jennings and Heuston, that manner and form provisions are treated differently because of the role that they play in the definition of valid legislation. This is further supported by an examination of both the case law that they relied on to support their theories and the most recent case law containing dicta in support of self-embracing theories of parliamentary legislative supremacy. The strongest evidence for this conclusion is found in the following statement by Jennings:

> 'Legal sovereignty' is merely a name indicating that the legislature has for the time being power to make laws of any kind in the manner required by the law. That is, a rule expressed to be made by the Queen, 'with the advice and consent of the Lords spiritual and temporal, and Commons in this present Parliament assembled, and by the authority of the same', will be recognised by the courts, including a rule which alters this law itself. If this is so, the 'legal sovereign' may impose legal limitations upon itself, because its power to change the law includes the power to change the law affecting itself.[7]

Parliamentary legislative supremacy vests in the Queen in Parliament because the law has granted the power to pass valid legislation to the Queen in Parliament. To be recognised as valid legislation, the measures in question must be passed according to the manner and form proscribed by the law. Were a purported legislative provision to be passed without the assent of the monarch, for example, then the measure in question would not be recognised as a valid statute. Ordinarily, in order to be valid legislation, the measure needs to comply with the manner and form requirements that necessitate the consent of the Commons, Lords and the monarch. Manner and form requirements differ from substantive requirements because they form part of the legal requirements of valid law. Were Parliament to change the legal requirements of a valid law by altering manner and form provisions, then statutes passed in breach of these manner and form requirements would not be recognised as legally valid legislation.

The connection between manner and form provisions and the definition of valid legislation explains why, under a theory of self-embracing parliamentary legislative supremacy, Parliament can bind its successors as to manner and form requirements. The doctrine of implied repeal does not apply to manner and form requirements because legislation passed in breach of manner and form requirements is not recognised as valid law. There is no conflict between an earlier statute and a later statute passed in breach of the manner and form requirements set out in the earlier statute because the later statute is not recognised as a valid statute.[8]

Further evidence of the relationship between manner and form requirements and the definition of valid legislation is found in the judgments of the High Court of Australia in *Trethowan*. The majority, who supported self-embracing parliamentary legislative supremacy, justified their conclusions through a discussion of manner and form provisions and the way in which the components of valid legislation can be redefined. Rich J, Dixon J and Starke J relied on manner and form arguments, stating that it was possible for Parliament to bind its

---

[7] Jennings, above n 2, at 152–3.

[8] Jennings makes a similar argument regarding legislation passed by a prince requiring all legislation in future to be approved of by a legislative committee, *ibid*, at 152.

successors as to the manner and form in which legislation is passed.[9] Rich J also specifically connected this discussion of manner and form requirements with the way in which legislation is defined, stating that:

> Two methods of controlling the operations of the Legislature appear to be allowed by the express terms of the section. The constitution of the legislative body may be altered; that is to say, the power of legislation may be reposed in an authority differently constituted. Again, laws may be passed imposing legal requirements as to manner and form in which constitutional amendments must be passed.[10]

In drawing this distinction between the two ways in which Parliament may bind its successors, Rich J provides an explanation for why manner and form provisions bind future legislatures. Were the New South Wales Parliament to alter its own constitution and transfer sovereignty to a new body, it would be redefining the law-making process by redefining the identity of the sovereign law-making body. Courts would no longer recognise as valid purported legislative acts passed by the old New South Wales Parliament. It would only recognise as valid those legislative measures passed by the new legislative body to which the old New South Wales Parliament had transferred its sovereignty. Were the New South Wales Parliament to legislate as to the manner and form required to modify certain substantive provisions of legislation, it would be redefining the requirements of valid legislation without redefining the identity of the sovereign law-making body. Legislation passed without the requisite manner and form requirement would not be recognised as valid legislation. As Dixon J explains:

> The power to make laws respecting its own constitution enables the legislature to deal with its own nature and composition. The power to make laws respecting its own procedure enables it to prescribe rules which have the force of law for its own conduct. Laws which relate to its own constitution and procedure must govern the legislature in the exercise of its powers, including the exercise of its powers to repeal those very laws.[11]

Dixon J argued that this principle would apply not only to the New South Wales legislature, but to other law-making institutions. If legislation of the Westminster Parliament required that approval of the electorate be obtained in order to legislate contrary to Convention rights, Dixon J would argue that, in these circumstances,

> the Courts might be called upon to consider whether the supreme legislative power in respect of the matter had in truth been exercised in the manner required for its authentic expression and by the elements in which it had come to reside.[12]

The most recent evidence of the connection between manner and form requirements and the definition of valid legislation is found in *R (Jackson) v*

---

[9] (1931) 44 CLR 394, 416–17 (Rich J), 423–24 (Dixon J) and 427–8 (Starke J).
[10] *Ibid*, at 407–8.
[11] *Ibid*, at 429–30.
[12] *Ibid*, at 426.

Attorney-General (Jackson).[13] Both Lord Steyn and Baroness Hale made statements in support of self-embracing parliamentary legislative supremacy. Lord Steyn explained self-embracing theories of parliamentary legislative supremacy by distinguishing between the static and dynamic elements of the definition of Parliament and legally valid legislative enactments. 'Static' refers to the composition of Parliament. 'Dynamic' refers to the process that these component elements of Parliament must use if they are to enact valid legislation. Dynamic elements are determined by the law and custom of Parliament. It is possible, therefore, for Parliament to alter the manner and form in which valid legislation is passed by modifying its laws and customs. This possibility exists not merely with regard to a modification of the manner and form in which legislation must be passed in general, but can also occur when Parliament decides to functionally redistribute power to legislate in different ways for different purposes. This redefinition, occurring through a modification of the law and customs of Parliament, cannot then be ignored by the courts. Courts would need to refer to such manner and form requirements to determine the validity of legislation.[14] In this way, Lord Steyn reached the conclusion that the Parliament Act 1911 was an example of a redefinition of the manner and form in which legislation is passed in order to achieve a specific purpose. It enables legislation to be passed without the consent of the House of Lords.[15]

Baroness Hale also concluded that the provisions of the Parliament Act 1911 bound Parliament as to the manner and form in which legislation is passed, setting out a way in which Parliament can enact valid legislation without the consent of the House of Lords. She based her conclusion on an analysis of the nature of sovereignty. If Parliament is sovereign and can do anything, then 'there is no reason why Parliament should not decide to redesign itself, either in general or for a particular purpose'.[16] Once such redefinition takes place, courts are required to recognise the new manner and form requirements of valid legislation.

B. Redefinition and Continuing Theories of Parliamentary Legislative Supremacy

Self-embracing parliamentary legislative supremacy recognises that Parliament can modify the definition of the sovereign law-making institution, or the nature of the law-making process, simply by enacting legislation. This explains why Parliament can bind its successors as to the manner and form of future legislation. Future Parliaments need to comply with the manner and form requirements set out in earlier legislation if they are to enact legislation that the courts will recognise as legally valid. Continuing parliamentary legislative supremacy also needs to ensure that valid legislation is only enacted by the sovereign

---

[13] [2005] UKHL 56, [2006] 1 AC 262.
[14] *Ibid*, at [86].
[15] *Ibid*.
[16] *Ibid*, at [160].

law-making body in the requisite manner and form required, in order to preserve the sovereignty of Parliament. However, it does not place a power to alter
this definition of the sovereign law-making institution, or the requirements of
valid legislation, in the hands of the legislature.

This conclusion is supported, in part, by Dicey's account of continuing parliamentary legislative supremacy. Dicey argued that the sovereign law-making
body could transfer or abdicate sovereignty, provided that the original sovereign law-maker ceases to exist.[17] Two distinctions can be drawn between
Dicey's account of the transfer or abdication of sovereignty and a redefinition of
sovereignty as explained by an alteration of manner and form provisions found
in self-embracing parliamentary legislative supremacy. First, Dicey is only concerned with provisions affecting the composition of the sovereign law-maker.
His argument does not extend to redefinitions of the law-making process itself.
If the Westminster Parliament were to legislate to the effect that legislation
amending or modifying the Human Rights Act needed to be passed by a two-
thirds majority of the Commons and Lords sitting together, self-embracing theories of parliamentary legislative supremacy would regard this as a manner and
form provision that bound future Parliaments. Dicey would not classify this
provision as a transfer of sovereignty. Consequently, he would argue that legislation which modified the Human Rights Act without the two-thirds majority
of both Houses would be valid legislation. The circumstances in which it was
passed would impliedly repeal the requirement to obtain a two-thirds majority.

Secondly, Dicey requires transfers of sovereignty to be complete. A sovereign
law-making body can delegate power to a non-sovereign body, or can transfer
its sovereign law-making power to another body, provided that the sovereign
law-making body then ceases to exist.[18] Self-embracing parliamentary legislative supremacy allows sovereignty to be shared between two sovereign law-
making institutions, each institution legislating on different matters and each
bound by the legislation establishing its existence and the manner and form
required to enact valid legislation.

These distinctions can be illustrated by the different ways in which self-
embracing and continuing parliamentary legislative supremacy would analyse
the decision in *Trethowan*. The legislation in *Trethowan* would be regarded by
self-embracing parliamentary legislative supremacy as creating a new sovereign
law-making institution. Sovereignty is shared between the New South Wales
legislature and a differently-composed sovereign consisting of the New South
Wales legislature and the electorate. The New South Wales legislature has

[17]   Dicey above n 1, at 69, fn 1.

[18]   Dicey reaches a similar conclusion when examining the Act of Union. If the Scottish and
English Parliaments had remained in existence, with the power to modify the Act of Union, leaving
the Westminster Parliament with the power to legislate on all other matters, the Westminster
Parliament would be a subordinate as opposed to a sovereign legislative body. However, given that
the transfer of power from the Scottish and English Parliaments to the Westminster Parliament was
complete, with the Scottish and English Parliaments ceasing to exist, the Westminster Parliament is
a sovereign legislative body. Dicey, *ibid*.

the power to enact legislation on all matters apart from the abolition of the Legislative Council. The sovereign law-making institution consisting of the New South Wales legislature and the electorate has the power to enact legislation abolishing the Legislative Council. Dicey, however, would regard the legislation in *Trethowan* as creating a new subordinate law-making body. The new legislative body—the New South Wales legislature plus the electorate—would be subordinate to the sovereign New South Wales legislature. Future reincarnations of the New South Wales legislature would not be bound by the rules of its predecessors regarding the composition of the sovereign legislature. The subordinate body would be bound by these rules. Consequently, if the subordinate body were to pass legislation outside its remit, the courts would be free to declare this legislation invalid. However, if the New South Wales Parliament were to abolish the legislative council without obtaining the agreement of the electorate, this would impliedly repeal the earlier legislation. Parliament would not be bound by the wishes of its previous incarnation.[19]

However, there are difficulties in drawing the distinction between continuing and self-embracing parliamentary legislative supremacy in this manner. First, it reduces the distinction between continuing and self-embracing theories of parliamentary legislative supremacy to a matter of degree. According to continuing parliamentary legislative supremacy, Parliament may create a new, limited law-making body, provided that the supreme law-making body transfers all its law making power to this new body and then ceases to exist. According to self-embracing parliamentary legislative supremacy Parliament can create a new limited law-making body merely by enacting legislation. It may divide its law-making power, as well as abdicate it. Secondly, it requires English law to classify legislation passed under the provisions of the Parliament Acts 1911–49 as delegated legislation, despite their form and appearance as ordinary legislation. This is because continuing parliamentary legislative supremacy would classify actions of the House of Commons and the monarch as those of a subordinate legislative body, as opposed to a sovereign body which shared the power to enact primary legislation with the Queen in Parliament. This would contravene *Jackson* which reached the opposite conclusion.[20]

Despite its weaknesses, the exploration of the differences between sharing and abdicating sovereignty points the way to a better understanding of the distinction between continuing and self-embracing parliamentary legislative supremacy. For self-embracing parliamentary legislative supremacy, the definition of legally valid legislation is determined by principles of the common law. Consequently, it can be altered by ordinary legislation, which overrides the common law.[21] For continuing parliamentary legislative supremacy, the definition of valid legislation cannot merely be determined by principles of the

---

[19] This is similar to the way in which HWR Wade regards the Parliament Acts 1911–1949. See,, HWR Wade, 'The Basis of Legal Sovereignty' [1955] *Cambridge Law Journal* 172, 193–4.

[20] *R (Jackson) v Attorney-General* [2005] UKHL 56, [2006] 1 AC 262.

[21] Jennings, above n 2, at 156–63.

common law. Consequently, it cannot be altered by ordinary legislation. For continuing parliamentary legislative supremacy to operate, the definition of the sovereign law-making body and the way in which legislation is enacted is found in a rule which is logically prior to the first Parliament to which the sovereign law-making power is granted. This logically prior rule cannot be altered by legislation.[22]

HWR Wade recognised the need for such a logically prior rule when defending continuing parliamentary legislative supremacy from the challenge posed by Jennings's account of self-embracing parliamentary legislative supremacy.[23] Wade recognised that Dicey's theory of continuing parliamentary legislative supremacy was in danger of collapsing into self-embracing parliamentary legislative supremacy, given that both Dicey and Jennings classified parliamentary legislative supremacy as a form of legal rule. Both were investigating the response of the courts to purported attempts of Parliament to entrench legislation. Both theories require that courts are bound to follow rules determining the process by which valid legislation is enacted. If courts do not adhere to this rule, then courts are in danger of failing to uphold parliamentary sovereignty, as they may recognise as valid legislation that is not enacted by the sovereign law-making institution in the correct manner required to enact valid legislation. If courts are required to adhere to this rule, then this requirement would appear to stem either from the common law, from legislation or as a matter of judicial custom.

Continuing parliamentary legislative supremacy collapses into self-embracing parliamentary legislative supremacy if the rule determining the manner in which legally valid legislation is enacted is classified as anything other than a rule of judicial conduct that does not have its source in either the common law or legislation. If we are to adhere to continuing parliamentary legislative supremacy, then this rule cannot stem from legislation, otherwise Parliament can bind its successors by using legislation to redefine the sovereign or the valid law-making process. If future parliaments were to fail to adhere to the rule establishing the procedure for enacting valid legislation, then courts would be bound to strike down such purported legislation as invalid. However, if the rule establishing the procedure through which valid legislation is enacted is part of the common law, then it is also capable of modification by statute, given that legislation overrides the common law. This is required to ensure parliamentary sovereignty.

Wade countered this argument by explaining that, although courts were bound to follow a legal rule that dictated the criteria by which courts were to recognise valid legislation, this rule was not a normal rule of the common law. Rather, it was a fundamental rule that was recognised by the common law and

---

[22] See, Wade, above n 19, at 187, who relies on Salmond and ECS Wade, in his introduction to the 9th and 10th editions of AV Dicey, above n 1, xxxviii and xli, which relies on the work of RTE Latham.

[23] Wade, above n 19, at 172.

whose existence depended on political facts.[24] Wade based his conclusion on Salmond's discussion of fundamental rules. The rule dictating the criteria that courts should use to recognise valid legislation is fundamental because it confers authority on Parliament to act. It cannot be changed by legislation as any legislation purporting to confer such a power would be assuming the very power that it was meant to confer.[25] By classifying the rule defining the sovereign law-making institution and the process by which it enacts valid legislation in this manner, continuing parliamentary legislative supremacy is preserved. Courts are bound to ensure that purported legislation adheres to the properly prescribed manner if it is to be recognised as legally valid. Thus, courts preserve the sovereignty of Parliament. However, this duty stems neither from common law nor from statute. It stems instead from a fundamental rule, the function of which is to identify what constitutes valid law in a given jurisdiction. As such, it is not capable of modification by Parliament acting alone. Although courts and Parliament are bound by this fundamental rule, they are not bound by legislation enacted by a previous Parliament. Consequently, continuing parliamentary legislative supremacy is preserved.

It is this distinction that provides the means through which to explain how Convention rights can be entrenched without violating continuing parliamentary legislative supremacy. If it is possible for the rule defining the sovereign or the procedures through which valid legislation is enacted to be changed such that valid legislation cannot contravene Convention rights, then Convention rights would be effectively entrenched. Future parliaments would be unable to enact legislation that was contrary to Convention rights, as such purported legislation would not be recognised by the courts as valid law. This entrenchment could be achieved without requiring future legislatures to be bound by earlier legislatures. All sovereign law-making institutions are bound by the rules establishing the enactment of valid legislation. However, this rule is neither created by nor modified through the sole actions of any sovereign law-making institution. Although legislatures are bound, they are bound by a logically prior rule, not by the actions of a previous legislature.

III. METHODS OF ENTRENCHMENT

This section will investigate two possible ways in which Convention rights could be entrenched without breaching continuing parliamentary legislative supremacy. In order to explain and evaluate these methods, we need first to draw three important distinctions. These distinctions help to clarify the way in which entrenchment may be possible, as well as evaluating the extent to which these methods achieve entrenchment without contravening continuing parliamentary legislative supremacy.

[24] *Ibid*, at 188.
[25] *Ibid*, at 187.

The first distinction is between rules defining the nature of the sovereign law-making institution and rules defining the way in which the sovereign must act. Rules defining the sovereign law-making institution describe the valid institution(s) that are recognised as having the power to enact valid legislation. In English law the sovereign law-making institution is the Queen in Parliament, consisting of the House of Commons, the House of Lords and the monarch. Rules explaining how the sovereign law-making body acts describe the process that the sovereign law-making institution must use if it is to enact legally valid legislation. In English law, avoiding for the moment the possible complications caused by the Parliament Acts 1911–1949, legislation is validly enacted when a measure receives the consent of the House of Commons, the House of Lords and the monarch.

The second distinction is drawn between power-conferring and duty-imposing rules. Power-conferring rules confer powers and duty-imposing rules impose duties. The rules determining the definition of the sovereign law-making institution and the procedures that it must follow to enact valid legislation can be regarded as both power-conferring and duty-imposing, depending on the perspective from which they are analysed. When assessed from the perspective of the sovereign law-making institution, these rules are power-conferring, conferring a law-making power on the legislature. Under the current provisions of the United Kingdom constitution, a power is conferred on the Queen in Parliament to enact legislation. This power may be subject to duties determining the way in which it is to be exercised. The Queen in Parliament must use the correct procedure to successfully enact legally valid legislation. When analysed from the perspective of the courts, the rule defining the sovereign law-making institution and establishing the procedures it must follow to enact valid legislation is duty-conferring. It places the courts under a duty to recognise laws passed in the correct manner by the sovereign law-making institution as legally valid. For the purpose of the United Kingdom constitution, the courts are placed under a duty to recognise laws properly passed by the Queen in Parliament as validly enacted legislation.

Thirdly, we need to distinguish between core and penumbral aspects of both the rule defining the sovereign law-making body and that establishing the procedures required to enact valid legislation. The core refers to those aspects of the rule that are sufficiently clear and precise and generally accepted. The penumbra refers to the vague periphery of the law, where it can be reasonable to disagree about the content of the law, and about how the content of the law is to be determined; where there may often be no clear legally established definition. The core definition of the sovereign law-making body in the United Kingdom constitution is the Queen in Parliament. An example of a penumbral issue arises from the enactment of the Parliament Acts 1911–1949. Do these legislative measures create two distinct sovereign law-making bodies in English law—the Queen in Parliament and the House of Commons and the monarch acting under the provisions of the Parliament Acts? Penumbral issues concerning the definition of the law-making process could arise, for example, regarding whether valid legislation has been passed if it is discovered that sufficient votes in favour of a particular statute were only obtained because some Members of Parliament walked through the 'aye' corridor more than once, thus meaning that votes were double-counted.

It will be argued that entrenchment can occur without contradicting Dicey's theory of continuing parliamentary legislative supremacy only when the rules relating to both the definition of the sovereign and the way in which the sovereign needs to act in order to pass legally valid legislation are classified as rules or standards that cannot be modified by Parliament acting alone. This is best explained through the classification of these rules as part of the rule of recognition. However, before reaching this conclusion, it is valuable to investigate a different possible method of entrenchment, both to rule this out as a possible method of entrenchment and to help to justify our conclusion.

A. Modification of Rules of Action

A possible method of entrenchment stems from Richard Ekins's analysis of the Parliament Acts 1911–1949 and the subsequent decision on the validity of the Parliament Act 1949 in *Jackson*.[26] First, Ekins argues that the Parliament Act 1911 is best understood not as a redefinition of the sovereign law-making institution, but as a change to the way in which the sovereign is obliged to act to pass valid legislation. Ekins bases this conclusion on the text of section 4 of the Parliament Act 1911, which sets out the distinctive wording used for Bills presented for the Royal Assent under the provisions of the Parliament Act. Section 4 requires that Bills must bear the following words, in order to be presented to the monarch and receive Royal Assent:

> Be it enacted by the King's most Excellent Majesty, by and with the advice and consent of the Commons in this present Parliament assembled, in accordance with the provisions of the Parliament Act, 1911, and by the authority of the same, as follows.

For Ekins, the placing of a comma after '1911' makes it clear that the 'authority' referred to in section 4 is not the authority of the Parliament Acts 1911, but rather the authority of the Queen in Parliament. Moreover, the words 'authority of the same' are also referred to in the wording used to enact statutes that do not utilise the provisions of the Parliament Acts. In this formulation 'authority of the same' is taken to refer to the authority of the Queen in Parliament to enact legislation. It would be odd, therefore, if the words 'authority of the same' were meant to refer to the authority of the Parliament Act 1911 as opposed to the authority of the Queen in Parliament when found in section 4. In addition, section 4 refers to the 'consent of the Commons in this present Parliament assembled'. Thus,

---

[26] R Ekins, 'Acts of Parliament and the Parliament Acts' (2007) 123 *Law Quarterly Review* 91.

section 4 recognises that the Commons is acting as part of Parliament, which includes the House of Lords as well as the House of Commons. These textual arguments lead Ekins to conclude both that measures passed under the Parliament Acts 1911–1949 are primary legislation and that the authority of such legislation does not derive from the Parliament Acts, but from Parliament itself. The Parliament Acts 1911–1949 do not purport to redefine Parliament, but rather to modify the way in which Parliament can act, specifically the way in which it can act to modify legislation.[27]

Secondly, having classified the Parliament Act 1911 as merely providing a mechanism by which Parliament can act, Ekins distinguishes between these rules and those defining the sovereign law-making body. Ekins argues that rules defining the sovereign law-making institution form part of the rule of recognition. He supports this conclusion by reference to the inherent jurisdiction of the Westminster Parliament. The authority of the Westminster Parliament to enact valid legislation does not derive from any legal document. As such, it stems from the rule of recognition.[28] Rules that prescribe how Parliament may act, however, are not part of the rule of recognition. They are instead part of the customs of Parliament. Although they are often referred to as legal rules, this description is inaccurate. A more accurate description is to recognise that these are non-legal rules that impose duties on the courts. Courts are required to recognise as legally valid only those measures enacted according to the proper procedures established by the customs of Parliament. This difference in classification has an impact on the way in which these rules can be modified. The rule of recognition cannot be changed by Parliament alone. The customs of Parliament can be changed by Parliament acting alone as customs are created and modified by Parliament. Parliament may adopt rules that determine the way in which Parliament must act to pass valid legislation and the Parliament Act 1911 is best understood as an example of Parliament formulating such a rule.[29]

These two steps enable Ekins to reach the conclusion that his analysis is consistent with continuing parliamentary legislative supremacy. Unlike self-embracing theories of parliamentary legislative supremacy, his theory does not assume that the definition of the sovereign law-making institution is established solely by legal rules. For Ekins, this is part of the rule of recognition and cannot be modified by Parliament alone. Ekins concludes, therefore, that his interpretation of *Jackson* does not conclude that Parliament is free to redefine itself or to bind its successors. It is merely an example of a modification of the customs of Parliament explaining how Parliament acts. Consequently, it is compatible with continuing parliamentary legislative supremacy.[30]

---

[27] R Ekins, 'Acts of Parliament and the Parliament Acts' (2007) 123 *Law Quarterly Review* 91, at 97–100.

[28] *Ibid*, at 101–2.

[29] *Ibid*, at 103–5.

[30] *Ibid*, at 108.

Ekins's interpretation of *Jackson* provides a possible means through which Convention rights could be entrenched without challenging continuing parliamentary legislative supremacy. This could occur through a modification of the procedures prescribing the way in which the sovereign law-making body acts when passing legislation. This form of modification may enable Parliament, for example, to enact a modified Human Rights Act which establishes that the consent of the House of Commons and the House of Lords is only obtained by a two-thirds majority when voting on legislation concerning the modification, repeal or amendment of Convention rights. Such a modification would be analysed by Ekins in a similar way to the provisions of the Parliament Acts 1911–49. Both regulate the way in which Parliament acts when passing legislation, albeit both prescribe how Parliament acts not in general but with regard to a specific type of legislation. If the Parliament Act 1911 succeeds in binding future Parliaments without challenging continuing parliamentary legislative supremacy, then so would our modified Human Rights Act.

There are difficulties, however, with this method of entrenchment. First, it is questionable whether this modified Human Rights Act would bind future Parliaments. Ekins's argument rests on the claim that a modification of rules of action is best understood as a modification of parliamentary custom. Consequently, it is not an example of Parliament enacting a statutory provision that binds its successors. Nevertheless, the courts would have to recognise legislation passed under the Parliament Acts 1911–1949 as legally valid, even though its validity would depend, at least in part, on whether the provisions of the Parliament Acts had been followed. If the provisions of the Parliament Act are not adhered to, then the courts would conclude that the sovereign had not acted in the manner prescribed for enacting valid legislation. Courts would effectively hold that the later Parliament was bound to adhere to the legislation of an earlier Parliament.

Ekins argues that this would not occur, as courts have no jurisdiction to question whether Parliament had acted in the manner prescribed. The Parliament Act 1911 grants a power to the Speaker to certify that legislation has been enacted in accordance with the provisions of the Act. Section 3 of the Act ousts the jurisdiction of the court to question the validity of the Speakers' certificate. Consequently, it is beyond the jurisdiction of the court to determine whether or not a statute was enacted according to the procedure established in the Parliament Acts. Even if section 3 is insufficient to oust jurisdiction, Ekins argues that the question as to whether Parliament has followed the correct procedures when enacting legislation is not an issue to be determined by the court. Such matters are best left for Parliament.[31] A modified Human Rights Act, therefore, could bind future parliaments in practice, in that future parliaments would have to follow the procedure found in the modified Human Rights Act to enact valid legislation. However, the entrenchment that occurs is not a form of legal entrenchment. Future parliaments are not legally bound by the decisions

---

[31] *Ibid*, at 111–14.

of their predecessors as courts do not have the jurisdiction to determine the validity of the legislation in question. Future Parliaments are bound by the statute as it forms part of the agreement of the institutions of Parliament as to the rules they need to follow to ensure that they enact valid legislation. Courts merely confirm that legislation was enacted according to the proper procedures, given that Parliament certifies that this is the case and the legislation is found on the parliamentary roll.

If successful, Ekins's argument provides an ingenious means of entrenchment without challenging continuing parliamentary legislative supremacy. Although a statute setting out the way in which legislation is to be passed would bind future Parliaments, this is a form of non-legal as opposed to legal entrenchment. Courts are not empowered to assess whether Parliament has followed the correct procedure to enact valid legislation set out in the statute and, therefore, they do not have the power to question legislation. However, even if this were to succeed, it would only provide for a weak form of entrenchment. Arguments for entrenching Convention rights stem from a need to ensure that Convention rights are more difficult to overturn and often recognise the need for the court to play a role in ensuring that Convention rights are protected to a greater extent. If we were to use Ekins's arguments to provide greater protection for Convention rights, then courts would be denied this role. It would be for the Speaker of the House to determine that legislation did or did not breach Convention rights and, therefore, did or did not require a two-thirds majority to be passed, as well as determining whether this two-thirds majority had been achieved.

Not only is this form of entrenchment weak, but Ekins's argument is in danger of collapsing into an argument for self-embracing as opposed to continuing parliamentary legislative supremacy. Continuing parliamentary legislative supremacy is only maintained as courts do not have the power to assess the validity of the Speaker's certificate under section 3 of the Parliament Act 1911 and, presumably, would not have the ability to assess the validity of legislation enacted under a modified Human Rights Act, were a similar ouster clause to be included in the modified legislation. However, Ekins's argument as to the success of such an ouster clause can be challenged. His argument rests predominantly on the scope of parliamentary privilege and his claim that the regulations governing how Parliament acts are for Parliament alone to determine. However, it is hard to see how courts would be questioning proceedings in Parliament were they to ascertain whether legislation had been validly passed under the provisions of the Parliament Acts. Although the Attorney-General conceded in *Jackson* that the court did have jurisdiction to determine this issue, and hence it was not a matter for decision by the court, some of their Lordships examined the jurisdiction of the court, concluding that the court would be engaged in issues akin to statutory interpretation and hence had jurisdiction to act.[32] Such

---

[32] *R (Jackson) v Attorney-General* [2005] UKHL 56, [2006] 1 AC 262, [27] (Lord Bingham), [49]–[51] (Lord Nicholls), [110] (Lord Hope) and [169] (Lord Carswell).

jurisdiction would not breach parliamentary privilege as the court would not be looking behind the wording of Parliament or questioning how Parliament acted.[33]

A further argument in support of the jurisdiction of the court stems from the long-established power of the court to determine the validity of legislation. Such validity does not turn merely on the definition of the sovereign, but on the way in which legislation is validly enacted. The Parliament Acts do enable legislation to be passed by the Queen in Parliament without the consent of the House of Lords, but it limits the circumstances in which such legislation can be passed. Section 2(1) of the Parliament Act expressly excludes Bills to extend the life of Parliament beyond three years from its provisions. If Parliament were to use the provisions of the Parliament Acts 1911–1949 to enact legislation to extend the life of Parliament beyond five years without the consent of the House of Lords, would the courts have the power to declare that this was not valid legislation, having been enacted in breach of the provisions of section 2(1) of the Parliament Act 1911? Ekins's answer to this question would depend on whether the Speaker had endorsed the Bill or not. If so, then courts would have no power to do anything other than to recognise the legislation as valid, illustrating the weakness of any form of entrenchment achieved through the modification of the way in which Parliament passes legislation. However, it is at least arguable that the courts would have the power to strike down this legislation, on the grounds that it was not a valid statute as passed in transgression of the Parliament Act 1911. Parliament would not have the jurisdiction to enact valid legislation to extend the life of Parliament beyond five years without the consent of the House of Lords because the 1911 Act expressly excludes such legislation from its provisions. The ouster clause would not succeed to remove the jurisdiction of the court in these circumstances. The certificate of the Speaker would be considered final with regard to the determination that the monarch and the Commons had assented to the legislation and as to whether the House of Lords had failed to agree to a Bill placed before it at least twice within the same session of Parliament. However, in questioning the validity of the purported statute, courts would not be questioning the finality as to whether the monarch, the House of Lords and the House of Commons had acted in the manner proscribed by the Parliament Acts 1911–1949, but would be questioning whether Parliament had the power to enact valid legislation in this manner. In investigating this issue, the courts would not be questioning Parliament's ability to determine its own internal procedures or the manner in which it should act.

The jurisdiction of the court to examine such issues is further reinforced when we examine the Parliament Acts 1911–1949 from the perspective of the courts. The Parliament Acts 1911–1949 can be construed as placing the courts under a duty to recognise as valid those measures that satisfy the conditions of the Acts. Construed in this manner, the jurisdiction of the court to determine whether

---

[33] *Ibid*, at [27] (Lord Bingham), [49]–[50] (Lord Nicholls) and [112] (Lord Hope).

legislation is valid does not interfere with the power of Parliament to determine for itself the way in which it should act. Given these arguments in favour of the jurisdiction of the court, it is difficult to rescue Ekins's theory from collapsing into a theory of self-embracing parliamentary legislative supremacy. Without the ouster of the jurisdiction of the court, it is hard to regard the entrenchment occurring through the Parliament Acts 1911–1949 as non-legal as opposed to legal. The court would be using the provisions of the Parliament Act to determine the validity of future legislation. In effect, the Parliament Acts 1911–1949 bind future legislatures wishing to enact legislation without the consent of the House of Lords.

A possible way in which Ekins's argument could be sustained would be if the laws and customs of Parliament, which govern the way in which Parliament acts, were incapable of being modified by Parliament alone. However, it is difficult to see how this argument can be sustained, given that Ekins argues that the Parliament Acts were able to modify these laws and customs of Parliament. It would appear that the laws and customs of Parliament operate in a similar manner to conventions as non-legally binding rules. As such, just as conventions can be replaced by statutes, meaning that the source of the previous convention-based power is now said to stem from the statute, the Parliament Acts 1911–1949 would replace the power to act derived from the laws and customs of Parliament with a power derived from a statute.[34]

Ekins's argument does not provide a stable method by which Parliament could entrench Convention rights without breaching continuing parliamentary legislative supremacy. This is because it is difficult to sustain a distinct classification of rules relating to the way in which Parliaments enact legislation and rules related to other customs and laws of Parliament governing their behaviour. Also, it may be difficult for Parliament to oust the jurisdiction of the court. Even if this were successful, it would only provide for a weak form of entrenchment. The next section investigates a stronger form of possible entrenchment through modification of the rule of recognition.

B. Modification of the Rule of Recognition

The rule of recognition was developed by HLA Hart.[35] It is similar to HWR Wade's fundamental rule which prevented continuing parliamentary legislative supremacy collapsing into self-embracing parliamentary legislative supremacy. Hart recognised the similarity between his rule of recognition and the ultimate legal principles identified by Salmond and, in turn, relied on by Wade when determining the nature of the fundamental rule establishing the identity of the sovereign law-making institution.[36] Hart also refers to Wade's analysis of the

---

[34] See *ibid*, at [81] (Lord Steyn) for a similar argument.
[35] HLA Hart, *The Concept of Law*, 2nd edn (Oxford, Oxford University Press, 1994) chs 2–6.
[36] *Ibid*, at 245, and 97, fn 1.

nature of the rule identifying that courts should obey Acts of Parliament, when discussing the nature of the rule of recognition and its classification as a political fact.[37] Hart's rule of recognition shares many characteristics of the logically prior rules of RTE Latham, which included rules regarding the authenticity of law, rules of succession, rules of procedure regarding the making of law and rules regarding the modification of these three rules.[38] It is also regarded as a logical pre-requisite of a legal system. Consequently, the logical pre-requisite describing the sovereign law-making institution and the procedures that it must use to enact valid legislation required by continuing parliamentary legislative supremacy could be found in Hart's rule of recognition. In particular, both Hart's rule of recognition and Wade's fundamental rule establish the criteria of validity of all forms of law, including legislation, and have a dual nature, being classified as a rule of the legal system and a political fact.

It is the dual nature of the rule of recognition as a political fact and a rule of the legal system[39] that explains why its modification may entrench substantive provisions, without contravening continuing parliamentary legislative supremacy. As a rule of the legal system, courts are bound to adhere to its provisions. Consequently the sovereignty of Parliament is preserved, as courts only recognise as valid those legislative measures passed by the sovereign law-making institution in the prescribed manner. Legal decisions help determine the content of the rule of recognition. The rule of recognition is characterised as a political fact as by asserting that the rule of recognition exists, we are asserting a fact about how law is identified in a particular system. Its existence is determined through an identification of shared practices used by legal officials that recognise purported legal rules as valid rules of a particular legal system. The statement describing the content of the rule of recognition is an 'external statement'. It can be made by an observer, observing the practises of those operating within a particular legal system and describing the criteria used to identify valid law. It requires no approval of such criteria.[40] In order for the rule of recognition to perform its function, determining what counts as law within a particular legal system, the officials of the system must regard the content of the rule of recognition 'as common standards of official behaviour and appraise critically their own and each other's deviations as lapses'.[41] In this sense, officials of the system accept the content of the rule of recognition, accepting it as providing the criteria by which valid law is identified. This acceptance need not be based on an acceptance of the moral

---

[37] *Ibid*, at 108, including fns, and 247.

[38] See, RTE Latham, 'The Law and the Commonwealth' in WK Hancock (ed), *Survey of British Commonwealth Affairs* Vol 1, *Problems of Nationality 1918–1936* (Oxford, Oxford University Press, 1937) 510–630; P Oliver 'Law, Politics, the Commonwealth and the Constitution: Remembering RTE Latham, 1909–1943' (2000) *King's College Law Journal* 153 and P Oliver, *The Constitution of Independence* (New York, Oxford University Press, 2005) 85–92.

[39] As a rule within the legal system, the rule of recognition creates duties for the judiciary. However, it is not a rule of law in the same sense as a statute or provisions of the common law. If it were, it would determine its own validity. It is probably best understood as a judicial custom.

[40] Hart, above n 35, at 107–8.

[41] *Ibid*, at 113.

validity of the rule of recognition. Nor does it require a complete justification according to a deep theory of values. It does require, however, that it be accepted as an appropriate means by which to identify legally valid rules, such that those who fail to use the proper criteria of the rule of recognition can be validity criticised.

Modification of the rule of recognition cannot be achieved by Parliament acting alone. It is only achieved where at least some of the officials in the legal system accept a change in its content. Even if the criteria used to identify valid law were included in a statute, this,

> would not reduce [the rule of recognition] to the level of a statute; for the legal status of such an enactment necessarily would depend on the fact that the rule existed antecedently to and independently of the enactment.[42]

Consequently, even if the current Parliament were to enact legislation to the effect that Acts of Parliament that did not comply with Convention rights were legally invalid, it would neither reduce the rule of recognition to a statute, nor modify the rule of recognition. Unless the officials in the system accepted this change in the rule of recognition—ie they regarded it as 'right' to identify the law according to these new criteria and as 'wrong' to identify the law in any other manner—the rule of recognition would not change.[43] It follows, therefore, that a change in the rule of recognition, even if prompted by a statute, does not require future parliaments to be bound by previous parliaments. Future parliaments are bound through the actions of officials in the legal system—when Members of Parliament, the courts and the officials administering the legal system accept a change in the rule of recognition—not just by the actions of Parliament alone. If officials did not accept the change to the rule of recognition initiated by statutory enactment, then this change would not succeed.

Entrenchment of Convention rights, therefore, could occur if the rule of recognition were to be modified, such that legislation that contravened Convention rights would not be regarded as legally valid legislation. However, there are three possible difficulties in the use of the rule of recognition to entrench Convention rights. The first arises from Hart's description of the rule of recognition as consisting both of a single rule and of a series of criteria.[44] This restricts the scope of entrenchment. It is only a modification of the 'supreme criterion' of the rule of recognition that would succeed in entrenching Convention rights without contravening continuing parliamentary legislative supremacy. Secondly, Hart recognised that the rule of recognition itself had a core and

---

[42] Hart, above n 35, at 108.

[43] It is hard to determine how many officials of the legal system need to accept a change in the rule of recognition for this change to occur. The precise number may depend on the circumstances surrounding a purported modification to the rule of recognition.

[44] See, eg the conclusions of K Greenawalt in his pursuit of the rule of recognition for the US legal system in 'The Rule of Recognition and the Constitution' (1986–1987) 85 *Michigan Law Review* 621.

penumbra of application.[45] Although modification of the core of the rule of recognition requires acceptance by officials in the legal system, modification of the penumbra can be achieved by the courts alone without the need to observe the conduct of other officials in the legal system to determine how they would resolve a penumbral issue as to the content of the rule of recognition. Consequently, entrenchment of Convention rights would require a modification of the core meaning of the rule of recognition if it is to occur without an ensuing danger of contravening continuing parliamentary legislative supremacy. Thirdly, due to the connection drawn between the rule of recognition and continuing parliamentary legislative supremacy, it may be difficult in practice to modify the rule of recognition without this also being interpreted as a modification of the theory of parliamentary legislative supremacy, shifting from continuing to self-embracing parliamentary legislative supremacy.

(i) Modification of the Supreme Criterion

Hart asserts that it is usual for the rule of recognition to contain 'several criteria, ranked in order of relative subordination and primacy' where one of these criteria is 'supreme'.[46] A criterion is supreme:

> if rules identified by reference to it are still recognised as rules of the system, even if they conflict with rules identified by reference to the other criteria, whereas rules identified by reference to the latter are not so recognised if they conflict with the rules identified by reference to the supreme criterion.[47]

There is, therefore, a hierarchical relationship between the supreme criterion and other criteria of the rule of recognition. Entrenchment will only occur where there is modification of the supreme criterion of the rule of recognition. If the need for compliance with Convention rights is recognised as a minor criterion of the rule of recognition, then legislation complying with the supreme criterion of the rule of recognition will still be recognised as valid even when it failed to comply with Convention rights.

This would appear to pose a problem for the entrenchment of Convention rights through the modification of the rule of recognition. Hart states that only one of the criteria of the rule of recognition is supreme.[48] It would appear odd for this criterion of our modified rule of recognition to be the compliance of legislation with Convention rights. If this were the case it would mean that, for example, Acts of Parliament that did not comply with Convention rights would not be recognised as valid law, but that resolutions of the House of Commons

---

[45] Hart, above n 35, at 119–20. Issues surrounding the core and penumbral meanings of the rule of recognition are discussed by P Oliver in 'Sovereignty in the Twenty-First Century' (2003) 14 *King's College Law Journal*, 137, 152–54.

[46] Hart, *ibid*, at 102.

[47] *Ibid*, at 103.

[48] *Ibid*, at 102.

which did comply with Convention rights, but which had not received approval by the House of Lords or the monarch, would be recognised as valid law. However, despite restricting superiority to one criterion of the rule of recognition, Hart argues that 'the formula "Whatever the Queen in Parliament enacts is law" . . . is accepted as an ultimate criterion for the identification of law'.[49] Although one criterion is expressed, it consists of different components—enactments by the Queen in Parliament require the agreement of the Commons, Lords and the monarch, or the Commons and monarch acting alone according to the provisions of the Parliament Acts 1911–49. It is theoretically possible, therefore, for the supreme criterion of the rule of recognition to be modified to include a further component—the compliance with Convention rights.

(ii) Core and Penumbra

Hart also claimed that the rule of recognition may be open-textured. Although possessing a clear core meaning there may be dispute at the penumbra surrounding whether a criterion is part of the rule of recognition. The core of the rule of recognition changes when officials in the legal system accept a modification to the content of the rule of recognition—officials are now criticised for failing to adhere to the new as opposed to the old rule of recognition. Consequently, entrenchment through modification of the core elements of the rule of recognition would not contravene continuing parliamentary legislative supremacy. Doubts surrounding the penumbra of the rule of recognition, however, are resolved through the actions of a person having sufficient authority to decide this issue—namely the courts.[50] However, if the courts decide this issue by merely examining provisions of the common law, without also ascertaining political reality through an analysis of the conduct of other officials in the legal system, then entrenchment through modification of the rule of recognition is in danger of collapsing into self-embracing parliamentary legislative supremacy. If courts can decide penumbral issues of the rule of recognition by merely modifying provisions of the common law, then it is possible that the legislature may also resolve these issues through statutory provisions, which override the common law. Were this to occur, Parliament would bind its successors, in contravention of continuing parliamentary legislative supremacy.

It is possible to argue that a dispute surrounding whether Convention-compatibility is a criterion of the validity of legislation is part of the penumbra of the rule of recognition. Indeed, the enactment of the Human Rights Act 1998 itself may be interpreted as creating or highlighting this issue. Although it is clear from the provisions of the Act that it does not require Convention-compatibility as a condition of legality, it has been interpreted as a constitutional statute.[51] It could also be regarded as marking a potential shift away from

---

[49] Hart, above n 35, at 145.
[50] *Ibid*, at 145–8.
[51] *Thoburn v Sunderland City Council* [2002] EWHC 195 (Admin), [2003] 1 QB 151.

the doctrine of continuing parliamentary legislative supremacy towards the establishment of a rights culture, limiting democracy and the sovereignty of Parliament.

This difficulty, however, is best understood as posing practical as opposed to conceptual problems. Courts are able to resolve complexities surrounding the penumbra of the rule of recognition because courts are the institution possessing the inherent authority to resolve these difficulties. However, it does not follow from this that the courts decide such issues merely by examining principles of the common law.[52] Therefore, it does not follow that legislation, which overrides the common law, could be used to overturn the resolution of the courts. It may well depend on how the courts react to such legislation. Even if Parliament were to resolve penumbral issues through the enactment of legislation, if Parliament is not deemed to have the authority to resolve such issues, it is open to the courts to reach an alternative authoritative resolution.

It can, however, be difficult to distinguish between a modification of the rule of recognition and a modification of the common law.[53] The difference occurs in the sources used by the courts to resolve the scope of the rule of recognition and of the authority of their resolution. When assessing the common law, courts examine legal sources, exercising a choice when legal sources fail to provide an answer. When ascertaining the scope of the rule of recognition, courts turn to political as well as legal sources, basing their authoritative choice on both political and legal facts.[54] In addition, when ascertaining the scope of the common law, the decision of the judiciary obtains its authority through the inherent jurisdiction of the court to determine the common law. The courts are the final arbiters of the scope of the common law. When ascertaining the scope of the rule of recognition, courts gain their authority through the acceptance of their conclusions—their authority derives from the success of their determinations.[55] Modification to both a core and penumbral element of the rule of recognition can provide for entrenchment that does not challenge continuing parliamentary legislative supremacy.

(iii) Rule of Recognition and Parliamentary Legislative Supremacy

Hart argues that 'the principle that no earlier Parliament can preclude its "successors" from repealing its legislation constitutes part of the ultimate rule of recognition used by the courts in identifying valid rules of law'.[56] Moreover, he considers that indeterminacies exist as to the rule of parliamentary sovereignty, citing as an example the issue as to whether Parliament would be allowed to

[52] But see Oliver, above n 45.
[53] This is recognised by Hart himself: Hart, above n 35, at 149.
[54] See, NW Barber, 'Sovereignty Re-examined; the Courts, Parliament and Statutes' (2000) 20 *Oxford Journal of Legal Studies* 131.
[55] Hart, above n 35, at 149.
[56] *Ibid*, at 145.

bind its successors as to manner and form. As a peripheral issue, its resolution would be determined by an authoritative choice made by the courts.[57] This poses difficulties for the entrenchment of Convention rights through a modification of the rule of recognition. If Convention rights are to be entrenched in this manner, the entrenchment will become effective when a court decision recognises that the rule of recognition has changed so as to entrench Convention rights. However, this decision may also be interpreted as a shift in the nature of parliamentary legislative supremacy. A decision of the court overturning legislation that contravened Convention rights could also be interpreted as a move from continuing to self-embracing parliamentary legislative supremacy. This is particularly pertinent given that a redefinition of valid legal sources can also be interpreted as a modification of the manner and form in which legislation is passed.[58] The difficulty arises, therefore, as to whether a modification of the supreme criterion of the rule of recognition to entrench Convention rights could take place without this also being recognised as a contravention of continuing parliamentary legislative supremacy.

The problem is illustrated by Wade's analysis of the *Factortame* litigation. Wade regards *Factortame II* as a judicial recognition, or creation, of a change in the fundamental constitutional rule determining the criteria used by the courts to recognise valid legislation. He argues that, prior to *Factortame II*, Parliament could not bind its successors. Post *Factortame II*, however, Parliament can now bind its successors, as it did through the 1972 European Communities Act which imposed restrictions on the 1988 Merchant Shipping Act. The provisions of the 1972 Act can only be overturned by express and not by implied repeal, imposing a specific manner and form requirement that binds future Parliaments. These restrictions could not be achieved within the constitutional arrangements prevalent at the time—ie those of continuing parliamentary legislative supremacy. Consequently, for Wade, the decision must mark a revolution, albeit a technical legal revolution. The courts have broken the line of continuing parliamentary legislative supremacy and have shifted to self-embracing parliamentary legislative supremacy.[59]

Neil McCormick offers an alternative explanation of *Factortame* which may resolve this difficulty. His explanation is based on the distinction between analysing the rule defining the sovereign as a duty-imposing rule, requiring the court to recognise as valid legislation that is enacted by the sovereign law-maker, or as a power-conferring rule, conferring powers on the sovereign law-making body to enact valid legislation. McCormick refers to the duty-imposing rule as the rule of recognition and the power-conferring rule as a rule of change.

---

[57] Hart, above n 35, at 146–8.

[58] See discussion above and P Mirfield, 'Can the House of Lords be Lawfully Abolished?' (1979) 95 *Law Quarterly Review* 36, 38–9.

[59] *Ibid.* See, N McCormick *Questioning Sovereignty: Law, State and Nation in the European Commonwealth* (Oxford, Oxford University Press, 1999) 80–81 and P Oliver, above n 38, at 301–02.

According to McCormick, Wade's analysis of *Factortame* conflates these two perspectives. Wade describes continuing parliamentary legislative supremacy in terms of the powers of the Westminster Parliament. It has the power to make laws on any subject, save that it cannot legislate to bind its successors. McCormick argues that this also entails that Parliament cannot enact laws that derogate from continuing parliamentary legislative supremacy. It is not only the case that a law purporting to bind its successors will not achieve its objective— its provisions being subject to the doctrine of implied repeal—but also that Parliament has no power to act in this manner.[60] McCormick classifies this rule as a rule of change—a rule regarding the (dis)ability of Parliament to change law. Hart, however, focused on a different aspect of the doctrine of sovereignty when he expressed his rule of recognition that 'whatever the Queen in Parliament enacts is law'.[61] This is a rule of recognition as it focuses on the issue of how we recognise valid law, it does not concern the powers of the legislature.[62]

McCormick uses the distinction between rules of change and rules of recognition to transform the issue facing Wade, challenging the idea that *Factortame* marks a legal revolution. The question now becomes one of ascertaining the scope of the rule of change: did Parliament have the power to modify the rule of recognition? The doctrine of continuing parliamentary legislative supremacy grants to Parliament the power to make law on any subject matter that it required, including the power to modify the rule of recognition, provided that it did not purport to bind future Parliaments when doing so. McCormick argues that the European Communities Act 1972 can be interpreted as marking a change in the rule of recognition, both with regard to recognising a new source of law—directly effective European Community law—and by changing the rules of priority between different valid sources of law, as directly effective European Community law overrides national law. However, the European Communities Act does not bind future Parliaments. Future Parliaments can also change the rule of recognition, provided that they do so expressly.[63]

McCormick's interpretation of *Factortame* does enable entrenchment, but it does so at the cost of a partial challenge to the doctrine of continuing parliamentary legislative supremacy. The continuing nature of parliamentary legislative supremacy is not challenged when analysed from the perspective of the rule of change, arguably the interpretation predominantly in focus in the work of Dicey. Parliament has only changed the rule of recognition. This change does not bind a future Parliament's law-making powers; it retains the ability to further modify the rule of recognition. Consequently, parliamentary legislative supremacy remains continuing as opposed to self-embracing. However, a shift has occurred when analysed from the perspective of the rule of recognition. Courts are under a duty to accept as valid only those laws that are recognised as

---

[60] McCormick, *ibid*, at 83.
[61] Hart, above n 35, at 148.
[62] McCormick, above n 59, at 84–6.
[63] *Ibid*, at 88–9.

legally valid by the rule of recognition, ie those statutes that are compatible with directly effective European Community law, unless the statute is such as to purport to require a shift in the rule of recognition no longer requiring compliance with the provisions of directly effective European Community law, which can only be achieved by express provisions. Parliament is binding its successors as to the manner and form required to change the rule of recognition. However, it still requires a shift in the nature of parliamentary legislative supremacy. Parliament is bound as to the manner and form of legislation altering the rule of recognition.[64]

A better answer to Wade's conundrum is to recognise that Parliament does not have the power to modify the rule of recognition acting alone. A statute provides an illustration of the wishes of the legislature. It may provide factual evidence of the desire of one section of the officials of the legal system, or at least members of this section of officials, to change the rule of recognition, but it cannot change the rule of recognition in and of itself. A change in the rule of recognition requires acceptance by officials representing different types of officials within the system—ie the legislature, the judiciary and those that police or administer the law. Although courts are in the position to make an authoritative legal declaration as to the content of the rule of recognition, the legal decision only succeeds in changing the rule of recognition if it is accepted. Courts examine political facts to determine the content of the rule of recognition, and can take statutory pronouncements into account in ascertaining these political facts. In the same manner, the pronouncement of the court is itself also, at the same time, a political fact to be taken into account regarding the nature of parliamentary legislative supremacy. This may occur through a process of evolution, showing evidence of a gradual change in the practice of the officials of the legal system.

(iv) Practical Problems

It is possible to entrench Convention rights through a modification of the rule of recognition. However, entrenchment in this manner faces a plethora of practical difficulties. Its success depends on our interpretation of the constitutional significance of the actions of Parliament and the courts, particularly when a purported modification of the rule of recognition is prompted by legislation. These difficulties can be aptly illustrated through emerging interpretations of the constitutional significance of the Parliament Acts 1911–1949 following the seminal House of Lords decision of *Jackson*.

Jackson concerned the validity of the Hunting Act 2004, a statute that banned hunting with dogs and hare-chasing. The Hunting Act had been passed under the provisions of the Parliament Act 1911, as amended by the Parliament Act

---

[64] For an excellent discussion of McCormick, particularly regarding its application to the Commonwealth, see P Oliver, above n 45, at 301–14.

1949, following the refusal of the House of Lords to assent to the Bill proposed by the House of Commons. It was argued that the Parliament Act 1949 was invalid, having been enacted without the consent of the House of Lords following the procedure established in the Parliament Act 1911. All nine of their Lordships agreed that the Parliament Act 1949 and therefore the Hunting Act 2004, was validly enacted legislation. In reaching this conclusion, all of their Lordships agreed that legislation enacted under the provisions of the Parliament Acts was primary legislation. In addition, there was unanimous agreement that legislation to extend the life of Parliament beyond five years could not be enacted under the Parliament Acts procedure without also including within the Bill a provision for the amendment of section 2 of the Parliament Act 1911.

These two conclusions pose a paradox for continuing parliamentary legislative supremacy, as they imply that section 2 of the Parliament Act 1911 cannot be repealed by implication but must be expressly repealed. Continuing parliamentary legislative supremacy would dictate that later legislation passed under the provisions of the Parliament Act to extend the life of Parliament beyond five years would in and of itself repeal section 2 of the Parliament Act 1911. One possible explanation of the conclusion is that enactment of the Parliament Act 1911 prompted a change in the rule of recognition. Although the statute in and of itself could not change the rule of recognition, its enactment could be taken to indicate an acceptance by Parliament of a change to the manner in which legislation is passed. This change could then also be accepted by other officials in the system, who would recognise legislation passed under the Parliament Acts procedure as valid legislation. The acceptance by Parliament and the courts would then be recognised as a shift in political fact—marking a change to the rule of recognition.

Statements by Lord Hope and Lord Nicholls lend credence to this possible interpretation of *Jackson*. Lord Hope referred to Hart's concept of the rule of recognition,[65] and concluded that parliamentary sovereignty was ultimately based on a political fact.[66] In addition, he assessed the validity of the Parliament Act 1949 at least in part due to the fact that the Act had been used and relied on both by Parliament and the courts. Lord Hope also remarked that it was not possible to conclude that the Parliament Act 1911 redefined law as such a conclusion was contrary to parliamentary legislative supremacy.[67] Lord Nicholls also concluded that the validity of the Parliament Act 1949 rested at least in part on the fact that Parliament had used the provisions of the Parliament Acts to enact further legislation and that such legislation had not been challenged by the courts.[68]

However, the fact that indirect support for the claim that the Parliament Acts 1911–1949 prompted a shift in the rule of recognition can only be found in two

[65] *R (Jackson) v Attorney-General* [2005] UKHL 56, [2006] 1 AC 262, [126] and [128].
[66] *Ibid*, at [120].
[67] *Ibid*, at [113].
[68] *Ibid*, at [67]–[69].

out of the nine judgments in *Jackson* illustrates that, although possible, it is neither the only nor necessarily the most attractive interpretation of the decision. This interpretation was expressly rejected by Lord Steyn,[69] who preferred to reach his conclusion by using self-embracing as opposed to continuing parliamentary legislative supremacy.[70] Baroness Hale also argued in favour of self-embracing as opposed to continuing parliamentary legislative supremacy.[71] Their judgments, moreover, are a much stronger endorsement of self-embracing parliamentary legislative supremacy than the indirect endorsement of an approach based on a modification of the rule of recognition found in the judgments of Lord Hope and Lord Nicholls.

Ekins also criticises the assessment of *Jackson* as marking a shift in the rule of recognition. Although he recognises that such a shift is possible, he argues that this did not take place as the current definition of the rule of recognition only extends to the definition of the sovereign law-making authority and does not include reference to the manner in which the sovereign law-making authority must act in order to ensure that its actions are recognised by the courts as validly enacted legislation. However, it is difficult to know how Ekins reaches this conclusion as to the nature of the rule of recognition. It is true that Hart refers to the content of the rule of recognition as including the simple statement that 'whatever the Queen in Parliament enacts is valid legislation'; but it is important to recognise that Hart later recognises that he is referring here to the ultimate criterion of the rule of recognition and that he is aiming to give as simple a picture as possible of how this may be expressed within the United Kingdom.[72] In reality, it is far more complicated to precisely delineate the content of the rule of recognition.

Despite these difficulties, examples can be provided where it is clearer to identify a successful modification of the rule of recognition. One such example is *Madzimbamuto v Lardner-Burke*.[73] Following the unilateral declaration of independence of Rhodesia, the Appellate Division of the High Court of Southern Rhodesia and later the Privy Council had to choose between two competing claims to sovereign power: that of the authorities of southern Rhodesia and that of the United Kingdom. In choosing between these two claims to sovereign authority, the courts were also choosing between two different ultimate criteria of the rule of recognition. It is easier to interpret this case as one where the courts choose either to change or retain the ultimate criterion of the rule of recognition as such a shift is accompanied by a purported change in political sovereignty. It indicates a revolution in more than the technical legal sense implied by Wade. This does not mean, however, that the rule of recognition can change only when political sovereignty changes. It merely illustrates that it may

---

[69] *R (Jackson) v Attorney-General* [2005] UKHL 56, [2006] 1 AC 262, at [99].
[70] *Ibid*, at [81]–[86].
[71] *Ibid*, at [160]–[66].
[72] Hart, n 35, at 104 and 117.
[73] [1969] 1 AC 645 (PC).

be easier to identify changes in the rule of recognition that derive from changes in political sovereignty.

IV. CONCLUSION

This chapter has examined the distinction between continuing and self-embracing parliamentary legislative supremacy. It has concluded that the distinction does not depend on the *possibility*, but on the *method* of entrenchment. Self-embracing theories of parliamentary legislative supremacy enable future Parliaments to bind their successors as to the manner and form of legislation. As such, Parliaments enjoying self-embracing parliamentary legislative supremacy can entrench legislative provisions merely by enacting legislation. Continuing parliamentary legislative supremacy does not allow Parliament to bind its successors as to the manner and form of legislation. This does not mean that it is impossible for entrenchment to occur in legal systems that have a principle of continuing parliamentary legislative supremacy. It merely means that this entrenchment cannot occur through the actions of Parliament alone.

We have argued that one of the ways in which this could be achieved is through a modification of the rule of recognition. A modification of the core meaning of the supreme criterion of the rule of recognition only occurs when officials in the legal system accept such a change. If the rule of recognition were to change, such that legislation were not recognised as legally valid unless it complied with Convention rights, this may succeed in entrenching Convention rights without contravening continuing parliamentary legislative supremacy. However, entrenchment in this manner is difficult to achieve in practice. In particular, it may be hard to distinguish the facts interpreted as instituting a shift in the rule of recognition from those used to indicate a change from continuing to self-embracing parliamentary legislative supremacy. Consequently, entrenchment may be difficult to achieve in practice.

4

Democracy and Rights

THIS BOOK HAS argued that it could be possible for the Human Rights Act to provide a stronger protection of Convention rights than is currently provided, without contravening continuing parliamentary legislative supremacy. First, an entrenchment effect may occur, given the narrow scope of the doctrine of implied repeal and the way in which later statues can be interpreted to remove an apparent conflict with an earlier statute. Secondly, Convention rights could be entrenched through a modification of the rule of recognition. Both methods, in theory at least, can be achieved without contravening continuing parliamentary legislative supremacy. However, entrenchment may be difficult to achieve in practice. In particular, it may be hard to entrench Convention rights through a modification in the rule of recognition. The facts that could be used to support a change in the rule of recognition may also be interpreted as evidence of a shift from continuing to self-embracing parliamentary legislative supremacy. These conclusions call into question the assumption that the Human Rights Act could not entrench Convention rights because of the need to uphold continuing parliamentary legislative supremacy.

There are two possible responses to this argument. First, it could be argued that the Human Rights Act should be modified in order to entrench Convention rights. Secondly, it could be argued that the Human Rights Act should be preserved, as it has value above and beyond its assumed ability to preserve continuing parliamentary legislative supremacy. The following chapters will argue that the current protection of Convention rights found in the Human Rights Act can be justified. It rests on the claim that the Human Rights Act provides a democratic dialogue model of rights protections. As such, it aims to balance the competing claims of the protection of human rights and the preservation of democracy.

In order to justify this conclusion, we will first return to Dicey's theory of continuing parliamentary legislative supremacy and the way in which Dicey appeared to be prepared to modify his theory. This account illustrates the way in which Dicey also recognised the need to balance rights and democracy, although perhaps drawing the balance in a different way from that found in the Human Rights Act. We will then analyse the arguments used both to support and reject a strong protection of rights, illustrating the way in which these

arguments rely, at least in part, on a conflict between the preservation of democracy and the protection of rights. The aim of this chapter is not to subject these
arguments to critical analysis, but to set out the main contours of the debate, to
be used in later chapters to find a model of interpreting the democratic dialogue
established in the Human Rights Act that responds to this debate, finding a
balance between rights and democracy.

I. DICEY AND DEMOCRACY

It is difficult to discern Dicey's precise justification for the legal principle of continuing parliamentary legislative supremacy. First, Dicey's main concern was to
assert the existence of continuing parliamentary legislative supremacy as a legal
fact as opposed to providing a political conception of sovereignty, justifying
vesting sovereignty in a particular institution. It can be harder, therefore, to
piece together his political theory of sovereignty. Secondly, it would appear that
Dicey's conception of and justification for continuing parliamentary legislative
supremacy changed in his later writings from the conception proposed in *The
Law of the Constitution*. Despite these difficulties, it is clear that Dicey based his
justification of continuing parliamentary legislative supremacy on its ability to
preserve democracy.

We can discern the connection drawn by Dicey between continuing parliamentary legislative supremacy and democracy in *An Introduction to the Study
of the Law of the Constitution*. Although Parliament faces no legal limits to the
legislation it can enact, it faces internal and external restrictions, both of which
work to preserve democracy. External limits placed on the Queen in Parliament
stem from the will of the electorate. Legislation passed by the legal sovereign is
'limited on every side by the possibility of popular resistance'.[1] Dicey argued, for
example, that it would be impossible for Parliament to enact legislation to pro-
long the life of Parliament, or to deprive electors of their vote or to engage in
'reactionary legislation'.[2] Although it would be legally possible for Parliament
to enact such legislation, the reaction of the electorate makes it impossible in
practice for Parliament to legislate in this manner. Internal limits stem from the
character of the sovereign itself. Even a tyrannical despot will have some limits
that his own character places on the legislation he is willing to enact—even
though others might consider these limits to be few and far between.

For Dicey, the special role of representative government was to ensure that
the internal and external limits placed on the sovereign law-making body were
coterminous. The sovereign law-maker, through its very composition, would
not wish to enact legislation that would meet with popular resistance.[3]

---

[1] AV Dicey, *An Introduction to the Study of the Law of the Constitution*, 10th edn (London,
Macmillan, 1959) 79.
[2] *Ibid.*
[3] *Ibid*, at 82–5.

Presumably to do so would lead to the electorate expressing its will through general elections to change the composition of the House of Commons to ensure that its will was better met by a differently-composed sovereign law-making institution. In this manner, Dicey was able to conclude that the,

> will of the electors shall by regular and constitutional means always in the end assert itself as the predominant influence in the country.[4]

Regular means existed as the House of Commons faced regular elections where the electorate was able to express its will regarding its composition. Constitutional means followed from the legal principle of continuing parliamentary legislative supremacy. Continuing parliamentary legislative supremacy ensures that legislation of constitutional importance can be modified in the same manner as other types of legislation. Consequently, general elections would provide the electorate with the opportunity to react to constitutional as well as other examples of legislation enacted by Parliament. The electorate would also have the ability to debate potential constitutional as well as legal reforms.[5]

The legal principle of continuing parliamentary legislative supremacy requires the courts to recognise the Queen in Parliament as the legislative sovereign, enjoying a law-making power unrestricted by legal limits. In doing so, it ensures that the limits over the sovereign law-making institution stem purely from internal and external political limits. The effect of these limits is to ensure that the law-making body does not legislate in a manner that would provoke popular resistance. The implication being that the House of Commons, as a democratically representative body, was better able to discern the will of the electorate than the courts, thus providing a better protection of democracy.[6] Dicey's account of the way in which continuing parliamentary legislative supremacy promotes democracy rests on an account of the United Kingdom constitution as a self-correcting unitary democracy. It is unitary as the United Kingdom is not a federal state. It is self-correcting due to its representative nature, helping to maintain the correlation between the internal and external limits placed on the sovereign law-making institution.[7]

Dicey's justification of continuing parliamentary legislative supremacy relies on an analysis of political facts. Continuing parliamentary legislative supremacy only preserves democracy to the extent that the political system works to ensure that the internal and external limits placed on the sovereign law-making body are identical, ensuring that the will of the electorate is adhered to. This places the legal principle of continuing parliamentary legislative supremacy on shaky foundations. First, Dicey's account can be attacked from a factual perspective. Is it really the case that there exists means which ensure that representative

---

[4] *Ibid.*

[5] *Ibid*, at 73, fn 1.

[6] *Ibid*, at 74.

[7] PP Craig, *Public Law and Democracy in the United Kingdom and the United States of America* (Oxford, Clarendon Press, 1990) ch 2.

democracy guarantees that legislation enacted by the Westminster Parliament is coterminous with the wishes of the electorate? Secondly, Dicey's theory fails to provide a deeper justification for the adoption of the model of a self-correcting unitary democracy, leaving the preference for this model open to further criticism. Is it really the case that the will of the electorate should prevail over other possible legal restrictions that could be placed on the power of the electorate, particularly those designed to protect human rights? These weaknesses were recognised by Dicey and his response to these criticisms help to explain, in part, Dicey's later divergence from the conception of sovereignty promoted in *An Introduction to the Study of the Law of the Constitution*, as well as providing further insight into his political justification for the legal principle of continuing parliamentary legislative supremacy.

A. Factual Accuracy

Dicey's account of the correlation between internal and external limits placed on Parliament can be criticised both as to its accuracy at the time of writing and as to its ability to provide an accurate account of the current working of the United Kingdom's constitution. Paul Craig provides an excellent account of these criticisms, focusing in particular on the way in which the development of party-politics restricted the ability of a representative democracy to ensure that the internal and external limits placed on Parliament were coterminous. As political parties developed, power transferred from Parliament to the executive. Members of Parliament became more concerned with ensuring they represented the wishes of the party than those of the electorate. Hence, it became more likely that legislation could be passed that did not represent the wishes of the people. This legislation, once passed, could remain on the statute books for a considerable time, further separating the will of Parliament, expressed in legislation, from the will of the electorate.[8]

Craig argues that Dicey was unaware of these developments, although they were recognised by political commentators contemporaneous to Dicey.[9] However, although Dicey did not mention the influence of party politics in *An Introduction to the Study of the Law of the Constitution*, he did incorporate these criticisms in his later work.[10] Dicey was critical of 'parliamentarianism'

---

[8] PP Craig, *Public Law and Democracy in the United Kingdom and the United States of America* (Oxford, Clarendon Press, 1990) ch 2, at 39–43.

[9] *Ibid*, at 43–7.

[10] AV Dicey 'Democracy in Switzerland' (1890) 113 *Edinburgh Review* 113, 143–5; 'Ought the Referendum to be Introduced in to England?' (1890) 57 *Contemporary Review* 489, 501–2 and 507–09; 'The Referendum' (1894) 23 *The National Review* 65, 65–8 and 70–72; 'Will the Form of Parliamentary Government be Permanent?' (1899) 13 *Harvard Law Review* 67, 77–9; 'The Referendum and its Critics' (1910) 212 *Quarterly Review* 538, 539–54 and *Introduction to the Study of the Law of the Constitution*, 8th edn (London, Macmillan, 1915) xci-ii and c. Further evidence is found in Dicey's lectures, the notes for which are held in the archives of the Codrington Library, All Souls College, Oxford.

deriving from the party system. He argued that 'the artificial supremacy of a Parliamentary majority, occasionally at any rate, deprives large minorities of their due political influence'.[11] Thus, he recognised that party politics may divorce the internal limits placed on Parliament from the will of the electorate. The recognition of 'parliamentarianism' was at least a partial influence on Dicey's later avocation of referenda. A referendum operates in a different manner from a general election, requiring voters to focus on issues as opposed to persons or policies. In addition, those who would not vote in a general election, either because they were unable to find a Member of Parliament who best represented their wishes or because they were part of a minority in a constituency with a large majority in favour of a particular political party, would feel empowered to vote on an issue arising in a referendum where votes on a particular issue were calculated on a national basis. The referendum was a better means of communicating the wishes of the electorate, such that:

> Even party managers and wire-pullers will be forced to remember that they owe obedience to the will of the country when the nation on a critical occasion utters with its own voice its undoubted command.[12]

Dicey's recognition of the potential factual inaccuracy of a correlation between the internal and external limits on Parliament undermines his justification for continuing parliamentary legislative supremacy as a political principle. Moreover, it has given rise to the accusation that Dicey himself was not Diceyan. This is based on the argument that Dicey modified his account of sovereignty in his later work, advocating entrenchment in breach of continuing parliamentary legislative supremacy.[13] When supporting the adoption of the referendum in England, Dicey agreed that this could be achieved through different mechanisms, including the passing of a Referendum Act. In particular, Dicey argued for the inclusion of a clause in his proposed Referendum Act to the effect that statutory provisions which 'repealed, changed, added to or otherwise affected' provisions of the highest constitutional importance should not become law unless approved by the electorate at a referendum and, moreover, that any Bill purporting to affect such changes which had not followed a referendum should be 'held invalid by every court of law'.[14] Dicey proposed that the Act of Settlement, the Union of Scotland Act 1707, the Union with Ireland Act 1808 the various Parliamentary Reform Acts and the proposed Referendum Act itself be counted as those provisions requiring a referendum were they to be altered in any manner.

Dicey's proposed Referendum Act challenges continuing parliamentary legislative supremacy in a manner similar to the challenge posed by section 19 of the Human Rights Act and the provisions of the Parliament Acts 1911–1949. It

---

[11] Dicey, 'The Referendum and its Critics', *ibid*, at 67.

[12] Dicey, 'The Referendum and its Critics', above n 10, at 559.

[13] See the criticism of R Weill, 'Dicey was not Diceyan' (2003) 62 *Cambridge Law Journal* 474.

[14] Dicey, 'The Referendum and its Critics', above n 10, at 554. and Weill, *ibid*.

requires that constitutional provisions are changed in a manner different from other statutory provisions and that courts should not recognise legislation that has not been passed according to the distinct manner and form required by the Referendum Act.[15] It would appear, therefore, that not only does the justification for continuing parliamentary legislative supremacy rest on factual inaccuracies, but that Dicey himself felt the need to reject continuing parliamentary legislative supremacy as a political theory. It will be argued, however, that while this may weaken Dicey's support of continuing parliamentary legislative supremacy, it demonstrates the importance of the protection of democracy to his support of continuing parliamentary legislative supremacy, both in his earlier and his later work.

First, it is not clear that Dicey is advocating a move away from continuing parliamentary legislative supremacy. Dicey still described English law as subscribing to this principle and also continued to support the legal principle of continuing parliamentary legislative supremacy, despite his commitment to the introduction of the referendum.[16] More fundamentally, a statutory provision proposing a different manner and form by which certain types of legislation should be enacted, which requires courts to recognise as valid only those statutes enacted in this specific manner and form, does not undermine continuing parliamentary legislative supremacy in and of itself. As Dicey recognised, one argument against his proposed Referendum Act would be that its provisions would be futile. It would always be possible for Parliament to evade its provisions, by adding words to the Bill exempting it from the provisions of the proposed Referendum Act.[17] Dicey's response to this criticism was to argue that political pressure from the electorate was such that Parliament would not be able to legislate contrary to the provisions of the proposed Referendum Act, unless it was politically expedient to do so.[18] He did not argue that the provisions of the proposed Referendum Act would be legally entrenched.

A further argument that Dicey is advocating a move away from continuing parliamentary legislative supremacy stems from the claim that Dicey appears to suggest that his proposed Referendum Act could only be overturned by express as opposed to implied repeal. This is because Dicey refers only to the possibility that Parliament could enact words to exempt it from the provisions of the Referendum Act, perhaps suggesting that repeal merely by implication would not suffice. Two arguments can be made in response to this accusation. First, this would be to punish Dicey for sins of omission as opposed to commission, especially given that earlier discussion of his proposed Referendum Act merely referred to the possibility that '[p]arliament might by a subsequent statute undo

---

[15] Weill, above n 13.

[16] See Dicey's commitment to this principle in the introduction to the 9th edn of *An Introduction to the Study of the Law of the Constitution*, above n 10, xviii–xxxvii.

[17] Dicey, 'The Referendum and its Critics', above n 10, at 555.

[18] *Ibid*. See also V Bogdanor, 'Dicey and the Reform of the Constitution' [1985] *Public Law* 652, 671.

its own handiwork',[19] suggesting that the provisions of the Referendum Act could be overturned by implied as well as express repeal. Secondly, as discussed earlier, the scope of the doctrine of implied repeal is narrower in scope than it first appears.[20] Even if Dicey did believe that only express words could contradict the provisions of his proposed Referendum Act, this may not challenge the doctrine of implied repeal. It may merely recognise that later legislation would only contradict the Referendum Act if, for example, its provisions were to state that the Act took effect regardless of the provisions of the Referendum Act.

Secondly, even if we do regard Dicey has having rejected continuing parliamentary legislative supremacy, it is clear that his motivation rests, at least in part, on the need to ensure that Parliament upholds the wishes of the electorate.[21] He advocates a referendum both to ensure that constitutional provisions are protected[22] and to overcome the deficiencies of the party system, aiming to ensure that Parliament is prevented from acting contrary to the wishes of the electorate.[23] The electorate remains factually sovereign, ensuring that it alone can change both normal and constitutional legislation.

B. Self-Correcting Unitary Democracy?

Dicey's justification for defending continuing parliamentary legislative supremacy as a political theory rests on the claim that the United Kingdom constitution is a self-correcting unitary democracy. We have argued above that this may be an inaccurate description, as Dicey himself recognised. In addition, Craig argues that there are flaws in this model of democracy. He argues that Dicey's justification of continuing parliamentary legislative supremacy is based on a model of popular sovereignty. However, this justification is incomplete as Dicey juxtaposes two different concepts—the wishes of the majority of the electorate and the wishes of the electorate as a whole. Even if we accept that the internal and external limits operate to ensure that legislation passed by our representatives in Parliament corresponds with the wishes of the majority of the electorate, it is not the case that this will ensure that legislation corresponds to the wishes of the electorate as a whole. Moreover, there is the danger that legislation will be passed that is contrary to the wishes of a particular minority,

[19] Dicey, 'Ought the Referendum to be Introduced in to England?', above n 10, at 499.
[20] See ch 2.
[21] See, Bogdanor, above n 18; I McLean and A MacMillan, 'Professor Dicey's Contradictions' [2007] *Public Law* 435 and V Bogdanor, 'The Consistency of Dicey: a Reply to McLean and MacMillan' [2008] *Public Law* 19.
[22] Dicey, 'Democracy in Switzerland', above n 10, at 141–3; 'Ought the Referendum to be Introduced in to England?', above n 10, at 505–6; 'The Referendum', above n 10, at 69–70; 'The Referendum and its Critics', above n 10, at 539 and 558–9.
[23] Dicey, 'Democracy in Switzerland', above n 10, at 143–5; 'Ought the Referendum to be Introduced in to England?', above n 10, at 507–8; 'The Referendum', above n 10, at 70–72; 'The Referendum and its Critics', above n 10, at 539 and 559–62.

running the risk that legislation may be enacted that damages their individual rights.[24]

Dicey is not immune to these concerns. He recognises the need to protect both democracy and human rights. However, as his discussion of the rule of law demonstrates, he believed that human rights were best protected through the common law. Dicey's three principles of the rule of law are well known. First, he argued that there shall be no punishment except through law, in contrast to punishments that may be meted out by arbitrary or discretionary powers. Secondly, all are subject to the same ordinary law administered by ordinary tribunals. Thirdly, the general principles of the constitution, which protect individual liberties, are found in decisions of the common law courts as opposed to legal proclamations.[25]

Dicey did not only believe that parliamentary sovereignty was compatible with the rule of law, but that his conception of parliamentary sovereignty furthered the maintenance of the rule of law. Continuing parliamentary legislative sovereignty meant that the will of the sovereign could only be expressed through legislation, requiring the consent of the monarch, Lords and Commons. This restricted arbitrary decision-making powers as courts would not recognise resolutions of either the House of Commons or the House of Lords as having legislative authority.[26] Moreover, courts would restrict the ability of the executive to take arbitrary decisions, as legislative powers could only be delegated to the executive by the legislature, with scrutiny by the courts to ensure that the executive did not act beyond the scope of the delegated power.[27] This scrutiny was not restricted to the determination of the will of the legislature, or to a strictly legal analysis of the meaning of the words of the statute. Instead, the courts were able to interpret legislation so as to uphold the general principles of the constitution.

This can be illustrated by the following statements:

> Powers, however extraordinary, which are conferred or sanctioned by statute, are never really unlimited, for they are confined by the words of the Act itself, and what is more, by the interpretation of the statute by the judges.[28]
>
> When interpreting legislation the judiciary are influenced 'by the general spirit of the common law'.[29]
>
> The courts 'are disposed to construe statutory exceptions to common law principles in a mode which would not commend itself either to a body of officials, or to the Houses of Parliament, if the Houses were called on to interpret their own enactments'.[30]

---

[24] Craig, above n 7, at 34.
[25] Dicey above n 1, at 183–203.
[26] *Ibid*, at 406–08.
[27] *Ibid*, at 408–11.
[28] *Ibid*, at 413.
[29] *Ibid*.
[30] *Ibid*, at 413–14.

The strongest role for the court is found in Dicey's later work, particularly in *Law and Public Opinion*, where Dicey recognises that courts may not override statute law, but that they 'may, by a process of interpretation, indirectly limit or possibly extend the operation of a statute'.[31] Dicey included the right to personal freedom, the right to freedom of discussion and the right of private meeting as part of the general principles of the constitution which were upheld by the common law; illustrating the connection between Dicey's conception of the rule of law and civil liberties, if not more modern, broader conceptions of human rights.

Our analysis of Dicey's arguments reveals a tension in his support for continuing parliamentary legislative supremacy as a political principle. Continuing parliamentary legislative supremacy preserves democracy. It aims to ensure that Parliament does not enact legislation that is contrary to the wishes of the electorate. Dicey is also sensitive to the need to preserve fundamental rights. However, he believes that the role of the court when interpreting legislation is sufficient to protect these rights. In a similar manner, the issue as to whether Convention rights should be entrenched, in order to override the wishes of the electorate wishing to restrict these rights, depends on the balance drawn between democracy and rights.

II. CONSTITUTIONAL RIGHTS

Dicey's justification for continuing parliamentary legislative supremacy favours democracy over a constitutional protection of rights. Dicey concluded that sovereignty should vest in Parliament as a democratic institution. Nevertheless, he recognised that the judiciary were, at least in part, better equipped to protect rights from accidental intrusion by legislation. He was sensitive to the claim that the majority may infringe minority rights, regarding the courts as better placed to preserve long-standing principles of the common law which protected fundamental rights.

The way in which Dicey draws the balance between rights and democracy depends on two related issues that help to ascertain how human rights should be protected by the legal system. First, we need to determine whether to preserve parliamentary sovereignty, thus promoting democracy, or to allow human rights to override the will of the democratic law-making institution. Secondly, we need to determine which institution should have the right to make authoritative determinations about rights. Are the courts or the legislature better equipped to reach the right answer as to the scope of human rights and their application to a particular situation?[32] The aim of this section is to show the

---

[31] AV Dicey, *Lectures on the Relation between Law and Public Opinion in England during the 19th Century*, 2nd edn (London, Macmillan, 1914) 486.

[32] This is similar to, but not the same as the separate questions of a theory of justice and a theory of authority discussed by Waldron in J Waldron, 'A Rights-Based Critique of Constitutional Rights' (1993) 13 *Oxford Journal of Legal Studies* 18, 31–2.

different ways in which those advocating a constitutional or a democratic protection of rights answer these two issues. In doing so, it aims to establish the groundwork to determine both whether it is possible to balance the competing claims of democracy and rights through proposing a democratic dialogue model of rights. This will be used in later chapters to provide a theoretical account of the democratic dialogue model of protecting rights found in the Human Rights Act and how sections 3 and 4 of the Human Rights Act should be interpreted to facilitate the right form of dialogue between the legislature and the courts.

The strongest argument in favour of a constitutional principle of rights grants primacy to rights over democracy, allowing courts to overturn legislation that overrides or restricts human rights, with courts having the final authority to determine the scope and application of human rights. Human rights are regarded as objective fundamental principles that either override, or underpin democracy. Hence, they should override legislation. The judiciary is regarded as the best institution to determine the scope of human rights as this depends on determining the scope of legal rights set out in constitutional documents. As such, this is firmly within the expertise of the judiciary. Not only do the skills of the judiciary lie in assessing legal arguments, but moreover the principle of judicial independence should ensure that the assessment of rights is not swayed by political opinion. The judiciary is therefore undeterred from protecting minority rights, even if to do so may necessitate reaching decisions that are detrimental to the majority.[33]

Theories of common law constitutionalism,[34] in particular that promoted by Sir John Laws, provide the closest example to this argument in favour of a constitutional protection of rights made in the context of the constitution of the United Kingdom. It differs, in that it grants primacy to rights found in the common law, as opposed to a document containing such rights. Laws bases his argument for a constitutional protection of rights on the underlying value of personal autonomy; as expressed in the Kantian maxim that individuals are to be treated as ends as opposed to means. Laws regards the principle of personal autonomy and the rights flowing from it as logically prior to democracy.[35] It is the proper constitutional role of the courts to act as guardians of these principles,[36] even to the extent of challenging statutes that are contrary to these fundamental rights.[37] The judiciary is the best institution to determine the content of fundamental rights. As these rights stem from principles of personal

---

[33] See, eg M Perry, 'Protecting Human Rights in a Democracy: What Role for the Courts?' (2003) 38 *Wake Forest Law Review* 635, 635–45; J Laws, 'Law and Democracy' [1995] *Public Law* 72. Arguments of this nature often rely on Ronald Dworkin's theory of adjudication, see M Loughlin, *Public Law and Political Theory* (Oxford, Clarendon Press, 1992) 207–8.

[34] For an excellent discussion of common law constitutionalism and its different permutations, see T Poole, 'Back to the Future? Unearthing the Theory of Common law Constitutionalism' (2003) 23 *Oxford Journal of Legal Studies* 435.

[35] *Ibid*, at 629.

[36] *Ibid*.

[37] J Laws, above n 33.

autonomy, they give rise to non-contentious principles that can guide the judi-ciary.[38] The judiciary is less likely to be swayed by political considerations when making judgments, focusing instead on ascertaining the scope of fundamental rights.[39]

Challenges to the justification of granting primacy to common law rights, as opposed to legislation or a constitutional document listing fundamental rights, can be made in two ways. First, it can be argued that human rights should not override legislation. Instead, democracy, as a more fundamental principle than the protection of human rights, would require that legislation overrides human rights. Secondly, the argument is made that allowing rights to override legisla-tion does not undermine democracy, but merely enables rights to take priority over the wishes of a particular democratic law-maker at a particular time. There may be good reasons for protecting rights from their inadvertent removal by a future parliament, particularly where the constitutional document in question is also created through a democratic law-making process. These reasons are not present if fundamental rights are found in the common law. The common law is not created through a democratically accountable process. Granting priority to common law rights may enable the wishes of the non-democratically accountable judiciary to override the wishes of the electorate, as expressed through the legislation of the democratically representative and accountable law-maker.

An example of the first criticism can be found in the work of John Griffith. Griffith regards rights as political claims. As such, there is no justification for allowing them to override democratic will. To do so is merely to replace a later democratic assessment of rights with an earlier democratic assessment of rights, where there may be no grounds for preferring the earlier account of rights. Moreover, courts should not be granted the authority to make determinative decisions as to the content of human rights. To grant courts this power would give power to a non-democratically elected institution, whose political opinions as to the content of rights would override the political opinions of Parliament.[40] Yet, Parliament should be granted the authority to determine the content of rights. This is not because Parliament is more likely to reach the correct answer as to the scope of a particular right, but because as a democratically accountable decision it is more legitimate for Parliament to determine the scope of rights, which is essentially the determination of the relative merits of different political claims.

However, to fail to regard rights as examples of objective, moral principles need not entail a rejection of a constitutional or legal protection of human rights. Conor Gearty, for example, draws a distinction between human and legal rights. Rejecting claims of the existence of human rights as anything other

---

[38] *Ibid*, at 78–9.
[39] *Ibid*, at 77–90.
[40] JAG Griffith, 'The Brave New World of Sir John Laws' (2000) 63 *Modern Law Review* 159, 165.

than political claims or desires, he argues that there may nevertheless be a range of legal rights which should be protected by the courts. The existence of these legal rights, once such rights are created, is a social fact. Courts may be better placed to protect these rights. Gearty's argument, however, still vests primacy in legislation. He advocates a legal as opposed to a constitutional protection of rights, thus preserving parliamentary sovereignty.[41] Rorty also rejects the claim that rights are objective, fundamental principles. Nevertheless, he would advocate a constitutional protection of rights, allowing rights to override legislation, if it were proved that a constitutional protection of rights would be more likely in practice to achieve the desires of a particular society to protect human rights than other means of protecting rights.[42]

An example of the second criticism can be found in the work of Bruce Ackerman. Ackerman distinguishes between two types of legislation: ordinary legislation and that passed at a 'constitutional moment' in history. The latter represents the decisions of the democratic majority at a moment in history where the electorate was more able to fully reflect on constitutional principles, producing a catalogue of fundamental rights underpinning their society. This is contrasted with ordinary legislation, where the electorate is tempted to limit the rights deemed so important at a constitutional moment, but where there is no full reflection on the constitutional values of the particular society in question. The decisions of the majority at a 'constitutional moment' should be able to override the decisions of the majority in ordinary legislation, in the same way that the decision of a sober individual not to drive after drinking alcohol should override his drunken request for his car keys.[43]

Waldron criticises this argument, relying on the contestable nature of rights. If we accept that rights are contestable, then it may not be possible to distinguish between moments of constitutional lucidity, where the electorate was able to pay special attention to constitutional values and reach better conclusions concerning the scope of constitutional rights and other moments where this lucidity was not present. What appears to be a distinction between ordinary legislation and that passed at a constitutional moment may in reality merely be two different, reasonable accounts of theories of rights. There may be no logical reason for regarding one as opposed to the other as being capable of providing the more legitimate or accurate account of rights that can justifiably override alternative accounts of rights.[44]

Debate surrounding whether the judiciary or Parliament is best placed to make authoritative decisions about the nature of rights focuses on whether

---

[41] CA Gearty, *Principles of Human Rights Adjudication* (Oxford, Oxford University Press, 2004) ch 2. For criticism of this distinction, see AL Young, 'A Peculiarly British Protection of Rights' (2005) 68 *Modern Law Review* 858.

[42] R Rorty, 'Human Rights, Rationality and Sentimentality' in S Shute and S Hurley (eds), *On Human Rights: the Oxford Amnesty Lectures 1993* (New York, Basic Books, 1993) 111.

[43] B Ackerman, *We the People: Foundations* Vol 1 (Cambridge, Mass, Belknap Press, 1991); B Ackerman, *We the People: Transformations* Vol 2 (Cambridge, Mass, Belknap Press, 1998).

[44] Waldron, above n 32.

issues surrounding the scope and application of Convention rights are contestable or non-contestable. Contestability occurs when it is reasonable to disagree as to the scope or application of a Convention right. Contestability may arise as rights are indeterminate, or because rights are incommensurable. The former refers to the difficulty of delineating the scope of particular rights and the latter to the impossibility of balancing rights when they contradict.[45]

If it is reasonable to disagree about the content of rights or their outcome in a particular case, then it may be hard to conclude that a judgment of the court provides a definitive account of the right that should be allowed to override the legislature's account. A constitutional protection of rights may not ensure the maintenance of fundamental principles that are logically prior to, or underpin democracy. Instead, it may allow the reasonable opinions of a non-democratically accountable judiciary to override the reasonable opinions of the democratically accountable legislature. This is not fatal to an argument for the constitutional protection of rights—but it does require substantive theories of rights to be bolstered by a theory of authority. Given that it is reasonable to disagree with the decisions of both the judiciary and the legislature, to whom should we grant the power to protect rights that we believe to be fundamental, if indeterminate?[46]

Advocates of the constitutional protection of rights argue that the courts are the best-placed institution to resolve indeterminacies as to the scope and application of human rights. Democratic institutions cannot be trusted to protect rights, as they are more likely to protect interests that are popular, have a high profile and are more lucrative. Human rights issues frequently require the protection of minority interests, with a low profile and little financial backing. The courts are the best institution to protect rights precisely because human rights are designed to protect minorities from the tyranny of the majority inherent to democracy.[47] In addition, it is argued that courts are more likely to reach the right/best answer concerning the scope of a right and its application. Courts applying common law reasoning examine principles inherent to their particular society, weighing up their relative strength and application. Their independence and legal training makes them ideally suited to protecting the legal principles underpinning fundamental rights.[48]

The most sophisticated presentation of this argument with regard to the constitutional protections of rights in the United Kingdom is found in the writings of Trevor Allan. Allan argues that the resolution of conflicts surrounding the interpretation and application of fundamental rights depends on the examination of

---

[45] See, J Waldron, *Law and Disagreement* (Oxford, Oxford University Press, 1999) 224–31.
[46] See, Perry, above n 33, at 645–51.
[47] *Ibid*, at 654–5.
[48] See, eg J Jowell, 'Beyond *Wednesbury*: Substantive Principles of Administrative law' [1987] *Public Law* 368; J Jowell, 'Of Vires and Vacuums: the Constitutional Context of Judicial Review' [1999] *Public Law* 448, 451–6; J Laws, 'Is the High Court the Guardian of Fundamental Constitutional Rights?' [1993] *Public Law* 59; J Laws, 'Law and Democracy', above n 33, at 72, 76–9; J Laws, 'The Limitations of Human Rights' [1998] *Public Law* 254, 256–57. See also Loughlin, above n 33, at 207–8.

principles underpinning a particular society. Tensions are resolved by informed debate analysing such principles. The common law is the exemplar of the type of public reasoning needed to resolve such issues. In order to succeed before a court, counsel needs to provide an appeal to a concept of justice and the common good within that particular society. The success of their argument depends on its moral and intellectual strength. Hence, discussion through the court is more likely to reach the best answer regarding the application of the right.[49]

In addition, Allan regards common law reasoning as an expression of a shared enterprise within a particular community. Precedent ensures that courts build on previous expressions of rights, analysing broad rights and their application to particular situations in order to determine the way in which they should apply to the situation before the court. He regards legal reasoning as a form of moral reasoning—regarding legal principles as those moral principles that have filtered into the legal system, becoming legally recognised rights.[50] Judicial reasoning is superior to that provided by the legislature. Legislation is the result of compromise and negotiation. It establishes broad rights, but does not provide clear guidance as to their specific resolution. Common law reasoning is able to provide greater clarity and deeper understanding, ensuring that specific applications of rights are developed in line with the fundamental principles in a particular community and their specific concept of the common good.[51] It has also been argued that entrusting the judiciary to provide authoritative determinations of rights issues promotes certainty and stability.[52]

Two criticisms can be made against the argument that courts should have the authority to determine the scope of rights. First, it can be argued that it is factually inaccurate that courts are best suited to protecting minority interests. Tushnet, for example, argues courts protect majority as opposed to minority interests, thereby failing to provide a sufficient protection of fundamental rights.[53] Although his analysis is based on the protection of rights provided by American courts, his concerns are echoed by academics examining the record of human rights protections provided by English courts.[54] Tushnet argues further that legislators are just as capable of protecting fundamental rights as the courts. He argues that legislators often have the relevant expertise to protect rights, given that legislative bodies frequently contain members who were former

---

[49] TRS Allan, *Constitutional Justice: a Liberal Theory of the Rule of Law* (Oxford, Oxford University Press, 2001) 289–90.

[50] *Ibid*, at 291–2.

[51] *Ibid*, at 292–4.

[52] L Alexander and F Schauer, 'On Extra-Judicial Constitutional Interpretation' (1997) 110 *Harvard Law Review* 1359 and L Alexander and F Schauer, 'Defending Judicial Supremacy: A Reply' (2000) 17 *Constitutional Comment* 455.

[53] M Tushnet, *Taking the Constitution Away from the Courts* (Princeton NJ, Princeton University Press, 1999) ch 6.

[54] See, eg KD Ewing, 'The Human Rights Act and Parliamentary Democracy' (1999) 62 *Modern Law Review* 79; KD Ewing, 'The Futility of the Human Rights Act' [2004] *Public Law* 829 and Gearty, above n 41.

lawyers.[55] Moreover, he criticises the argument that legislators will not protect human rights given that it is never politically rewarding to do so. If a legislative body is part of a society that wishes to promote human rights, then a legislative body will not maintain its popularity unless it protects human rights. Consequently, it may not be factually accurate to describe the legislature as unwilling to protect human rights.[56]

A further criticism as to the factual accuracy of entrusting the authoritative resolution of rights issues to the judiciary focuses on the way in which this may have a negative impact on the goals underpinning democracy and rights, leading to democratic debilitation and policy distortion.[57] Legislative bodies may disregard issues surrounding the scope of fundamental rights, becoming apathetic to such issues if they are to be resolved authoritatively by the courts. Consequently, money may be diverted away from supporting grass-roots politics to funding legal actions, thus damaging political participation. In addition, the technical jargon developed by the courts when interpreting constitutional protections of rights may exclude non-lawyers, including the legislature, from debates surrounding the scope of human rights. This may result in rights-holders reaching the conclusion that they are no longer responsible for the protection of their rights, giving rise to general apathy.[58] In addition, the court process is bivalent and adversarial, focusing on balancing the competing arguments of two parties to determine which party wins the particular dispute. This process may damage tolerance and community values, leading to rights-extremism and divisiveness.[59] Policy distortion occurs when the legislature pursues a policy different from its ideal policy, purely because it is easier to defend from potential judicial review. This occurs when courts produce clear guidance as to the scope of constitutional rights and their application which the legislature takes account of when it enacts legislation. Instead of weighing up arguments in favour and against a particular policy pursued by proposed legislation, the legislature gives too much weight to the predicted reaction of the court, choosing the path of least resistance.[60]

Secondly, a challenge is made to the ability to use factual evidence to assess whether the judiciary or the legislature is more likely to reach the right answer as to the scope and application of contestable rights. Waldron argues that the contestable nature of rights makes it impossible to determine the relative ability of different institutions to reach the right answer concerning the scope and application of human rights. To answer the question requires an ability to know the right answer to a particular question. Once this is ascertained, the answers

---

[55] Tushnet, above n 53, at 62.

[56] *Ibid*, at 66–7.

[57] M Tushnet, 'Policy Distortion and Democratic Debilitation: Comparative Illumination of the Counter-Majoritarian Difficulty' (1995–96) 94 *Michigan Law Review* 245.

[58] J Goldsworthy, 'Judicial Review, Legislative Override and Democracy' (2003) 38 *Wake Forest Law Review* 451, 459–62.

[59] *Ibid*, at 462–3.

[60] Tushnet, above n 57, at 250–75.

of the two institutions can be assessed to determine which institution reached the right answer. However, if rights are contestable, then it is reasonable to disagree about the right answer to a question concerning the scope and application of the Convention right in question. Therefore, it is not possible to determine which institution is more likely to reach the right answer.[61]

Waldron argues further that any assessment as to which institution is best placed to take authoritative decisions concerning the scope and application of human rights depends, at least indirectly, on a theory of rights. Yet, theories of rights are also contestable. Allan, for example, argues that the judiciary is better suited to determining issues of rights because the principles of common law reasoning used by the judiciary are more suited to such issues than the reasoning processes of the legislature. The common law reaches decisions based on the moral and intellectual strength of arguments related to the particular conception of the common good in a distinct political society. Allan reaches this conclusion because of his conception of rights. Allan argues for the protection of the rule of law based on equal citizenship, this requires that differential treatment between citizens should be justified according to a conception of the common good. Each political society derives a more precise conception of the common good from the principles on which it is based, these principles evolving over time as precedents are developed. Given his conception of rights, it is rational to argue that courts are best suited to determining the nature of individual rights.

However, if we disagree with Allan's conception of individual rights, then we are also likely to disagree with his assertion as to the best placed institution to take authoritative decisions concerning those rights. If, for example, we regard human rights as merely political claims, then we would regard the legislature as a better institution than the judiciary to make authoritative decisions regarding individual rights. Waldron classifies assessments of the relative institutional merits of the legislature and the judiciary to resolve rights issues as a 'rights-instrumentalist' account.[62] He argues that rights-instrumentalist accounts fail to provide a valid theory of authority. Rights-instrumentalism requires a resolution as to the best theory of rights, in order to grant the power to make authoritative determinations to the institution that is best able to reach the correct conclusion as to the scope and application of a particular right. However, there would be no need to determine which institution should be granted the ability to make authoritative decisions on rights issues unless theories of rights are regarded as contestable.[63]

Waldron argues instead for a different rights-based solution to the question of authority, based on what he terms the 'right of rights'—the right to participation.[64] Disagreements about the nature of rights should be settled by those who are the subject of that disagreement. Individuals, as bearers of rights,

[61] Tushnet, above n 57, at 245.
[62] Waldron, above n 45, at 252.
[63] *Ibid*, at 252–54.
[64] *Ibid*, ch 11.

are those who are subject to disagreements about the nature of rights. Consequently, individuals should participate in decisions determining the scope and application of human rights. In addition, Waldron argues that the very notion of human rights incorporates the idea of individuals as thinking agents, capable of deliberating morally.[65] Waldron derives further support for this view from theories of natural and human rights, which are based on the inherent characteristics of individuals as humans, regarding them as capable of determining for themselves decisions regarding the nature of rights.[66] This provides at least a prima facie justification for regarding rights-bearers as the appropriate person to decide issues as to rights. To do so is to respect the capacity of a rights-bearer to make such decisions—a capacity that is inherent to allocating rights-bearers with fundamental rights in the first place. Consequently, the institution best suited to taking authoritative decisions as to the scope and application of rights is the legislature—an institution accountable to the majority of rights-bearers.

Raz criticises Waldron's arguments against rights-instrumentalism, arguing that it is possible to determine whether the legislature or the courts would be better placed to take authoritative decisions without resorting to contestable theories of rights. Raz provides two examples: arguments based on evidence as to whether an institution will indeed endeavour to establish what rights people have when making decisions about rights; or arguments based on which institution is best placed to take decisions that are not based on factors that are known to cloud one's judgment, for example institutions that are biased in favour of or against particular interests. The conclusions reached above concerning the relative abilities of the courts and the legislature to reach conclusions as to the nature of rights are arguments of this type. Courts decide issues based on the evidence of the parties before the court, referring back to previous cases to help determine the legal answer to the specific case before the court. Legislatures decide issues of general application, responding to new situations that require resolution. These features explain both why the courts are more likely to determine what rights individuals have than the legislature, ensuring that specific rights are not overruled or reduced by general legislative provisions, and how the courts can protect long-standing principles of rights from erosion by the legislature. Legislatures make decisions according to majority voting processes, where it may be more difficult for minority groups to find sufficient support to participate effectively in the political process. Minorities have easier access to the courts. Hence it may be the case that the courts are more able to hear and respond to the arguments of minorities than the legislature.[67]

---

[65] *Ibid*, ch 10 and Waldron, above n 32.

[66] Waldron, above n 45, at 250–51.

[67] J Raz, 'Disagreement in Politics' (1998) 43 *American Journal of Jurisprudence* 25. See also: A Kavanagh, 'Participation and Judicial Review: A Reply to Jeremy Waldron' 22 *Law and Philosophy* 451, 466–7.

Waldron is critical of this approach, arguing that it too requires an analysis of the nature of rights.[68] For example, the argument that the judiciary is best placed to protect rights because it is more likely to make logical decisions, based on general principles, which it applies to the actual facts of the case, is more likely to be correct if rights are based on arguments of principle stemming from morality, but not if rights are political claims which are resolved through political compromises.

The debate as to whether rights should be constitutionally protected discusses whether rights or democracy should be given priority. Democratic dialogue models of rights protections balance rights and democracy in a different manner. In particular, democratic dialogue arguably compensates for the claim that a constitutional protection of rights is anti-democratic by providing the legislature with opportunities to respond to the assessment of rights by the courts. The next section analyses how democratic dialogue models of rights protections provide for this balance, illustrating how the Human Rights Act can be interpreted as providing for a democratic dialogue model of rights protection.

III. DEMOCRATIC DIALOGUE

The Canadian Charter of Fundamental Rights and Freedoms is regarded as the seminal example of a democratic dialogue model of rights protection. The Charter enables courts to strike down legislation that is incompatible with the Charter. However, section 33 and section 1 of the Charter enable the legislature to respond to or modify these decisions of the judiciary. Section 33 of the Charter provides for a legislative override. The legislator can insert an express clause into legislation enabling its provisions to take effect notwithstanding certain rights found within the Charter. This enables the legislature to respond to a decision of the court as to the unconstitutionality of legislation by re-enacting its provisions subject to a notwithstanding clause. Such clauses only have effect for five years.[69] Section 1 enables the legislature to limit the application of the provisions of the Charter, stating that rights in the Charter are subject to 'such reasonable limits prescribed by law as can be demonstrably justified in a free and democratic society'. This enables the legislature to respond to court decisions by modifying legislation, facilitating dialogue as to the reasonable limits of a Charter right required to further other purposes of a free and democratic society. It allows the legislature to modify legislation in response to court decisions, in order to reach a conclusion shared by the courts and the legislature regarding the correct balance between the Charter right and other rights and goals necessary for a democratic society.[70]

---

[68] Waldron, above n 32, at 253–4.
[69] PW Hogg and AA Bushell, 'The *Charter* Dialogue between Courts and Legislatures (or perhaps the *Charter of Rights* isn't such a bad thing after all)' (1997) 35 *Osgoode Hall Law Journal* 75, 83–4.
[70] *Ibid*, at 84–7.

It is these two features of the Canadian Charter that have been most frequently referred to when discussing the democratic dialogue model. Hogg and Bushell also refer to two further provisions: the qualified rights contained in the Charter, which facilitate dialogue in a similar manner to section 1,[71] and equality rights. Equality rights only require that individuals in comparable situations are treated equally. It is open to the legislature to determine how this equality is achieved. For example, a law requiring women to retire at an age younger than men would breach principles of equality as it discriminates between men and women. Equality requires that men and women are subject to the same retirement age. This may be achieved either by allowing men to retire at the younger age currently provided for women, or by raising the retirement age of women to that currently in place for men, or by chosing a completely different retirement age. The legislature is left with a choice as to the age that should be set and is only required to ensure that it is the same for men and women. This consequently enables the legislature to respond to the decision of the court in equality decisions.[72]

It is easy to conclude that the Human Rights Act 1998 provides for a democratic dialogue model of rights protection. First, section 14(1)(b) of the Act enables the Secretary of State to derogate from the provisions of the Convention, subject to approval by a resolution of both the House of Commons and the House of Lords approving the order within 40 days of its being passed.[73] The duration of a derogation order is restricted to five years[74] and can be renewed for a further five years.[75] The Secretary of State is also required to review the derogation, laying a report before Parliament concerning the need for it to be retained beyond the original five-year period. This has a similar purpose to the notwithstanding clause found in section 33 of the Canadian Charter. Dialogue is facilitated between the courts and the legislature as courts can review derogation orders, prompting parliamentary dialogue in response.[76] The qualified rights found in articles 8–11 of the ECHR also facilitate dialogue in a manner similar to section 1 of the Canadian Charter and the specific qualified rights contained within it.

Dialogue is also facilitated through the provisions of sections 3 and 4 of the Human Rights Act. When the courts use section 3 to construe statutes in a manner compatible with Convention rights, the legislature is able to respond by re-enacting the statute in terms that cannot be interpreted in a manner compatible

---

[71] *Ibid*, at 87–90.
[72] *Ibid*, at 87–92.
[73] Human Rights Act 1998 s 16(3) and s 16(5).
[74] Human Rights Act 1998 s 16(1)(b).
[75] Human Rights Act 1998 s 16(2).
[76] See, *A and others v Secretary of State for the Home Department; X and another v Secretary of State for the Home Department* [2004] UKHL 56, [2005] 2 AC 68, where the House of Lords overturned the derogation order made by the Human Rights Act 1998 (Designated Derogation) Order 2001 SI 2001/3644. The Home Secretary responded to the judgment in a statement to the House: see Hansard HC vol 428, col 151WS (16 December 2004).

with Convention rights. When the courts use section 4 of the Act to declare statutes to be incompatible with Convention rights, the legislature is able to respond to such declarations, either by modifying the provisions of the statute or by refusing to do so. The lack of a legal obligation to modify the provisions of the statutes enables the legislature to respond according to political will, ensuring that the judiciary is unable to override the wishes of the people as represented by the legislature.[77]

IV. CONCLUSION

Dicey regarded continuing parliamentary legislative supremacy as both a legal and a political principle. From the perspective of political theory, continuing parliamentary legislative supremacy is justified as it preserves democracy, while recognising the claim that courts may need to reinterpret legislation so as to protect human rights from inadvertent legislative intrusion. In the same manner, the Human Rights Act can be defended not because it aims to provide a protection of human rights that does not contravene the legal principle of continuing parliamentary legislative supremacy, but because it seeks to provide a protection of rights that is also sensitive to the need to preserve democracy.

Although we have recognised that the Human Rights Act may be interpreted as providing a democratic dialogue method of rights protection, this is not enough in and of itself to justify this form of rights protection. First, a more in-depth analysis is needed of the way in which democratic dialogue models of rights protection aim to balance democracy and the protection of fundamental rights. Secondly, having established the way in which the Human Rights Act facilitates dialogue, we need to investigate the way in which courts should use sections 3 and 4 to ensure that dialogue is facilitated between the legislature and the courts in the correct manner. These issues will be discussed in the following two chapters.

---

[77] See, R Clayton, 'Judicial Deference and "Democratic Dialogue": the Legitimacy of Judicial Intervention under the Human Rights Act 1998' [2004] *Public Law* 33 and T Hickman, 'Constitutional Dialogue, Constitutional Theories and the Human Rights Act 1998' [2005] *Public Law* 306. Waldron also refers to the Human Rights Act as a model of democratic dialogue; J Waldron, 'Some Models of Dialogue between Judges and Legislators' (2004) 23 *Supreme Court Law Review* (2d) 7, 33–4.

5

Democratic Dialogue and the Human Rights Act 1998

T HE PREVIOUS CHAPTER concluded that the Human Rights Act 1998 may be justified as providing a democratic dialogue model of human rights protection. As such, it aims to balance the competing values of democracy and human rights. It is argued that dialogue models of human rights protection do not harm democracy: by enabling the legislature to respond to the decisions of the judiciary, democratic institutions can override or modify the decisions of the courts, should they wish to do so.

A democratic dialogue model of rights protection is also found in Canada's Charter of Fundamental Rights and Freedoms, however, there are differences between the way in which Canada protects human rights and the protection of rights found in the Human Rights Act. The Canadian judiciary is granted the power to overturn legislation that is contrary to the fundamental rights found in the Charter. The legislature can respond to judicial decisions overturning legislation by exercising its powers under section 33 to enact legislation notwithstanding the provisions of the Charter. The English judiciary does not enjoy the same power to overturn legislation and may only read and give effect to its provisions so as to ensure, so far as it is possible, that they are compatible with Convention rights, or declare legislation incompatible with Convention rights. These differences call into question the defence of the Human Rights Act, as do criticisms that the democratic dialogue model in the Canadian Charter is anti-democratic.[1]

---

[1] See, eg M Perry, 'Protecting Human Rights in a Democracy: What Role for the Courts?' (2003) 38 *Wake Forest Law Review* 635; M Tushnet, 'New forms of Judicial Review and the Persistence of Rights—and Democracy-based Worries' (2003) 38 *Wake Forest Law Review* 813; B Friedman, 'Dialogue and Judicial Review' (1993) 91 *Michigan Law Review* 577; J Waldron, 'Some Models of Dialogue between Judges and Legislators' (2004) 23 *Supreme Court Law Review* (2d) 7; K Roach, 'Constitutional and Common Law Dialogues between the Supreme Court and Canadian Legislatures' 80 (2001) *Canadian Bar Review* 481; K Roach, 'Dialogue, Judicial Review and its Critics' (2004) 23 *Supreme Court Law Review* (2d) 49; L Tremblay, 'The Legitimacy of Judicial Review: the Limits of Dialogue between Courts and Legislatures' (2005) 3 *International Journal of Constitutional Law* 617; J Goldsworthy, 'Judicial Review, Legislative Override and Democracy' (2003) 38 *Wake Forest Law Review* 451; PW Hogg and AA Bushell, 'The *Charter* Dialogue between Courts and Legislatures (or perhaps the *Charter of Rights* isn't such a bad thing after all)' (1997) 35 *Osgoode Hall Law Journal* 75; CP Manfredi and JB Kelly, 'Six Forms of Dialogue: a Response to Hogg and Bushell' (1999) 37 *Osgoode Hall Law Journal* 513; PW Hogg and AA Thornton, 'Reply to "Six Degrees of Dialogue"' (1999) 37 *Osgoode Hall Law Journal* 529.

This chapter will investigate whether democratic dialogue models of rights protection provide a justifiable balance between the protection of rights and the preservation of democracy. It will argue that the Human Rights Act lends itself to a democratic dialogue model that focuses on the relative strengths and weaknesses of the legislature and the courts when protecting human rights.

This chapter will argue that legislatures may fail to realise that its general measures restrict individual rights in certain specific situations, or that its legislation challenges or undermines long-standing rights found within the legal system. In addition, the democratic credentials of the legislature may mean that it fails to provide an adequate protection of minority rights. It will not argue that courts should be given the power to override the decisions of the legislature when they feel that a mistake has been made. Nor will it argue that courts are always performing this correcting function when they reach a conclusion that the legislature has harmed human rights. Rather, it will argue that it is only reasonable to assume that courts are performing this correcting function when faced with *non-contestable rights issues*.

In order to make this argument, we need first to clarify the meaning of democratic dialogue models of rights protection and the particular features of the democratic dialogue model found in the Human Rights Act. Only then can we investigate how such models may provide an effective balance between democracy and rights.

I. MODELS OF DIALOGUE

The meaning of 'democratic dialogue' almost seems to fail to warrant investigation. The term 'democratic dialogue' derives from the seminal work of Hogg and Bushell (now Thornton), who describe dialogue as occurring 'if judicial decision is open to legislature reversal, modification or avoidance'.[2]

It is for this reason that we reached the conclusion that the Human Rights Act contained a democratic dialogue model of rights protection. Judicial decisions taken under both section 3 and section 4 are open to 'reversal, modification or avoidance' by the legislature. If the legislature disagrees with the way in which the judiciary has interpreted section 3, then the legislature has the opportunity to enact legislation to ensure that its view prevails. If the judiciary exercises its powers under section 4, then even though declared incompatible with Convention rights, the legislation in question continues to exist, have legal validity and enjoy legal force: the legislature has the *opportunity* to legislate, should it wish to make the legislation in question Convention compatible and, when doing so, it has the freedom to disagree with the conclusions of the court as to the modifications required to ensure Convention compatibility.

---

[2] Hogg and Bushell, *ibid*, at 79.

A. Defining Democratic Dialogue

Despite the apparent simplicity of democratic dialogue models of rights protection, further clarification is useful. First, democratic dialogue is interinstitutional (between the judiciary and the legislature). So, for example, a constitutional model describing dialogue that takes place within the court, where individual applicants have the opportunity to discuss their case and members of the judiciary are able to discuss the outcome of the case with each other before reaching their own separate conclusions, is not a form of democratic dialogue[3]: such discussions constitute a form of intra- as opposed to inter-institutional dialogue. Nor does democratic dialogue refer to dialogue between members of the judiciary and the legislature that is not part of an inter-institutional exchange (for example when members of the judiciary write academic articles).[4]

Secondly, it is important to be clear what institutions are involved in the democratic dialogue. The model found in the Human Rights Act, and under consideration in this book, is a *legal mechanism* for interaction between the judiciary and legislature. Other writers have described the interaction between the legislature and the judiciary in the political arena as democratic dialogue. They note that such dialogue can be valuable and may result in a change to legislation or a modification of the constitution[5]: democratic dialogue in this sense may also seek to preserve democracy, but uses political rather than legal mechanisms.

Thirdly, democratic dialogue differs from deference.[6] The concepts are related as they both aim to restrict the criticism that a strong protection of rights damages democracy. The difference stems from the manner in which they seek to achieve this aim. Democratic dialogue achieves this by restricting the power of the judiciary and providing legal means to the legislature to respond to judicial decisions. Deference does not modify the powers granted to the judiciary, but advocates instead that the judiciary should exercise these powers in a restrained manner, in order to preserve democracy.[7]

---

[3] Friedman above n 1, at 655–6.

[4] Waldron, above n 1, at 21–5. It may, however, be an example of democratic dialogue, or be used as part of a dialogic interpretation of different models of rights protection.

[5] Friedman, above n 1, at 653–80.

[6] James B Thayer presented one of the first arguments in favour of judicial deference in the exercise of the power to strike down legislation that contravenes constitutionally protected human rights. Thayer advocated a minimalist interpretation of constitutional rights and argued that courts should only strike down legislation where there was a clear mistake as to the constitutionality of the law—'a mistake so clear that it is not open to rational question'. By exercising its powers in this way democracy is preserved because the court is respecting the opinions of the legislature concerning the interpretation of open-textured constitutionally protected human rights. See, JB Thayer, 'The Origin and Scope of the American Doctrine of Constitutional Law' (1893–4) 7 *Harvard Law Review* 129, 144. The relationship between deference and dialogue will be discussed further in ch 6, pp 145–6.

[7] For a discussion of the use of deference in English administrative law, see M Hunt, 'Sovereignty's Blight: Why Contemporary Public Law needs the Concept of "Due Deference"' in N Bamforth and P Leyland (eds), *Public Law in a Multi-layered Constitution* (Oxford, Hart

Finally, a distinction is made between dialogue as conversation and dialogue as deliberation.[8] Dialogue as conversation is informal, spontaneous and has no practical purpose other than 'the general goal of exploring or creating a common world and body of meanings, learning something new about others or discovering new perspectives'.[9] Dialogue as deliberation is more formal and less spontaneous and has 'specific mutual practical purposes'.[10] For example:

> it aims at taking decisions in common; reaching agreement; solving problems or conflicts collectively; determining together which opinion or thesis is true, the most justified or the best; or which particular practical view should govern actions or decisions.[11]

Democratic dialogue models of rights protection require dialogue as deliberation. Democratic dialogue has a specific aim—to provide for a protection of rights that does not damage democracy. The achievement of this aim requires dialogue that reaches conclusions as to the scope of human rights and the extent to which they should be protected in particular situations. The legal provisions facilitating democratic models of rights protections also provide a formal structure to this dialogue.[12]

II. JUSTIFICATION OF DEMOCRATIC DIALOGUE

Hogg and Bushell provide a *practical account* of how dialogue may alleviate the criticism that constitutional protections of rights are anti-democratic: democracy is protected because the legislature has the opportunity to modify or amend the decision of the court overturning legislation that contravenes human rights. Their account can be criticised however: it fails to provide sufficient guidelines as to when and how the legislature should react to judicial decisions, or how the judiciary should react to the legislature. This lack of guidance not only undermines the way in which democratic dialogue may achieve its objective, but it may also give rise to further practical problems.

Publishing, 2003) 337. For a critique, see TRS Allan, 'Human Rights and Judicial Review: a Critique of "Due Deference"' (2006) 65 *Cambridge Law Journal* 671.

   [8] Tremblay, above n 1.

   [9] *Ibid*, at 630.

   [10] *Ibid*, at 631.

   [11] *Ibid*. A conversation between two academics concerning the relative merits of articles about democratic dialogue would be an example of dialogue as conversation. There is no practical purpose to the conversation other than to learn of the opinions of others or to discover new perspectives on the way in which constitutions do or should protect human rights. A discussion in a faculty meeting, concerning whether to include democratic dialogue as part of the syllabus of constitutional law, would be an example of dialogue as deliberation. There are, albeit informal, rules concerning the contributions to this debate and the purpose of the debate is to reach a practical outcome, aiming to reach agreement and determine action that should be taken on the basis of this agreement.

   [12] This conclusion is shared by Tremblay, although for reasons different from the ones advocated in this chapter, *ibid*, at 632.

A. Practical Problems

If exercised in the wrong way, democratic dialogue may fail to provide an effective balance between rights and democracy. Democratic dialogue may fail to protect *democracy* if despite having the opportunity to respond, the legislature is convinced that the judiciary has greater authority to determine decisions of rights. This may give rise to policy distortions, as the legislature tailors its legislation to meet the response of the court, as opposed to reaching its own conclusion as to the scope and application of Convention rights.[13] Democratic dialogue may fail to protect *rights* if courts exercise restraint, considering that the legislature has greater authority to determine the content of more political rights. As such, courts may be persuaded to seek to find compromises, protecting rights in a manner that immunises their decision from a possible legislative response.[14]

The lack of guidance as to how the legislature and the courts should exercise their powers leads Tushnet to the conclusion that democratic dialogue is unstable. He argues that the democratic dialogue model found in the Human Rights Act is in danger of collapsing into a system of parliamentary sovereignty,[15] or regenerating into a system of strong-review.[16] The latter outcome may be particularly pertinent with regard to the Human Rights Act, given that cases where a declaration of incompatibility has been made may be referred to the European Court of Human Rights. Given the existence of a declaration of incompatibility, it may be hard for the European Court of Human Rights to conclude that Convention rights had not been breached in this situation, creating an obligation in international law on the United Kingdom to modify its laws to ensure that Convention rights are upheld.[17]

This tension is illustrated in the academic commentary as to the manner in which sections 3 and 4 of the Human Rights Act should be interpreted. Commentators advocating a strong protection of Convention rights advocate a wide application of section 3, thus strengthening the ability of the courts to protect Convention rights. Gavin Phillipson, for example, argues that section 3(1) should be interpreted in a self-referential manner. The scope of section 3(1) must be read and given effect to, so far as possible, to ensure its compatibility with Convention rights. Consequently, courts should apply section 3(1) as frequently as possible to ensure that courts provide as great a protection of Convention

---

[13] See, Manfredi and Kelly, above n 1.

[14] See, J Cameron, 'Dialogue and Hierarchy in Charter Interpretation: A Comment on *R v Mills*' (2001) 38 *Alberta Law Review* 1051.

[15] If the courts were to interpret section 3 as adding little to their powers of interpretation existing before the Act and if Parliament frequently and consistently failed to respond to declarations of incompatibility made under s 4.

[16] If the legislature believed that it was under a non-legally binding obligation to modify its legislation to match the decision of the court following every possible declaration of incompatibility.

[17] Tushnet, above n 1.

rights as possible.[18] Klug, by contrast, advocates a more restrictive use of section 3 and a greater use of section 4, regarding the latter as the principle means of promoting dialogue between the legislature and the judiciary. By strengthening Parliament (who have the opportunity to decide whether, and if so how, to respond to declarations of incompatibility) there is more democratic debate surrounding the balance to be drawn between the protection of Convention rights and the promotion of other social goals and values.[19]

Our analysis would appear to suggest that democratic dialogue models of rights protection need to ensure against inequalities arising between the power of the legislature and that of the courts if they are to be sustainable and achieve their aim of providing an effective balance of democracy and rights. This conclusion is supported by the work of Hickman and Roach.[20] One possible solution may be to require that the relative powers of the legislature and the judiciary are distributed equally. As such, neither institution will be able to gain ascendancy over the other, thus helping to maintain a balanced protection of democracy and rights.

Achieving this balance lies at the root of 'co-ordinate constitutionalism'. Co-ordinate constitutionalism was promoted by Jefferson and Madison and advocates a democratic dialogue interpretation of the constitutional protection of rights found in the US Constitution. Their theory provides the courts with the power to overturn legislation that is contrary to the provisions of the constitution, but also refutes the judicial supremacy of constitutional interpretations by enabling the legislature to ignore the interpretations of the court.[21] This would appear to redress the difficulties faced by the legislature granting too much authority to the determinations of the courts.

The disadvantage of such an approach is that it may give rise to further constitutional problems. First, it may produce a series of constitutional crises, as opposed to dialogue. This may undermine the stability of the constitution as a whole as well as the stability of democratic dialogue approaches to rights protection.[22] In addition, it challenges the principle of the separation of powers. The separation of powers is interpreted not merely as requiring the distribution of different aspects of governmental power to different institutions, but as requiring that this distribution be based on the different characteristics of these

---

[18] G Phillipson, '(Mis)representing section 3 of the Human Rights Act 1998' (2003) 119 *Law Quarterly Review* 183, 187.

[19] F Klug, 'Judicial Deference under the Human Rights Act 1998' [2003] *European Human Rights Law Review* 125, 131.

[20] T Hickman, 'Constitutional Dialogue, Constitutional Theories and the Human Rights Act 1998' [2005] *Public Law* 306 and K Roach, *The Supreme Court on Trial: Judicial Activism and Democratic Dialogue* (Toronto, Irwin Law, 2001).

[21] Roach, *ibid*, at 490–93. Hickman refers to this as 'principle-posing dialogue', *ibid*, at 316.

[22] Tremblay, above n 1, at 637. The need for finality is cited as the principle justification for judicial sovereignty by Schauer and Alexander. See, L Alexander and F Schauer, 'On Extra-Judicial Constitutional Interpretation' (1997) 110 *Harvard Law Review* 1359 and L Alexander and F Schauer, 'Defending Judicial Supremacy: A Reply' (2000) 17 *Constitutional Comment* 455.

institutions. Co-ordinate constitutionalism may undermine the different institutional roles of the legislature and the judiciary.[23] The ability of the legislature to ignore court decisions also undermines the rule of law.[24]

More is needed to justify democratic dialogue, therefore, than the simple assertion that the mere provision to the legislature of a means of responding to judicial determinations of rights ensures that democracy is not undermined. To see how democratic dialogue models of rights protection could provide an effective balance of democracy and rights, we need to build on our analysis in chapter four of the arguments in favour of and rejecting a constitutional protection of rights.

B. Finding the Right Balance

To ascertain how democratic dialogue can provide an effective balance of democracy and rights we need to return to the debate surrounding whether courts should be given the power to override legislation where this contravenes human rights. We argued that the debate revolved around two separate issues. The first concerned whether primacy should be granted to democracy or to the protection of rights. The second issue concerned the identification of the institution that was best placed to take authoritative decisions as to the content of rights. This assessment can be made on both process and outcome grounds. Either the legislature or the courts could be regarded as more likely to reach the right answer as to the scope and application of a particular human right, or the way in which each institution reaches its conclusions could be regarded as the more legitimate procedure through which to ascertain the content of legal rights.[25]

There is no scope for a democratic dialogue model of rights protection if we accept that rights always override democracy and that the judiciary are always best placed, in terms of both outcome and process, to determine the scope and application of human rights. In the same way, there is no scope for democratic dialogue models of rights protection where it is argued that democracy always overrides rights and that the legislature is always best placed to take decisions about the content of rights. A democratic dialogue model of rights protection, therefore, can only be justified if it is capable of delineating a middle ground between these two theories.

The establishment of this middle ground relies on two assumptions. First, rights need to be regarded as sufficiently important to override democracy in certain circumstances, but not as so important that they always override democracy, or as so unimportant that they can always be overridden by legislation.

---

[23] Roach, above n 21, at 493. See also: J Leclair, 'Reflexions critiques au sujet de la métaphore du dialogue au droit constitutionnel canadien' [2003] *Revue du Barreau (Numéro special)* 379.
[24] Roach, *ibid*.
[25] See discussion in ch 4, pp 103–112.

Secondly, it must be possible to conclude that either the legislature or the court is best placed to make authoritative determinations of the scope or application of rights, depending on the circumstances of the case.

These two assumptions are met if we accept both that rights have value and that rights are contestable. If rights are regarded as valuable, then there is a justification for allowing rights to override democracy. If we regard rights as contestable, then there may also be good reasons for failing to regard the judiciary or the legislature as being capable of reaching the right answer as to the scope and application of Convention rights. A third factor is also needed. Rights must not be so contestable that it is impossible to reach conclusions concerning the relative suitability of the legislature or the courts to make authoritative determinations about the scope and application of human rights.

C. Justifying the Assumptions Underlying Democratic Dialogue: Jeremy Waldron

One possible basis for a justification of democratic dialogue models of rights protection stems from Waldron's argument against a constitutional protection of rights. Waldron clearly asserts that his argument does not rest on any form of scepticism regarding the existence of objective human rights, being based instead on scepticism as to whether the scope of rights can be precisely delineated. He asserts both that rights have objective value and that they are contestable.

The core of Waldron's argument against a constitutional protection of rights rests on four assumptions. First, he assumes that the democratic institutions are in reasonably good working order, in order to provide factual justification of the claim to democratic legitimacy made by the democratic law-making institution. The second assumption is similar, concerning the judiciary as opposed to the legislature. Again, it requires there to be sufficient facts to support the claims of the judiciary to institutional legitimacy, including its ability to uphold the rule of law and sufficient judicial independence to ensure that it takes decisions on a non-representative basis. The third assumption is the relative commitment in a particular society to the protection of minority rights on the part of most of the members of society and most of the officials within that society. The fourth assumption is the existence of substantial, good faith disagreement about the nature of rights.[26]

The third and the fourth assumptions are of particular relevance. The third assumption satisfies our requirement for a commitment to a protection of rights. The fourth assumption explains both why rights should not always override democracy and why it cannot be conclusively proved that either the legislature

---

[26] J Waldron, 'The Core of the Case against Judicial Review' (2006) 115 *Yale Law Journal* 1346, 1360.

or the judiciary is always the best placed institution to take authoritative decisions concerning the scope and application of human rights. This appears to provide both the necessary consensus and dissensus regarding the identification of rights.

Waldron argues that rights dissensus can arise in three distinct ways.

1. There can be disagreement about the philosophical nature of rights. These disagreements concern the nature of rights and their identification.
2. There can be disagreement about the way in which abstract principles of rights apply to general legislative provisions. One possible example would be disagreement surrounding whether legislation promoting equal access to education requires exceptions to enable the establishment of exclusive religious schools.
3. Rights dissensus can arise when determining how a general right applies in a specific case. An example of this type of rights dissensus arises when determining whether freedom of expression should be restricted in order to prevent speech that may be used to promote terrorism, or whether speech should only be restricted where there is incitement to commit terrorist activities.[27]

D. Consensus, Dissensus and *Prolife*: an Example

The possibility of the co-existence of both consensus and dissensus surrounding the identification, scope and application of human rights appears to be supported by case law. One such example is the disagreement between the decisions of the Court of Appeal and the House of Lords in *R (Prolife Alliance) v British Broadcasting Corporation (Prolife)*.[28] *Prolife* concerned a decision of the BBC to refuse to broadcast a party political election broadcast for the Prolife Alliance Party. The broadcast contained graphic footage of aborted foetuses. The BBC concluded that were it to broadcast the material, it would contravene its obligation under section 6(1)(a) of the Broadcasting Act 1990 not to broadcast programmes that offend against good taste and decency.

The case provides sufficient evidence of rights consensus, given that all the judgments confirmed the importance not only of freedom of expression, but of the particular importance of the freedom of political speech.[29] Disagreements between the judiciary concerning the validity of the broadcasting ban turned, at least in part, on disagreements on the relative importance of these rights and their application to the specific facts before the court, providing evidence of rights dissensus.[30]

[27] *Ibid*, at 1366–7.
[28] [2002] EWCA Civ 297, [2002] 3 WLR 1080 (CA) and [2003] UKHL 23, [2004] 1 AC 185 (HL).
[29] *Ibid*, CA [36] (Laws LJ), [56]–[59] (Simon Brown LJ), *ibid*, HL [6] (Lord Nicholls), [54] (Lord Hoffmann) and [93], [97] (Lord Scott).
[30] Another area of disagreement concerned the role of the court and the degree to which the court should scrutinise the decision of the BBC.

Laws and Simon Brown LJJ, as well as Lord Scott, placed particular importance on the context of political speech, concluding that political broadcasts
could only be censored on grounds of taste and decency if the information that
was deemed to be in bad taste was false or gratuitously sensational. The particular importance of imagery in conveying the political message of Prolife Alliance
and the factual, non-sensational nature of the images led to the conclusion that
to censor such information would breach the Convention right to freedom of
expression found in article 10 ECHR.[31]

The majority of the House of Lords focused on the duty of the BBC not to
broadcast offensive material, as well as the cumulative impact of the images
used.[32] Lord Hoffmann also relied on the relatively weak connection between
this broadcast and political speech in general, recognising that the broadcast
concerned a single issue that may not have as much impact on decision-making
at the ballot box as party political broadcasts that focused on a broader range
of policies.[33]

A justification of democratic dialogue models of rights protection, however,
requires more than factual support for the co-existence of rights dissensus and
rights consensus. It also requires a method by which to distinguish between the
two. This helps to determine, for example, whether the decision of the House of
Lords in *Prolife* is an example of a situation where it was reasonable or unreasonable for the House of Lords to disagree with the conclusion of the Court of
Appeal. When looking at democratic dialogue, this helps to discern how the legislature or the judiciary should exercise their relative powers to ensure that
democratic dialogue models of rights protection provide for an effective balance
between democracy and rights without leading to instability that may cause the
theory to collapse into an argument for a constitutional or a democratic protection of rights.

E. Distinguishing between Consensus and Dissensus: Core and Penumbral Applications of a Human Right

One possible way in which this distinction may be drawn is to use Hart's distinction between a core and a penumbral application of the law. Applications of
the law that are plain to all are part of the core meaning of the right. Penumbral
applications lie on the debatable border of the legal term in question.[34] *Prolife*
may provide an example of a penumbral issue, requiring a discussion of the
scope of freedom of expression and its application to a borderline case of speech
that was deemed to offend public taste and decency. This can be contrasted with

---

[31] Above n 28, CA [39]–[45] (Laws LJ), [57]–[63] (Simon Brown LJ), HL [93]–[100] (Lord Scott).
[32] *Ibid*, HL [12]–[15] (Lord Nicholls) and [68] (Lord Hoffmann).
[33] *Ibid*.
[34] HLA Hart, *The Concept of Law*, 2nd edn (Oxford, Oxford University Press, 1994) 119 and
141.

a core issue that could have arisen in the case, whether the right to freedom of expression included the right to base a party political broadcast on the single issue of a campaign against abortion.

The facts in *Prolife* provide an example of a reasonable disagreement between the Court of Appeal and the House of Lords. The legislature would have been justified in responding to this judicial determination, if it disagreed with the conclusion of the court concerning the scope and application of the right to freedom of expression and the way in which it was to be balanced with the protection of the moral sensitivities of the audience.

However, the distinction between core and penumbral applications does not fully encapsulate the way in which we reason about rights. Disagreements about rights concern not just the way in which the right should be applied, but the justification of the right itself. The dissensus evident in the application of freedom of expression arguments to penumbral issues in *Prolife* concerned not only the way in which freedom of expression is applied, but the justification of freedom of expression. A variety of arguments are used to justify the right to freedom of expression. Freedom of expression is justified through the way in which it promotes truth, enhances democracy, promotes the personal autonomy of the speaker and/or the recipient of speech, furthers tolerance, or provides an alternative non-violent means of protest promoting stability. These theories in turn give rise to different core meanings of the right to freedom of expression, which in turn impact on the determination of penumbral applications of the right.

The existence of rights dissensus, therefore, may apply to the core as well as to penumbral issues of rights applications. Consequently, the distinction cannot be used as a means by which to determine when the reaction of the legislature to modify or amend a rights determination made by the court is an example of a justified use of democratic power, illustrating reasonable disagreement between the legislature and the judiciary, as opposed to providing an example of a misuse of the powers of the legislature that may fail to provide an effective balance between rights and democracy.

F. Distinguishing Between Consensus and Dissensus: Ronald Dworkin's Easy and Hard Cases

A further distinction that may be used to guide the legislature and the judiciary in the exercise of their powers is that between easy and hard cases drawn by Dworkin. To understand the manner in which Dworkin draws this distinction, we need to examine a further distinction used by Dworkin—the distinction between propositions of law and grounds of law.

Propositions of law are statements that establish what the law requires in a particular situation. Grounds of law are the legal arguments that are used to justify propositions of law. For example, the statement that it is unlawful to park on double yellow lines is a proposition of law. The grounds of law stem from traffic regulations governing parking restrictions. Applied to the facts of *Prolife*, the proposition of law is the conclusion reached by a majority of the House of Lords that it was lawful for the BBC to prevent the party political broadcast of Prolife Alliance. The grounds of this legal proposition stem from the meaning of article 10 ECHR and the statute requiring the BBC to ensure that it protected the moral sensitivities of its audience.

Disagreements surrounding propositions of law stem not only from empirical disagreements (about the facts before the court), but from theoretical disagreements (concerning the scope and application of the grounds of law). In a similar manner, disagreements concerning whether legislation is incompatible with Convention rights is a product not merely of empirical disagreements but of theoretical disagreements. Disputes arise both as to the facts before the court and with regard to the nature and content of rights.[35] Easy cases arise when the proposition of law is obvious. Any competent interpretation applying different theoretical accounts of the grounds of law would reach the same conclusion as to the proposition of law. Hard cases arise when there is no such agreement surrounding the proposition of law.[36]

The distinction between easy and hard cases is a better reflection of the way in which we reason about rights. In particular, it is compatible with the widely-accepted interest theory of rights. Raz, for example, argues that an individual has a right where she has a sufficient interest to place another under a duty to act.[37] The conclusion *as to the existence of such a right* represents an intermediate conclusion, drawn between values and duties (analogous to Dworkin's 'grounds' of law). Different values produce different interests, providing diverse justifications for a particular right. These particular rights, in turn, form *the foundation of different duties* (analogous to Dworkin's 'propositions' of law).

Applying this to *Prolife*, the values of personal autonomy, truth and democracy underpin the existence of a right to freedom of expression: the right to freedom of expression plays a role in promoting these values. In turn, the right to freedom of expression founds specific duties. The right to freedom of expression produces a duty on the state not to restrict political expression unless such a restriction serves other legitimate grounds and the restriction on freedom of political expression is limited to the restriction required to promote these legitimate grounds.

This understanding of rights helps to explain the existence of both a rights consensus and a rights dissensus. The intermediary nature of rights facilitates the formation of a common culture, explaining why consensus emerges regarding the rights to be legally protected in a particular society's Bill of Rights. However, rights are intermediary conclusions, explaining how an understanding of the right in and of itself may not provide a clear answer to the question of

[35] R Dworkin, *Law's Empire* (London, Fontana, 1986) 3–6.
[36] *Ibid*, at 266.
[37] J Raz, *The Morality of Freedom* (Oxford, Clarendon Press, 1986) 166.

whether particular legislation is or is not contrary to Convention rights. A full answer to this question may well require an analysis of the values underpinning the right, giving rise to a situation in which it is reasonable to disagree whether legislation breaches Convention rights. The stronger the nature of the intermediary conclusion, the more likely it is that there is little disagreement surrounding the nature of the right. Consequently, the issue will be classified as an easy case. The weaker the nature of the intermediary conclusion, the greater is the need to investigate values underpinning the right. This leads to the conclusion that the issue before the court is a hard case.[38]

The distinction between easy and hard cases itself is not clear-cut and depends on the expertise and experience of those determining propositions of law.[39] Although the distinction may help to meet the *assumptions* underlying a democratic dialogue model of rights protection, it may not provide a clear line that will ensure that the legislature and judiciary exercise their relative powers in a way that achieves the *right balance* between democracy and rights. Although this problem might be fatal to some conceptions of democratic dialogue, it will be argued that it does not undermine the model of democratic dialogue that is most suited to the Human Rights Act; furthermore, structuring our enquiry in this way may provide sufficient guidance to ensure that this model achieves an effective balance between democracy and rights.

III. JUSTIFICATION OF THE HUMAN RIGHTS ACT 1998

We have argued that democratic dialogue models of rights protection can be justified if we accept that there is both value in protecting those rights around which we have a sufficient consensus, and if there exist reasonable disagreements about the nature of rights and their scope and application to specific situations. We have also discussed the practical problems that may arise if democratic dialogue is not exercised in the proper manner, looking for a clear line that can be used to determine when the legislature should exercises its legal power to modify judicial determinations of rights issues so as to ensure an effective balance between rights and democracy.

This section will use the connections between justifications of a constitutional protection of rights to illustrate different models of democratic dialogue. It will argue that the model best suited to the Human Rights Act is that which relies on the *different institutional features* of the legislature and the courts: this model is able to overcome both the practical difficulties in justifying democratic dialogue, as well as the problems posed by the lack of a clear line between easy and hard cases.

---

[38] *Ibid*, at 180–83.
[39] *Ibid*, at 449, fn 14.

A. Justifications of Democratic Dialogue

First, democratic dialogue may be used to supplement arguments that vest primacy in a constitutional document that was enacted by a democratically-accountable body Such documents aim to balance democracy and rights by enabling the judiciary to overturn legislation that contravenes human rights, while recognising that the document containing these human rights has a democratic pedigree. Such protections were criticised as prioritising the wishes of an earlier democratically composed body over those of a later democratically composed body.

Democratic dialogue may respond to this criticism. By allowing the legislature to respond to the decisions of the judiciary, it provides the legislature with the opportunity to replace decisions as to the scope and application of human rights made by the democratic law-making institution of an earlier generation with the conclusions of a more recently composed democratic decision-maker. Moreover, a democratic dialogue model may protect such theories from criticisms that, as constitutional protections of rights are drafted in vague terms, granting the power to the judiciary to overturn legislation may empower the judiciary to replace the decisions of the legislature with the decisions of the court. This is because the interpretations of the constitutional document provided by the court may not reflect the wishes of the original authors, or reflect the current opinions of the democratic law-making body. Democratic dialogue would enable the legislature to re-establish the balance between democracy and rights, by modifying judicial decisions that the democratic decision-maker found to be out of line with the wishes of the electorate.

Two further justifications of democratic dialogue respond in different ways to the challenge posed to constitutional protections of rights by the contestable nature of rights. The second justification of democratic dialogue regards dialogue as a method through which the right answer can be reached as to the scope and application of a human right. The third justification argues that dialogue is a more legitimate process by which to resolve disputes about rights. The third justification does not require that democratic dialogue reaches the right answer, being based instead on an assessment of legitimate processes by which to reach justifiable conclusions as to the scope and application of human rights in the face of contestable rights issues.

B. Applying Justifications of Democratic Dialogue to the Human Rights Act

The Human Rights Act is best understood as combining elements of both the second and third justifications of democratic dialogue. It requires an examination of institutional features of the legislature and the judiciary, both to determine whether (i) arguments can be made as to whether the judiciary or the legislature is more likely to reach the right answer as to the scope and application of human rights, and whether (ii) this answer would be reached by a more legitimate process.

The Human Rights Act does not grant primacy to human rights, or to a document containing these rights. It preserves parliamentary sovereignty, as judicial decisions cannot override legislation that contravenes human rights. Parliament has the final authority to determine both whether specific legislation will be amended or be capable of being read to ensure its compatibility with Convention rights and to delineate the content of these Convention rights, as well as the authority to overturn the provisions of the Human Rights Act by either implied or express repeal.

The first justification of democratic dialogue, therefore, is not applicable to the provisions of the Human Rights Act. There are also difficulties with the first justification. It requires a clear line to be drawn between those measures where there is and is not sufficient consensus regarding Convention rights if it is to ensure that the legislature only act when required to ensure an effective balance between democracy and rights. The first model requires the legislature to intervene to challenge the decision of the judiciary only when the legislature can be certain that it is correcting an out of date interpretation of Convention rights. Given the difficulty of drawing a bright line between easy and hard cases, this may cause instability.

The second and third justifications may fit the provisions of the Human Rights Act, given that they do not rely on the existence of a document containing rights which has the power to override legislation. It will be recalled that the Human Rights Act establishes two different forms of democratic dialogue. First, the legislature has the ability to respond to the way in which the court exercises its powers under section 3 of the Human Rights Act by enacting different legislative provisions. Secondly, the legislature can respond to the decision of the court to issue a declaration of incompatibility under section 4. It can do so either by agreeing that the legislation is incompatible and modifying its provisions to ensure Convention-compatibility, or by disagreeing with the decision of the court, leaving the legislation as it stands. Such disagreement may occur either if the legislature disagrees with the scope and application of Convention rights, or if they disagree with the court that there are no justifications to override the Convention right.

Moreover, section 3 and section 4 give different degrees of relative authority to the legislature and the courts. Section 3 tips the balance of power in favour of the court. The court is able to provide a remedy that protects rights. The legislature needs to enact legislation that is incapable of being interpreted in the manner wished by the courts if it is to modify this judicial decision. Section 4 tips the balance of power in favour of the legislature. Rights are not protected unless and until the legislature chooses to act to modify the legislation declared incompatible with Convention rights, or enact different legislation in order to protect Convention rights.

The Human Rights Act, therefore, is suited to a model that focuses on the different institutional features of the legislature and the judiciary. Section 3 is more suited to situations where the *judiciary* is more likely to reach a correct conclusion as to the scope and application of Convention rights. Section 4 is more suited to cases where the *legislature* is more likely to reach a correct conclusion concerning the scope and application of Convention rights.

Moreover, the Human Rights Act does not require that the judiciary and the legislature have the same power to authoritatively resolve dialogue between the two institutions. This is important because there are two problems with models of democratic dialogue that depend on this form of equality between the legislature and the judiciary. First, instability occurs. If we accept the assumption of the contestable nature of rights, it may be difficult in practice for the legislature and the judiciary to reach an agreement as to the content of a particular right. Consequently, the possibility arises that the legislature will frequently use its power to modify the resolution of the judiciary, given that the legislature disagrees with the court's decision and it is reasonable for the legislature to hold this belief. In turn, it will also be reasonable for the judiciary to hold its belief as to the scope and application of a particular human right. This may lead to a series of constitutional crises, as each institution acts to overturn the resolution of the other and each believes that it is reasonable for it to act in this manner.

Alternatively, the equality of power between the legislature and the courts required by this form of dialogue may further undermine its justification. It may encourage the different institutions to exercise their powers to reach a compromise in order to avoid the instability caused by a series of constitutional crises. Yet dialogue is only justified when both institutions strive to reach the right answer, ensuring (i) a better ability to find the right answer as to the scope and application of human rights, or (ii) the legitimacy of the process through which the authoritative determination of the scope and application of human rights is discovered.

C. The Human Rights Act, 'Definitive Conclusions' and Theories of Rights

The Human Rights Act does not require that definitive conclusions are made as to whether the judiciary or the legislature is more likely to reach the correct conclusion as to the scope and application of Convention rights, or that either institution uses a better process. Instead, it requires that conclusions can be drawn as to whether it is reasonable to assume that the legislature or the courts has made a mistake when reaching a conclusion as to the scope and application of Convention rights (given (i) the nature of the right in question, and (ii) the process used by both institutions when taking decisions involving Convention rights). This feature helps to overcome a possible criticism of the use of different institutional features of the legislature and the courts to determine whether dialogue should be instituted through section 3 or section 4 of the Human Rights Act.

Waldron argues that determinations as to the relative ability of institutions to determine the scope and application of rights collapse into arguments about theories of rights. As theories of rights are contestable, then conclusions concerning the relative ability of institutions to resolve rights issues are also contestable. Waldron argues, therefore, that these arguments cannot be used alone to resolve issues as to the determination of rights, referring to this as the danger of 'rights instrumentalism'.[40]

Waldron's argument, however, only criticises the use of institutional factors to reach definitive conclusions as to whether a particular institution is best placed to reach the right answer as to the scope and application of human rights: the democratic dialogue model of rights protection found in the Human Rights Act does not require a definitive conclusion to be reached, however. It requires instead that institutional features be used to determine whether it is reasonable to assume that the courts or the legislature have reached the right answer concerning the scope and application of a Convention right, or that the process used by the courts or the legislature to reach these conclusions is more legitimate. This helps to determine when the court should exercise its powers under section 3 and when, instead, it should leave the matter to the legislature to resolve under section 4.

Where it is reasonable to assume that the judiciary is better placed to reach the right answer as to the scope and application of a right, or has a more legitimate process through which to reach this answer, then prima facie courts should exercise their powers under section 3. Where institutional features suggest that the legislature is more likely to reach the right answer, or use a more legitimate process, then courts should exercise their powers under section 4 as opposed to section 3.

The way in which the Human Rights Act provides for two different forms of dialogue also explains why stability can be preserved, despite the lack of a clear line between easy and hard cases. The Human Rights Act does not require a clear distinction between easy and hard cases in order to ascertain whether and how the courts or the legislature should exercise their powers under the Act. This is because sections 3 and 4 only give relatively greater authority, as opposed to a definitive authority, to resolve a human rights issue to either the legislature or the courts. It requires an assessment of whether it is reasonable to assume that the court is performing its correcting function,[41] given its better ability to reach a right answer as to the scope and application of Convention rights, or the greater legitimacy of the process used to reach that conclusion. When the court is faced with an easy case, it is reasonable to assume that the court is performing its correcting function; the same assumption may not be appropriate where the court is faced with a hard case. As assessment of reasonableness does not require a definitive answer as to whether the court is faced with an easy or a hard case.

---

[40] See ch 4, pp 109–112. See also Waldron, above n 26.
[41] When the court exercises its powers under s 3 to provide a Convention-compatible interpretation of legislation.

The democratic dialogue model of rights protection found in the Human Rights Act is able to overcome both the practical and theoretical difficulties of justifying democratic dialogue models of rights protection. However, to succeed, it relies on an ability to distinguish between institutional features of the legislature and the courts as to their relative abilities to reach correct conclusions, and the relative legitimacy of the process through which they reach such conclusions, concerning the scope and application of particular Convention rights.

IV. DIALOGUE AND INSTITUTIONAL COMPETENCES

We have concluded that the democratic dialogue model of rights protection found in the Human Rights Act 1998 requires an analysis of different institutional features of the legislature and the courts.[42] The focus of this investigation is on those features that govern whether courts should use section 3 or section 4. This is because the Human Rights Act grants a greater protection to democracy than to rights, reserving from the courts the power to override legislation that contravenes Convention rights. The Human Rights Act does not provide powers to the legislature to ensure that democracy is protected from unwarranted intrusion from an overly strong protection of rights, but instead provides courts with duties and powers to protect rights from unwarranted intrusion by the legislature.

There are three main areas where the courts are regarded as better at protecting human rights than the legislature. First, courts are arguably better at protecting the rights of minorities than legislatures. Secondly, courts are better suited to ensuring the preservation of long-standing principles of rights inherent to a particular legal system. Thirdly, courts are better able to protect specific individual rights from intrusion from more general provisions. The main limitation of the courts stems from the different way in which the legislature and the courts can act to provide a remedy for those whose rights have been harmed. Courts can only make interstitial changes to the law. They cannot provide broad, general, remedies.

A. Protection of Minority Rights

Arguments that courts are better placed to protect the rights of minorities can be found in a variety of sources. First, arguments focus on the inherent flaws of democratic law-making institutions, which favour majority as opposed to minority interests. This influences what Calabresi classifies as type II models of rights protections, which he refers to as the 'judicial enforcement of the anti-

---

[42] Hickman reaches a similar conclusion, see Hickman, above n 20.

discrimination principle'. Type II models of rights protection allocate the task of ensuring that fundamental rights are protected to the legislature. However, it argues that the legislature is unable to protect the rights of distinct minority groups, which have been significantly under-represented or excluded from the legislative process in a particular society. Consequently, when faced with legislation that imposes a burden on an under-represented minority, it is the role of the court to provide a closer scrutiny of this legislation, ensuring that it does not restrict the fundamental rights of the under-represented minority. Courts are empowered to overturn such legislation. This model of human rights protections draws on inherent flaws found in the democratic law-making processes, which, by definition, favour majorities. The concern is that, by pursuing policies that match the opinion of the majority, the rights of minorities may be ignored by the legislature. Courts, therefore, should restrict their role to protecting the rights of significant minority groups, correcting inherent flaws in the democratic law-making process.[43]

Ely's model of representation-reinforcing judicial review provides a further example of a model of judicial review that relies on the claim that the legislature is ill-equipped to protect minority rights.[44] Ely's theory requires the courts to intervene to protect the rights of minorities who are effectively cut off from the law-making process and to protect the rights of those who are disadvantaged by laws, where the court suspects that this disadvantage is motivated by prejudice of the majority towards the minority. The court is also required to closely scrutinise restrictions of rights that may facilitate participation in the democratic process by minority groups, for example restrictions placed on freedom of expression.

The assessment of whether there are such flaws in the democratic process requires an analysis of the composition of the democratic law-making body. The Westminster Parliament is elected through an electoral system of first past the post. Parliamentary seats are allocated to those individuals who obtain the most votes within a particular constituency, on the basis of a relative as opposed to an absolute majority of votes cast. In addition, a government is formed from the political party obtaining the most seats in the Westminster Parliament. It is the government that initiates most legislation, which requires only a simple majority of votes cast in each House (or failing that, in the House of Commons should the procedure of the Parliaments Acts 1911–49 be used) in addition to the consent of the monarch, to become legally valid. Given the operation of the party whip system, it is rare for a government to be defeated on the legislation that it has initiated.

Given these features of the Westminster Parliament, we can make a prima facie argument that the predominant law-making institution within the United

---

[43] G Calabresi, 'Antidiscrimination and Cultural Accountability (What the Bork-Brennan Debate ignores)' (1991) 105 *Harvard Law Review* 80, 91–103.

[44] JH Ely, *Democracy and Distrust: A Theory of Judicial Review* (London, Harvard University Press, 1980).

Kingdom constitution[45] may be less likely to take account of minority rights than the courts. The government may be drawn from members of a political party that holds a large majority of seats in Parliament, but which does not enjoy a majority of the votes cast as a whole across the country. This disparity may mean that there is less of an incentive for political parties to engage with the rights of minorities in society. The electoral system may also make it difficult for newly emergent political groups to obtain proportionate representation in the Westminster Parliament. Even when seats are obtained, the fact that legislation can be enacted through a simple majority of votes cast in the House of Commons, provided that at least the consent of the monarch is obtained, means that it may be hard for minority groups who are represented in the House of Commons to ensure that legislation does not erode their rights. There are also some groups for whom it may be extremely difficult in practice to raise sufficient political support to enter into political debate—eg the rights of prisoners.

As well as recognising the possible flaws in the democratic law-making process, arguments can also be made explaining why the courts may be better placed to protect minority rights. Raz recognises the way in which the courts play a role in constitutional politics which may be more suited to protecting minority interests, focusing on practical reasons that explain why it may be easier for minorities to protect their rights through the courts as opposed to through the legislature. It is those whose rights have been infringed that initiate legal action; there is no need to generate sufficient support from others as would be required in order to enter a political debate. It may also be easier for minorities to succeed in protecting their rights, given that success is more likely to be determined by persuasion through logical and reasonable argument as opposed to the forming of a political coalition.[46]

Aspects of English administrative law also suggest that it may be easier for minorities to protect their rights through judicial as opposed to legislative means. Standing is granted to a 'victim', which can include groups representing the interests of potential victims.[47] Those whose rights are harmed by legislation satisfy this legal requirement. Therefore, they are able to bring a legal action, asking for a statute to be reinterpreted so as to protect Convention rights, or seeking a declaration of incompatibility. It may be harder, however, for groups formed to represent the interests of particular minorities to obtain the same remedy, as a suggestion has been made that only actual or potential victims of

[45] The discussion will not touch on the composition of the Scottish Parliament, the Welsh Assembly and the Northern Ireland Parliament. This is because our investigation concerns the justification of the democratic dialogue model of rights protections found in the relationship between the courts and the Westminster Parliament. The devolved law-making institutions are not granted the power to legislate contrary to Convention rights. See Scotland Act 1998 s 57(2); Government of Wales Act 1998, s 22 to s 33 and Government of Wales Act 2006 s 81 and Northern Ireland Act 1998 s 24(1)(a).
[46] J Raz, 'Rights and Politics' (1995) 71 *Indiana Law Journal* 27, 42–3.
[47] Human Rights Act 1998, s 7(1), s 7(3) and s 7(7).

legislation should be able to obtain a declaration of incompatibility.[48] Even if this were the case, the court may still interpret legislation to ensure Convention compatibility. Moreover, even if a declaration of incompatibility were not issued, democratic dialogue may still be initiated, as the lack of a declaration of incompatibility will stem from the inappropriate nature of the remedy, given that there is no victim before the court, as opposed to the compatibility of the legislation in question with Convention rights.

These differences may not be sufficient to support the assertion that courts will always be better placed to reach correct conclusions concerning the nature of rights. However, it raises a suspicion that legislatures, in particular the Westminster Parliament, may take decisions without taking full account of minority rights. Judicial action provides a means by which minorities may be more able to raise these issues, enabling courts to correct mistakes where Convention rights have been breached. It may thus provide support for a prima facie conclusion that the judiciary are able to correct potential mistakes of the legislature in this area.

B. Protection of Long-standing Principles

The different institutional features of the legislature and the courts are also used to support the conclusion that courts are better placed to protect long-standing principles than the legislature. Arguments made to support this conclusion are similar to those used to support the assertion that the judiciary should be granted the power to make authoritative resolutions as to the nature of rights, given that correct determination of the scope and application of a human rights derives from principles of moral reasoning, a process reflected in the legal reasoning of the judiciary.

The difference stems from the way in which institutional differences are used. The different institutional features of the courts are not used to provide conclusive evidence that courts will reach the right answer determining the scope of rights. Rather, the argument is made that institutional features affecting the way in which courts and the legislature reason make it less likely that courts will ignore information relevant to the determination of the scope and application of rights than the legislature. Courts are more able to protect long-standing principles and rights inherent to the constitution than the legislature because its decision-making process is more specifically focused on determining the scope of rights, often through reference to long-standing principles of rights. The legislature is less focused on determining the scope and content of rights, being more concerned to regulate more immediate matters which may indirectly restrict rights.[49]

---

[48] *Re S(Minors)(Care Order: Implementation of Care Plan)* [2002] UKHL 10, [2002] AC 291, [88].

[49] It is the lack of the use of these institutional features to reach definitive conclusions that makes these arguments immune from criticisms of rights-instrumentalism and of the relative institutional

Bickel's theory of judicial review, advocating restraint in the role of the judiciary within a constitutional protection of rights that grants supremacy to the judiciary to resolve rights issues, draws on the way in which the judiciary is selected and the processes used to reach conclusions in legal arguments to support the assertion that the judiciary is better equipped to protect long-standing principles. The independence of the judiciary ensures that it is buttressed from political pressures and from giving way to emotional responses, as it is required to reach reasoned conclusions.[50] The judiciary is trained to tackle problems in the same manner as a scholar, looking to precedent to discern common principles running through the law. This methodology favours the development of long-term general principles over short-term policies. The legislature, on the other hand, is more concerned with the resolution of immediate problems in response to short-term political demands, may be more likely to respond emotively to garner political support and in addition may be less likely to pay attention to long-standing principles of rights that may be eroded by their legislative solution to the immediate problem before them.

Bickel is not claiming here that the reasoning of the court is akin to moral reasoning, or that the principles discovered by the courts are correct and therefore should override decisions of the legislature. He is merely recognising that, given their institutional differences, courts are more likely to focus on rights issues and long-term principles than the legislature.[51] Consequently, the judiciary may be able to preserve rights and long-standing principles from accidental erosion by the legislature.

Dicey reaches a similar conclusion, drawing on three distinctions between judicial and legislative law-making. Again, his focus is on the methodology used by these different institutions to reach conclusions as to the scope and application of human rights. Courts are more concerned with discerning principles, using logic to apply legal principles to resolve practical problems.[52] They are also more likely to create certainty, applying a chain of reasoning through precedent.[53] Courts are also more likely to rely on older currents of opinion, using more general, established principles as opposed to relying on the current strain of opinion.[54] The legislature is influenced by current political pressures, whereas the courts are better insulated from such pressures. All these features lead Dicey to the conclusion that the role of the court is to preserve general fundamental principles from hasty erosion by the legislature. As the legislature seeks to produce expedient results that accord with the wishes of the prevailing majority, it

---

features of the legislature and the courts to reach correct conclusions concerning the nature and scope of human rights. See Waldron, above n 26, at 370.

[50] AM Bickel, *The Least Dangerous Branch: the Supreme Court at the Bar of Politics* (Indianapolis, Bobbs-Merrill, 1962) 25–6 and AM Bickel, *The Supreme Court and the Idea of Progress* (New York, Harper and Row, 1970) 82 and 177.

[51] See, Hickman, above n 20.

[52] *Ibid*, at 364–7.

[53] *Ibid*, at 366–7.

[54] *Ibid*, at 367–71.

may lose sight of long-standing principles of rights which the judiciary may be more likely to recognise and protect.

These institutional differences are reflected in the constitutional arrangements of the United Kingdom. There is a constitutional principle preserving the independence of the judiciary.[55] The English legal system is based on principles of common law reasoning and courts do pay attention to binding precedents, preserving long-standing principles found in the common law. In addition, sections 3, 4 and 6 of the Human Rights Act strengthen this role of the courts, as the judiciary is obliged to focus on human rights when interpreting legislation, as well as when faced with arguments that actions of the executive are unlawful as they are contrary to Convention rights. Section 6(3)(b) further reinforces this obligation of the court, classifying the court as a public authority for the purposes of the Act.

A possible argument against this assertion is the role of section 19 of the Human Rights Act 1998. Section 19 requires a ministerial statement to be made concerning the compatibility of proposed legislation with Convention rights. By making these statements, the attention of the legislature is drawn to human rights, making it less likely that the legislature will ignore the implications of its legislation for human rights.[56] This may call into question the correcting function of the courts. However, even though the legislature will have human rights drawn to their attention, there is no guarantee that this will directly influence the content of legislation. Danny Nicol has presented evidence which suggests that rights discourse is rarely used by the legislature and that, frequently, section 19 statements prompt more general reactions from the legislature concerning the desirability of the need to protect human rights, as opposed to prompting critical reflection on the way in which general legislation may potentially erode human rights.[57] It is at least arguable, therefore, that the judiciary is able to focus more precisely on rights issues, ensuring that legislation does not accidentally erode human rights, even in instances where the legislature may now be more likely to consider human rights when enacting legislation.

C. Protection of Specific Individual Rights

The court is institutionally suited to protecting specific applications of rights to the facts of the situation presented before the court by a particular applicant. Bickel refers to this as the concern of the court with the actual flesh and blood of the case, looking at how the decisions of the legislature affect the specific rights of the applicant before the court. The legislature is more concerned with abstract general principles, the nature of legislation requiring a broader

---

[55] See in particular, Constitutional Reform Act 2005, s 3 and s 4.

[56] See, D Feldman, 'The Impact of the Human Rights Act on the United Kingdom Legislative Process' (2004) 25 *Statute Law* 91.

[57] See, D Nicol, 'The Human Rights Act and the Politicians' (2004) 24 *Legal Studies* 451.

approach.[58] These differences stem from the nature of the judicial function itself. Courts are better equipped to apply general legislative provisions of rights to specific situations because of the nature of the judicial function; they are required to resolve individual disputes.

The claim here is not that the court is more likely to reach the right answer than the legislature on the content of a specific right because it is more focused on individual as opposed to general issues. Rather, the argument is made that the legislature, focusing on general issues, may be unaware that its general measures may harm specific individual rights. Legislatures are not capable of considering the possible impact of legislation on every individual who may be affected. Those whose rights are affected by general measures can have access to the courts. The courts will focus on the specific issue raised before them to determine whether specific rights have been infringed.

D. Interstitial Changes

The ability of the judiciary to remedy situations where the legislature fails to sufficiently protect rights is limited by its ability to only make interstitial changes to the law. The judiciary deals with the case before it, looking at the issues raised by the parties appearing before the court. Consequently, it is not as suited to resolving complex social problems as the legislature. The legislature is more capable of resolving problems that touch on many different groups in society, or that are of greater magnitude with pervasive ramifications.[59]

These differences stem from the nature of the judicial reasoning process. The judiciary is able to make changes to the law through a process of interpretative reasoning, fitting new developments into previous case law. Consequently, it can only make interstitial changes to the law. In addition, the judiciary may only make partial and piecemeal changes. The judiciary is not able to initiate changes, but responds to the case before them. The case is presented in a bivalent manner. Courts hear the arguments of the parties before them, but may not be in a position to recognise the consequences of their decisions on other parties not represented before the court. The legislature is more able to make broad sweeping changes, having the ability to make these changes at its own initiative. It is able to carry out root and branch reform, and has a greater ability to understand the impact of its legislation on a wide variety of groups and individuals.[60]

These differences are reflected in the United Kingdom constitution. The doctrine of precedent operates to constrain the actions of the judiciary. Even though the House of Lords is not bound by its own previous decisions, it exercises its power to overturn past decisions rarely and cautiously. Although the broaden-

---

[58] Bickel, *The Least Dangerous Branch*, above n 50, at 26.

[59] Bickel, *The Supreme Court and the Idea of Progress*, above n 50, at 91 and 175–77.

[60] See, A Kavanagh, 'The Elusive Divide between Interpretation and Legislation under the Human Rights Act 1998' (2004) 24 *Oxford Journal of Legal Studies* 259, 271–74.

ing of standing requirements, particularly relating to the admission of *amicus curiae* briefs, may enable courts to have greater awareness of the impact of their judicial decisions beyond the immediate impact on the applicants before the court,[61] restrictions as to remedies limit the extent to which the judiciary may provide for these consequences. These restrictions are not faced by Parliament.

This institutional difference does not provide an example of where the judiciary may be best placed to correct potential errors made by the legislature in the protection of rights. Rather, it provides a restraint as to the extent to which the judiciary may remedy breaches of rights. As such, it may limit the circumstances under which the judiciary may use section 3 to read legislation in order to provide a remedy for the party before them whose rights have been breached.

V. TOWARDS A THEORY OF ADJUDICATION

In order to achieve an effective balance of democracy and rights, sections 3 and 4 must be interpreted in a manner that produces the dialogue required by our justification of the democratic dialogue model of rights protection established by the Human Rights Act 1998. This analysis provides us with our first component of a theory of adjudication for the Act. In addition, we need to take account of two further features of the Act.

A. Institutional Competencies and the Remedial Consequences

Sections 3 and 4 provide different remedies for the applicant and place the responsibility for providing that remedy on different institutions. The court provides a remedy for the particular applicant through section 3. The legislature needs to act if a remedy is to be provided for the applicant following a section 4 declaration of incompatibility. The institutional features of the legislature and the court provide limits as to the type of remedy that can be provided by the court, suggesting a further restraint on the use of section 3. In addition, the institutional features of the legislature and the court are reflected in the restriction found in section 3 that courts can only read and give effect to legislation 'so far as possible' to ensure its compatibility with Convention rights. Courts must not transgress the scope of their powers in providing a Convention-compatible reading of legislation. A theory of adjudication, therefore, most take into account the limits of interpretation. These limits also promote the dynamic element of dialogue, defining the manner in which the legislature can respond to a section 3 declaration of incompatibility.

Our justification of democratic dialogue relies on the different institutional features of the legislature and the courts. Courts are in a position to correct

---

[61] See, C Harlow, 'Public Law and Popular Justice' (2002) 65 *Modern Law Review* 1.

mistakes that may be made by the legislature. First, courts are better able to protect the rights of minorities than the legislature. Secondly, courts are able to correct potential errors made by the legislature when the general focus of legislation overrides a specific individual right. Thirdly, courts are able to correct the potential erosion of long-standing legal rights and principles of a particular legal society.

However, the democratic dialogue required by the Human Rights Act does not rely on courts exercising their powers under sections 3 and 4 solely according to an analysis of the relative institutional capacities of the legislature and the courts. This is because of the assumptions that underpin our justification of democratic dialogue: democratic dialogue models of rights protection assume that there is both sufficient consensus surrounding the need to protect rights and sufficient dissensus surrounding the scope and application of Convention rights. It also requires the ability to draw a distinction between those situations in which it is reasonable and unreasonable to disagree about the scope and application of rights. Where it is reasonable to disagree about the scope and application of a particular Convention right, it is not reasonable to assume that the court is performing its correcting function. Consequently, the issue is best suited to resolution by section 4, which provides the legislature with greater authority to definitively resolve the issue. Where there is no scope for reasonable disagreement concerning the nature and application of rights, then it is reasonable to assume that the court is performing its correcting function. As such, the issue is more suited for resolution by section 3 as opposed to section 4.

B. Identifying Cases where it is Reasonable to Disagree about Rights Issues

The different institutional features of the legislature and the courts, as well as the assumptions required for a justification of a democratic dialogue model of rights protection, combine to provide the first feature of a theory of adjudication required to ensure that the Human Rights Act provides an effective balance of democracy and rights.

The court needs to distinguish between cases where it is and is not reasonable to disagree about rights issues. When faced with a non-contestable issue, courts should, prima facie, exercise their duty under section 3 of the Act. When faced with a contestable issue, courts should exercise their powers under section 4 of the Act. These features may also provide guidance to the legislature. The legislature should be more cautious about exercising its powers to modify or amend the conclusions of the court when faced with a situation where the court determines that Convention rights have been breached due to the erosion of important minority rights, or the undermining of a specific or a long-standing individual right by general legislative measures. Greater justification is required of the legislature in these circumstances, particularly when determining whether to override a section 3 reading of legislation by enacting new legislative provisions.

C. Institutional Features and Remedies

The legislature is better placed to provide remedies for some breaches of rights. In particular, courts can only make interstitial changes, providing a solution to the particular issue before the court. Courts are not able to make broader, prospective changes, nor are they suited to establishing complex procedures that may be required to be adhered to by public bodies in order to ensure an effective protection of Convention rights. The legislature is better placed to provide a remedy in these situations. These institutional differences concerning the relative ability of the legislature and the courts to provide an effective remedy place a further limit on the use of section 3. Courts should not use section 3 where a Convention-compatible reading of legislation requires the courts to create a remedy that it is beyond the scope of its institutional capacities to provide. In these circumstances, it is better to issue a declaration of incompatibility, enabling the legislature to produce the remedy required for an effective protection of rights.

This feature also influences the way in which the legislature responds to decisions of the court. Where it is clear that the court was faced with a non-contestable rights issue and the only reason that the court issued a declaration of incompatibility was because institutional features would prevent it from providing an effective remedy, this theory of adjudication entails that the legislature has a strong obligation to enact legislation to protect the Convention right in question. This obligation is even stronger when faced with a conclusion by the court that the legislation in question has eroded a minority right, or is an example of the unintended erosion of specific individual rights at the hands of general legislative measures.

D. Democratic Dialogue and Principles of Interpretation

Principles of interpretation are also relevant to our interpretation of sections 3 and 4. Not only does this stem from the wording of section 3, which requires courts to read and give effect to legislation to achieve Convention-compatibility so far as it is possible to do so, but interpretation provides a means by which the Human Rights Act ensures that the legislature can respond to decisions of the court taken under section 3 of the Act. If the legislature wishes to successfully respond to the decision of the court, then it needs to be able to produce legislation that will not be reinterpreted by the courts so as to overturn the legislature's assessment of the Convention right in question. Interpretation helps to achieve this limit. It restricts the ability of the court to read legislation in order to achieve Convention-compatibility and enables the legislature to achieve its objective of establishing a different interpretation of a Convention right than the one proffered by the judiciary. Principles of interpretation, therefore, provide a further limit to the powers of the courts. They cannot use section 3 where a Convention-compatible reading of legislation would be beyond the scope of acceptable principles of interpretation.

When the court uses section 4 as opposed to section 3 purely because of the restrictions of principles of interpretation, there is a strong obligation placed on the legislature to respond to the declaration of incompatibility by modifying legislation so as to protect Convention rights. This obligation is enhanced when the legislature is faced with a conclusion of the court that legislation harms minority rights, or is an example of general legislation that erodes specific or long-standing principles of rights. This is not the case where the legislature has enacted legislation in order to overturn a previous reading of legislation by the court under section 3.

E. Conclusion

These components combine to provide an outline of a theory of adjudication of the Human Rights Act, based on its ability to provide a justifiable democratic dialogue model of rights protection. First, courts need to distinguish between easy cases (where the rights issue before the court is not contestable and it is not reasonable to disagree about its outcome) from hard cases (where it is reasonable to disagree about the outcome). When faced with a hard case, courts should apply section 4. When faced with an easy case, courts should apply section 3. However, courts should not use section 3 where a Convention-compatible interpretation of legislation requires the provision of a remedy that is beyond the institutional capabilities of the court. In addition, section 3 should not be used where principles of interpretation would dictate that it is impossible for the court to provide a Convention-compatible reading of legislation. In these circumstances courts should issue section 4 declarations of incompatibility.

The legislature has the freedom to modify conclusions of the court both in response to sections 3 and sections 4. It has the greatest liberty when faced with a section 4 declaration that is made solely on the basis that the court was faced with a hard case, where it is not reasonable to assume that the court is performing its correcting function. However, the legislature has a greater obligation to respond to a declaration of incompatibility when faced with a court decision that finds a Convention right has been breached because the rights of a particular minority have been harmed, or because general legislation has inadvertently overridden a specific or long-standing right. This does not mean that the legislature should respond in all such situations, but that a stronger justification is needed should the legislature choose not to respond to the decision of the court to protect the Convention right in question. If courts use section 4 when faced with a non-contestable right, but one which the court is unable to remedy or where it is not possible for the court to provide a Convention-compatible interpretation of the right, then the legislature is faced with an even stronger obligation to intervene so as to protect the Convention right in question, requiring an even stronger justification should it fail to do so. When courts exercise their powers under section 3, the legislature should not exercise its ability to overturn the decision of the court unless it can provide strong reasons for doing so. The political process should scrutinise the decisions of the legislature to ensure that it exercises its powers in a legitimate manner.

VI. CONCLUSION

Our analysis has concluded both that the Human Rights Act 1998 provides for a democratic dialogue model of rights protection, and that it is possible to justify this model as aiming to provide a stronger protection of rights balancing with the need to preserve democracy. The Human Rights Act achieves this by creating different forms of dialogue that enable either the judiciary or the legislature, in practice, to authoritatively resolve disputes as to the specific application of Convention rights, while at the same time facilitating dynamic dialogue between the institutions that preserves the ultimate legal authority of the legislature with regard to the protection of Convention rights.

The chapter has also argued that the different institutional features of the court and the legislature should be used to determine when dialogue should be instituted through the provisions of section 3 and when it should be instituted through the provisions of section 4, providing a theoretical model of adjudication. This investigation will continue in the next chapter when we analyse how far the current legal test produces the democratic dialogue needed to justify the Human Rights Act.

6

A Theory Of Adjudication

THE HUMAN RIGHTS ACT 1998 provides for a democratic dialogue model of rights protection. As such, it aims to balance the need to protect human rights and democracy. The Act tips the balance in favour of democracy. It preserves parliamentary sovereignty, in that Parliament has the final say over the content of Convention rights and also has the ability to overturn the current provision of the Human Rights Act either expressly or through implied repeal. Sections 3 and 4 of the Act provide a means by which courts can protect rights. Section 3 provides the courts with greater relative power to resolve an issue as to the scope and application of a Convention right. Courts are empowered to read and give effect to legislation to ensure its Convention-compatibility, providing a remedy for those whose rights have been harmed. The legislature can respond by enacting new legislation to modify or amend the outcome of the court, although this may be difficult to achieve in practice. Section 4 provides greater relative power to the legislature. A statute that has been declared incompatible with Convention rights still has legality, validity and force. If rights are to be protected, the legislature needs to respond to repeal or amend the statute. The two forms of dialogue found in the Human Right Act were best suited to a model of democratic dialogue that rested on the different institutional features of the legislature and the courts, both as to the relative ability to reach the right answer concerning the scope and application of a right and also as to the relative legitimacy of the process that they use to determine rights issues.

However, in order to ensure that the Human Rights Act achieves this balance in practice, we need to determine how the courts and the legislature should exercise their powers and duties under the Act to generate the right form of dialogue between these institutions. The previous chapter mapped out the theoretical basis for such a test. The current chapter investigates the current legal test. It will explain how the current legal tests may fail to promote the dialogue needed to justify the Human Rights Act and suggest an alternative test, building on both the current law and academic criticism.

I. THE CURRENT LEGAL TEST

The current legal test is found in the House of Lords decision of *Ghaidan v Godin-Mendoza* (*Ghaidan*)[1] which rejected a predominantly linguistic approach to section 3(1).[2] Section 3(1) requires the court to make Convention-compatible interpretations of legislation even when faced with a statute that does not contain ambiguous language. In addition, section 3(1) empowers courts to use expansive and restrictive principles of interpretation. Courts may supply words missing from the statutory provision in order to render it Convention-compatible.[3] They may also read words down, narrowing the scope of application of general provisions to ensure that they do not override Convention rights.

There are two limits to possible Convention-compatible readings of legislation. First, it is not possible to read and give effect to a statute to ensure its provisions do not contravene Convention rights where to do so would defeat a fundamental feature of the statute. This may occur where a statute is given a meaning that is incompatible with the underlying thrust of the legislation.[4] Courts need to ensure that they do not repeal the entire scheme of the statute[5] or furnish the statutory provision with a meaning that is intellectually indefensible.[6]

Secondly, courts should ensure that, when applying section 3(1), they do not make decisions for which they are institutionally ill-equipped. Three possible examples are provided in *Ghaidan*. First, courts should not make a legislative deliberation when choosing between several possible Convention-compatible readings of a statutory provision.[7] Secondly, courts should not provide a Convention-compatible reading of a statute where this would entail large practical repercussions.[8] Thirdly, courts should be reluctant to use section 3(1) when faced with complex issues of social policy.[9]

---

[1] [2004] UKHL 30, [2004] 2 AC 557.

[2] *Ibid*, at [30]–[31] (Lord Nicholls), [38]–[41] (Lord Steyn) and at [110] (Lord Rodger). Although dissenting, Lord Millett appears to agree that language should not provide as great a restriction on possible interpretations as was once thought, stating that a court 'can do considerable violence to the language of the statute as it finds it and give it a meaning which, however, unnatural or unreasonable, is intellectually defensible' [67].

[3] *Ibid*, at [32] (Lord Nicholls) and [67] (Lord Millett).

[4] *Ibid*, at [35] (Lord Nicholls), [110] (Lord Rodger).

[5] *Ibid*, at [65] (Lord Millett).

[6] *Ibid*, at [67] (Lord Millett).

[7] *Ibid*, at [33] (Lord Nicholls).

[8] *Ibid*, at [115] (Lord Rodger), [34] (Lord Nicholls).

[9] *Ibid*, at [65] (Lord Millett), [50] (Lord Steyn).

A. Analysis: Compatibility of the Current Law with a Democratic Dialogue Model of Adjudication

The current legal test does reflect, in part, the theory of adjudication required by the democratic dialogue model of rights protection found in the Human Rights Act. It directly incorporates two of the elements required. First, it provides an account of the scope of interpretation, which can be used to provide further detail to our theory of adjudication. In particular, it provides a definition of interpretation that is able to facilitate dialogue between the legislature and the courts. Secondly, it takes account of the institutional features of the legislature and the courts that determine which institution is best able to provide the specific remedy required to protect Convention rights. However the current law only focuses indirectly on the distinction between easy and hard cases. This indirect focus means that the current legal test may fail to produce the dialogue required to justify the Human Rights Act. In addition, the indirect focus fails to provide an adequate account of the features that can be used to provide a more detailed account of the distinction between contestable and non-contestable rights.

The current test provides a more detailed account of the way in which interpretation restricts the ability of the court to use section 3(1), even when faced with a non-contestable Convention right. The main focus of the restriction in *Ghaidan* is the extent to which a reading of legislation by the courts undermines a fundamental feature of the legislation in question. Not only does this provide a means of clarification of the scope of interpretation, but it provides a test that helps to facilitate dialogue. As Lord Steyn recognised in *Ghaidan*:

> If Parliament disagrees with an interpretation by the courts under section 3(1), it is free to override it by amending the legislation and expressly reinstating the incompatibility.[10]

Parliament can achieve this objective by making their intention to override the interpretation of the court a fundamental feature of its legislation. Not only will this ensure that the legislature is able to respond to the decision of the court, but by ensuring that this intention is a fundamental feature it furnishes a means through which to facilitate democratic debate within Parliament, providing a way in which the legislature can ensure that it meets the responsibility of providing a justification for override the wishes of the court.

It is also clear that the current legal test is sensitive to institutional features which limit the ability of the court to grant an effective remedy, providing a further means through which to add necessary detail to our theory of adjudication. This is illustrated by the second limit of Convention-compatible interpretations found in *Ghaidan*, which illustrates the concern that courts should not use section 3 to provide Convention-compatible interpretations where such interpretations

---

[10] *Ibid*, at [43].

have far-reaching practical ramifications.[11] Parliament, as opposed to the court, is better suited to resolving these issues.

A clear illustration is found in *In re S (Minors)(Care Order Implementation of Care Plan): In re W (Minors)(Adequacy of Care Plan) (S and W)*,[12] which concerned the compatibility of provisions of the Children Act 1989 with article 8 ECHR. The Act governed the way in which the local authority could make a care order removing a child from the care of his guardian. In providing a Convention-compatible interpretation of the Act's provisions, the Court of Appeal created a new 'starred' system for care. Under these provisions, unless certain milestones were met within a set time frame, it was open to the guardian of the child to contest the measure before the court, allowing the court to intervene with the decision of the local authority. Lord Nicholls concluded that this measure created practical repercussions which the court was not well placed to assess, particularly regarding the way in which the starred system would create administrative costs which in turn may create knock-on effects for the way in which local authorities manage their budgets, potentially reducing other services provided by local authorities. In addition, the need to submit reports and to await the decision of the court under the new 'starred' system would have further practical implications for the way in which the local authority discharged its parental responsibilities with regard to children who were the subject of care orders. The court is not best placed to assess these practical ramifications.[13] Therefore, it was better for the court to make a section 4 declaration of incompatibility as opposed to providing a Convention-compatible interpretation of the statute.

Ghaidan does not require that a distinction be drawn between easy and hard cases, analysing when courts are faced with contestable rights issues. However, factors relevant to contestability do influence decisions of the courts. In particular, courts refer to facts that influence contestability when determining whether the issue raised by the case is suitable for resolution by the courts. This connection becomes more evident when we analyse case law discussed in *Ghaidan* which were regarded as providing illustrations of the institutional limits of the courts, in particular the decision of *Bellinger v Bellinger (Bellinger)*[14]

B. An Example: *Bellinger v Bellinger*

Both Lord Nicholls and Lord Millett concluded that *Bellinger* was an example of a case unsuited to resolution by the courts.[15] The case concerned the interpretation of section 11(c) of the Matrimonial Causes Act 1973 which defined

---

[11] [2004] UKHL 30, [2004] 2 AC 557, at [34] (Lord Nicholls), [115] (Lord Rodger).
[12] [2002] UKHL 10, [2002] 2 AC 291.
[13] *Ibid*, at [43]–[44].
[14] [2003] UKHL 21, [2003] 2 AC 467.
[15] *Ibid*, at [34] (Lord Nicholls) and [65] (Lord Millett).

legal marriages as, inter alia, a union between a 'male' and a 'female'. Mrs Bellinger was a female trans-sexual, who was correctly registered as 'male' at birth but who had since undergone gender reassignment surgery and treatment and who was living as a woman. The issue arose as to whether 'male' and 'female' could be interpreted to enable gender to be ascertained by means other than biological factors used to assign gender at birth. In *Bellinger*, Lord Nicholls recognised the difficulty of using criteria other than biological features present at birth to determine gender. Given the range of possible surgical and other medical procedures, and the need to take into account social acceptance and way of life, there was no clear criterion that the court could use to distinguish between 'male' and 'female' individuals that would prevent discrimination against transgender individuals. In addition, the case required an analysis of transgender issues for the purpose of marriage, which raised religious and social issues. Consequently, it was unsuitable for section 3(1), as it raised issues of social policy and administrative feasibility that carried wide practical ramifications.[16]

Lord Nicholls's conclusion is based on issues that are relevant to determining contestability. The plethora of medical evidence surrounding the determination of gender creates a situation in which it can be reasonable to disagree with conclusions as to the criteria of a Convention-compatible interpretation of 'male' and 'female'. In addition, the question was raised in the context of marriage. There is a range of justifications for regulating marriage in society, which are related in turn to conflicting underlying principles. For example, marriage is regarded as valuable both as a particular expression of a relationship defined in religious terms and as a means of promoting and regulating stable relationships in society. These deeper principles could reach different, reasonable, conclusions concerning the definition of gender for the purposes of a legally recognised marriage.

The assessment of whether the issue before the court raises complex issues of social policy when determining whether it is possible to interpret legislation to render it Convention-compatible, gives rise to inaccuracies. Consequently, the current legal test does not facilitate the dialogue required to justify the Human Rights Act. These inaccuracies are explained, at least in part, by the way in which the court's approach to determining whether complex issues of social policy arise resembles the distinction between core and penumbral applications of rights. The court merely determines whether the scope and application of the Convention right raises issues of wide social policy. However, even if the Convention right before the court raises issues of social policy, this is not coterminous with the conclusion that the issue before the court is contestable. The determination of contestability relies on whether the specific issue before the court is contestable.

Although *Bellinger* concerned complex issues of social policy, the issue before the court was not contestable. It was clear that a definition of gender based

---

[16] *Ibid*, at [28]–[49].

solely on that assigned at birth failed to protect Mrs Bellinger's Convention rights under article 8 ECHR. In addition, it was clear that any of the other possible medical definitions of gender which took account of the rights of transgender individuals would have included Mrs Bellinger within its provisions. *Bellinger* is best understood not just as a case raising complex social policy issues, but as a case where the court was faced with a non-contestable rights issue, coupled with a choice from a range of possible Convention-compatible readings. It is not the rights issue, but the issue as to the best Convention-compatible reading of the legislation that raises contestable issues for the court. To understand further how these inaccuracies arise, we need to analyse *Bellinger* in more detail.

In *Ghaidan* Lord Nicholls refers to the case as raising issues that are ill-suited for the courts given their 'exceedingly wide ramifications'.[17] However, there are three different types of argument used by Lord Nicholls in *Bellinger* to explain its unsuitability for judicial resolution:

1. The vagueness inherent in determining the meaning of 'male' and 'female' to ensure Convention-compatibility.[18]
2. Practical and administrative problems that may arise from determining a Convention-compatible interpretation. A clear definition of gender is needed given the practical consequences of the determination of gender, not merely with regard to marriage, but also with regard, for example, to childcare provisions, employment situations and some gender-specific criminal offences.[19]
3. The facts raise important issues of social policy that are difficult to resolve, given the social and religious context of marriage.[20] The criteria used to determine the meaning of 'male' and 'female' may also carry policy implications. For example, selecting a particular surgical procedure as a criterion of gender may force those with gender orientation disorder to undertake painful and expensive surgical procedures in order to ensure that they were recognised as having a particular gender.[21]

The intermingling of these three distinct issues has two consequences that affect the accuracy of the test used to delineate between section 3 and section 4. First, inaccuracy may occur as social policy implications may be counted twice. When faced with a complex issue of social policy, the courts defer to the legislature when defining the scope of a Convention right, recognising the better suitability of the legislature in resolving this issue.[22] Courts also refer to the existence of complex issues of social policy to justify using section 4 as opposed to section 3. A consideration of the existence of a complex issue of social policy is

[17] *Ghaidan v Godin-Mendoza*, above n 1, at [34].
[18] *Bellinger v Bellinger*, above n 14, at [40].
[19] *Ibid*, at [42].
[20] *Ibid*, at [45].
[21] *Ibid*, at [42].
[22] See the later discussion at pp 156–8.

therefore used twice, both to narrow the scope of the application of a Convention right and to justify a use of section 4 and not of section 3. This may cause the balance between democracy and rights to be tipped too far in favour of the protection of democracy.[23]

This can best be explained by means of a fictitious example, combining the facts of *Bellinger* and *Ghaidan*. For the purposes of our example, Mrs Bellinger, a transgender, lived with Mr Bellinger, to whom she was married in a religious, but non-legally recognised, ceremony. Mr Bellinger rented a house in his own name from Mr Godin-Mendoza. Following Mr Bellinger's tragic death, Mrs Bellinger wishes to remain in what she considers to be her family home. Mr Godin-Mendoza, however, wishes to terminate the tenancy. A statute provides surviving tenancies for a spouse, defined as 'a person living with the original tenant as his or her wife or husband'. The court needs to determine whether this statute can be interpreted so as to include Mrs Bellinger, thereby protecting her Convention rights under articles 8 and 14 ECHR.

Ascertaining whether the definition of a 'spouse' includes Mrs Bellinger raises broad issues of social policy with wide practical and social ramifications. However, in this case the court is not faced with the difficult task of providing a definition of 'male' and 'female' to ensure that the law does not discriminate against transgender individuals. Instead, the court can read 'spouse' so as to include a transgender individual who is a 'person living with the original tenant as his or her wife or husband'. The wide social and policy ramifications were taken into account when determining the Convention right, limiting its scope to the specific issue before the court. For the court to fail to provide this Convention-compatible reading, arguing that the issue is more suited to an application of section 4 as it involves complex issues of social policy, would be to defer twice over. The existence of complex issues of social policy has already been taken into account to provide a narrower definition of the right.

There are situations, however, when the existence of complex social policy issues may provide a reason for the courts to use section 4 as opposed to section 3. This is where complex issues of social policy provide evidence of the better suitability of the legislature as opposed to the courts to provide a remedy for the breach of Convention rights. This may occur in two situations. First, where, despite the narrow definition of a particular Convention right, the court is still faced with a choice from a range of possible Convention-compatible readings. If complex social policy issues create contestability at this level, such that it is reasonable to disagree as to the interpretation that would provide the best protection of Convention rights, then the legislature may provide a better process through which to resolve this contestable issue. In addition, if the existence of complex social policy issues is coupled with possible wide practical ramifications, such that a better protection of Convention rights would be achieved

---

[23] For further discussion, see AL Young, '*Ghaidan v Godin-Mendoza*: Avoiding the Deference Trap' [2005] *Public Law* 23 and J Van Zyl Smit, 'The New, Purposive Interpretation of Statutes: HRA section 3 after *Ghaidan v Godin-Mendoza*' (2007) 70 *Modern Law Review* 294.

through general law as opposed to specific, interstitial development of the law, then the legislature is more able to provide an effective remedy for the breach of the Convention right.

C. Conclusion

Our analysis of the current legal test has provided further clarification of the criteria needed to develop a theory of adjudication for sections 3 and 4 of the Human Rights Act. The democratic dialogue required for a justification of the Act is facilitated if courts ensure that Convention-compatible interpretations do not undermine fundamental features of legislation, issuing declarations of incompatibility in these situations as opposed to striving to find a Convention-compatible reading of legislation. This facilitates dialogue through providing a means by which the legislature can modify or amend judicial decisions taken under section 3 in a manner that provides a check that the legislature would only amend legislation in this manner when there were good reasons to do so.

Our analysis has also provided further clarification surrounding the circumstances in which institutional features determine whether a remedy is best provided by the legislature or the courts. Not only is the legislature better placed to provide a remedy when faced with issues with large practical ramifications, but it provides a better process through which to protect Convention rights when it is reasonable to disagree as to the reading of legislation that will provide the best protection of Convention rights. However, we have also concluded that the current legal test may produce inaccuracies that may undermine the justification of the Human Rights Act.

II. A NEW THEORY OF ADJUDICATION

Two further clarifications to our theory of adjudication can be found in the literature and case law. Aileen Kavanagh's analysis of interpretation and its application to sections 3 and 4 of the Human Rights Act provides further analysis of the way in which institutional features of the legislature and the courts may influence the assessment of which institution is best suited to providing a remedy for the breach of a particular Convention right. Theories of deference may also help to clarify the way in which courts can ascertain whether the rights issue it is determining is contestable, although there are dangers with the use of this concept that could damage the justification of the democratic dialogue model of rights protection found in the Human Rights Act. These further additions will be discussed, before we present a complete account of the theory of adjudication, using *Bellinger* as an example to explain its application.

A. Interpretation

Kavanagh's analysis of interpretation shares one of the assumptions of our justification of democratic dialogue.[24] She recognises that Convention rights are vague and unclear, giving rise to interpretative pluralism where it is reasonable to disagree about possible meanings of Convention rights and their application. Moreover, disputes concerning Convention rights and their application turn on deep meanings, involving the values underpinning these rights as opposed to shallow meanings that depend more on linguistic conventions.[25]

This recognition is similar to our assumption of the need for sufficient rights dissensus, recognising that rights issues may be contestable and that the resolution of rights issues may not be found merely by searching for the meaning of the right. This assumption leads Kavanagh to reject a purely linguistic approach to interpretation, providing further confirmation of our approach to interpretation which focuses on whether a Convention-compatible reading of legislation breaches a fundamental feature of that legislation. Instead, Kavanagh argues that the scope of possible interpretations under section 3(1) of the Act is best understood as reflecting the distinction between legislative and judicial law-making.

Her distinction between judicial and legislative law-making is based on institutional features similar to the ones used above to determine whether the legislature or the courts would be best placed to remedy a breach of Convention rights. She argues that judicial law-making develops law in a partial and piecemeal fashion, looking back to previous cases in order to provide for possible future developments of the law. Legislative law-making is able to provide for more root and branch reform. The legislature only needs to look forward; it need not look back to previous legislative measures in order to ensure that new legislation fits the pattern of older legislation.[26]

Her conclusion is supported by her analysis of case law, which can help to furnish further clarification of when courts should use section 4 as opposed to section 3, even when faced with a non-contestable right, because the court is not able to provide an appropriate remedy through the application of section 3. Courts should not use section 3 where a Convention-compatible reading would require a radical alteration of a statutory scheme, given the inability of the courts to make root and branch changes to legislation.[27] Neither should courts use section 3 where a Convention-compatible reading of legislation would produce large practical ramifications which cannot be regulated by the interstitial approach of the court.[28]

[24] A Kavanagh, 'The Elusive Divide between Interpretation and Legislation under the Human Rights Act 1998' (2004) 24 *Oxford Journal of Legal Studies* 259.
[25] *Ibid*, at 263–64.
[26] *Ibid*, at 270–74.
[27] See, *International Transport Roth GmBh v Secretary of State for the Home Department* [2002] EWCA Civ 158, [2003] 1 QB 728 (Simon Brown LJ).
[28] See, In *Re S*, above n 12 (Lord Nicholls).

B. Deference and Adjudication

The concept of deference has been developed predominantly in the context of section 6 of the Human Rights Act, determining the extent to which public authorities should be allowed to determine the scope and application of Convention rights. As discussed above,[29] deference is motivated by the same concerns as democratic dialogue models of rights, aiming to ensure that a protection of rights is sensitive to the argument that contestable rights issues may be better suited to resolution by the executive than by the judiciary. Factors determining the scope of deference can help to furnish further criteria to help ascertain whether courts are faced with a contestable or a non-contestable issue. An illustration of the way in which judicial and academic discussion of the criteria of deference may further clarify the theory of adjudication of the Human Rights Act is found in the judgments of their Lordships in *A and others v Secretary of State for the Home Department; X and another v Secretary of State for the Home Department (A and X).*[30]

The decision concerned the detention of non-national terrorist suspects in Belmarsh Prison. Section 23 of the Anti-terrorism, Crime and Securities Act 2001 enabled the Home Secretary to detain non-nationals whose presence was believed to present a risk to the security of the United Kingdom due to a belief that they were involved in terrorist activities. This detention was permitted where the individuals in question could not be deported, either due to a fear for their safety should they be deported, or due to practical considerations. Section 23 clearly breached article 5(1) ECHR. Consequently, an executive order was passed to derogate from the ECHR. The issue of deference arose in *A and X* when determining the degree to which the courts could scrutinise the decisions of the executive both as to the existence of a threat to the life of the nation and as to whether the provisions of section 23 of the 2001 Act were necessary in order to protect national security. This was a complex issue, given both the importance of the right to liberty and of the protection of national security.

When discussing the scope of deference to be afforded to the government, three of their lordships appeared to base their conclusions, at least in part, on the contestable nature, or otherwise, of the particular issue before the court. This is most evident in the judgments of Lords Bingham and Hope. Lord Bingham argued that greater deference should be owed to the executive when faced with political as opposed to legal decisions. In particular, determining the nature of a threat to the life of a nation was a political issue. To determine this issue, the executive would need to predict human behaviour, which was less predictable than other events. Consequently, this political matter was best understood as an issue on which '[r]easonable and informed minds may differ',[31] thus

---

[29] See ch 5, p 117.
[30] [2004] UKHL 56, [2005] 2 AC 68.
[31] *Ibid*, at [29].

making it an issue more suited to the executive and the legislature than the courts. Lord Hope also concluded that there were good reasons for the court to defer to the decision of the executive. However, he argued that less deference was owed to the government, not merely because of the importance of the right to liberty, but because the issue before the court was not one of social or economic policy,

> where opinions may reasonably differ in a democratic society and where choices on behalf of the country as a whole are properly left to government and to the legislature.[32] The judiciary's experience of using the concept of deference demonstrates that the judiciary is aware of criteria that influence the determination of contestability. However, although case law and academic commentary discussing the scope of deference could be used to provide further clarification of the theory of adjudication required by the Human Rights Act, it should not be incorporated into our theory of adjudication.

First, there is a risk that a consideration of deference will encourage the judiciary to classify certain subject matters as contestable, as opposed to analysing whether the specific issue before the court is contestable, thus damaging the democratic dialogue required by the Human Rights Act. This may be countered by adopting a non-spatial as opposed to a spatial approach to deference. A spatial approach to deference occurs when the court is influenced by the general area of the judgment when determining whether to exercise deference. A non-spatial approach occurs when the court performs a more specific analysis, taking account of the area of the judgment and the particular context in which it is applied, when determining the scope of deference.[33] However, it can be difficult to stop a non-spatial approach to deference from collapsing into a spatial approach to deference, particularly when the court focuses on factors that may make an issue more or less contestable, as opposed to focusing on whether it is reasonable to disagree about the application of the Convention right to the specific issue before the court.[34] Consequently, errors may occur, hindering dialogue.

In addition, a consideration of deference may lead to further problems of double counting. A democratic dialogue model of rights protection allows the legislature to respond to the conclusions of the court. There is no need for the court to defer to the wishes of the legislature when defining the scope of the right. Should the judiciary do so, this would disturb the balance of the Human Rights Act, tipping it in favour of democracy as opposed to the protection of human rights. Dialogue is furthered, and a correct balance maintained, when the court provides its own reasoned conclusion as to the scope and application

---

[32] *Ibid*, at [108].

[33] M Hunt, 'Sovereignty's Blight: Why Contemporary Public Law Needs the Concept of Due Deference' in N Bamforth and P Leyland (eds), *Public Law in a Multi-layered Constitution* (Oxford, Hart Publishing, 2003) 337, 344–6.

[34] TRS Allan, 'Human Rights and Judicial Review: a Critique of "Due Deference"' (2006) 65 *Cambridge Law Journal* 671.

of a particular Convention right. This reasoned conclusion needs to be taken into account by the legislature seeking to overturn a judicial decision taken under section 3, or when determining whether to respond to a declaration of incompatibility enacted under section 4.

C. An Emerging Legal Test

Our analysis leads us to the following legal test. Courts need to assess whether the rights issue before the court is contestable. To determine this issue, courts assess the scope of the Convention right and its application to the specific facts. In assessing this issue, courts can have regard to previous decisions discussing the scope of deference, but they must ensure that these features are used to help determine the contestable nature of the issue faced by the court, as opposed to determining contestability in terms of broader provisions.

For example, in *Bellinger* the issue before the court was not contestable. It was not reasonable to disagree with the conclusion that Mrs Bellinger's Convention rights were breached by legislation that only determined gender according to that assigned to an individual at birth. Such legislation made it impossible for transgender individuals to be recognised as belonging to their new gender, in breach of article 8 and article 14 ECHR. This conclusion is not altered by the fact that the determination of the rights of transgender individuals requires an assessment of complex issues of social policy, or that the conclusion of the court would entail large practical ramifications. If the issue before the court is contestable, then the court should use section 4 as opposed to section 3. Where the issue before the court is not contestable, there is a strong prima facie reason to use section 3 as opposed to section 4. This presumption can be rebutted in two ways.

First, section 4 should be used in those situations where the legislature is better placed to provide an effective remedy for the breach of a Convention right. This may occur in three situations. The first situation occurs where a Convention-compatible reading of legislation may require more than a merely interstitial change to the law. An example may be found in *S and W*,[35] where the creation of the 'starred system' required more than a merely interstitial change to the law, requiring a radical departure from the legislative scheme.

In addition, any Convention-compatible reading of legislation that would require an express contradiction of the wording of legislation would be more than an interstitial change to the law. For example, in *R (Anderson) v Secretary of State for the Home Department*[36] section 29 of the Crime (Sentences) Act 1997 provided that:

---

[35] [2002] UKHL 10, [2002] 2 AC 291.
[36] [2002] UKHL 46, [2003] 1 AC 837.

1. If recommended to do so by the Parole Board, the Secretary of State may, after consultation with the Lord Chief Justice together with the trial judge if available, release on licence a life prisoner who is not [a discretionary life prisoner].
2. The Parole Board shall not make a recommendation under subsection (1) above unless the Secretary of State has referred the particular case, or the class of case to which that case belongs, to the Board for its advice.

The court concluded that this section breached article 6 ECHR, as the setting of the compulsory component of a life sentence was a judicial function that required performance by an independent and impartial adjudicator, not the Secretary of State. However, it was not possible to read this legislation so as to preclude the Secretary of State from setting any date for the release on licence of a life prisoner other than that recommended by the trail judge. To do so would contradict the express words of section 29 which granted a complete discretion to the Secretary of State.

The second situation where the legislature may be better able to provide an effective remedy for a breach of a Convention right occurs when a Convention-compatible reading of legislation would require the development of procedural or administrative mechanisms that, in turn, may have knock-on consequences for other areas of the law. *S and W*, again, provides an example of this limit. The starred system developed by the court created procedural mechanisms, which enabled the parents and guardians of children subject to care orders to initiate court proceedings to scrutinise the actions of local authorities with regard to children placed into its care under care orders.

The third situation occurs when courts are faced with a choice between different possible Convention-compatible statutory interpretations, where it is reasonable to disagree about this choice. This may occur, for example, when faced with legislation that breaches article 14 ECHR, requiring equal treatment. If, for example, legislation relating to the payment of pensions discriminates between men and women, it is possible to resolve this lack of equality either by (i) ensuring the amount currently paid to men is also paid to women, or (ii) by ensuring that the amount currently paid to women is also paid to men, or (iii) by choosing a completely different amount of money that is to be paid to both men and women.

In these situations, courts should remedy this breach of Convention rights by a declaration of incompatibility, enabling the legislature to decide from amongst the range of different possible Convention-compatible interpretations. *Bellinger* provides a further example. It was reasonable to disagree about the precise reading of 'male' and 'female' required to ensure Convention-compatibility, given the range of medical and other procedures used to change gender and the policy implications that may ensue from this choice.

In addition, section 4 should be applied where a Convention-compatible interpretation would breach a fundamental feature of the legislation in question. This limit facilitates dialogue by enabling the legislature to respond to correct a perceived mistake of the court in its application of section 3 to provide a Convention-compatible reading of legislation. An example of this limit is found in *S and W*. The Act had marked a policy change from prior legislation, in particular by instituting a general policy on non-interference by the courts into the decisions taken by local authorities exercising its parental authority for children placed under their care under care orders. The 'starred system', read into the legislation by the court, breached this general principle of intervention by providing the court with greater powers of oversight than the limited powers found under the provisions of the Children Act 1989. Consequently, it was not possible for the court to remedy a breach of a Convention right by reading this starred system into the Children Act 1989. The proper remedy for the court was a section 4 declaration of incompatibility.

When applying this test, courts should reach their own conclusion concerning the scope and application of the Convention right in question. There is no need for them to exercise deference when faced, for example, with complex issues of social or moral policy. The concern to ensure a democratic resolution to these issues is met with by the democratic dialogue model of rights protection, which enables the legislature to respond to decisions of the court taken both under section 3 and section 4 of the Act.

Our understanding of the Act also provides guidelines as to how the legislature should exercise its powers. There is a strong assumption that the legislature should not overturn the conclusion of the court which has found that broad legislative provisions have harmed minority rights, or the rights of a specific group, or has undermined a Convention right that mirrors a long-standing principle of the United Kingdom constitution. This presumption is even stronger when the legislature is determining whether to respond to section 3, or where the court has issued a declaration of incompatibility when faced with a non-contentious rights issue which is better resolved by the legislature, or where a Convention-compatible reading of legislation would breach a fundamental feature of a statute.

The presumption is weaker when the legislature is determining how to respond to a section 4 declaration of incompatibility where the rights issue before the court was contestable.

III. CONCLUSION

We have argued that the Human Rights Act can be justified through its provision of a democratic dialogue model of rights protection. Having established a justification for this model of democratic dialogue, this chapter has sought to provide guidance to both the judiciary and the legislature as to how this dialogue should be exercised, so as to maintain the delicate balance between maintaining democracy and protecting human rights.

It is important to realise two limits to our conclusion. First, it is not argued that the Human Rights Act provides an ideal protection of rights, or that it provides a perfect example of a democratic dialogue model of rights protection. Our analysis has sought merely to explain a possible interpretation of the Human Rights Act that justifies its adoption of a weak as opposed to a strong protection of rights. Secondly, our analysis of a theory of adjudication has sought to determine how courts should interpret sections 3 and 4 of the Act to facilitate the dialogue required by the Act. It has not focused on determining whether it was Parliament's intention to protect rights in this manner. Nor has it focused on providing an interpretation of the provisions of sections 3 and 4 of the Human Rights Act.

Our analysis has sought to illustrate, however, how the current interpretation of these provisions provides evidence that there are legal principles that could guide the court in its application of this theory of adjudication. This should ensure that the democratic dialogue model of rights protections provided in the Act does not collapse into either a strong protection of rights—where the legislature feels obliged to approve all judicial decisions determining the scope of Convention rights—or a predominantly political protection of rights—where courts defer too greatly to the legislature.

7

Conclusion

T HE AIM OF the book has been twofold. First, it has investigated the assumption that English law can only provide a weak as opposed to a strong protection of human rights because of the principle of parlia- mentary sovereignty. A strong protection of human rights entails entrenchment of rights provisions, enabling courts to overturn legislation that contravenes human rights. However, this would appear to be impossible in a legal system that adheres to Dicey's conception of continuing parliamentary legislative supremacy. Dicey's theory prohibits Parliament from passing laws that bind its successors, making it impossible to entrench human rights. In addition, it requires Parliament to be the sovereign law-making institution, whose legisla- tive provisions cannot be questioned as to their legal validity by any other insti- tution. If courts were able to strike down legislation that was incompatible with human rights they would be questioning the legal validity of legislation.

The first part of this book challenged this assumption. It analysed both whether the Human Rights Act itself could be said to challenge parliamentary legislative supremacy, as well as providing an account of how the Act could have provided for a stronger protection of human rights, without contravening con- tinuing parliamentary legislative supremacy. The second half of the book analysed whether the Human Rights Act should be modified, in order to provide for a stronger protection of human rights. It argued that there was validity in the protection of human rights provided by the Act. The Act facilitates dialogue between the legislature and the courts, thus aiming to adopt the strengths of a judicial protection of rights, while guarding against its possible anti-democratic consequences.

The book does not seek to provide an argument in favour of entrenching rights, but merely points out possible ways in which this can be achieved while preserving parliamentary sovereignty. Nor has it been argued that a democratic dialogue model of protecting human rights is better than a purely democratic or a strong constitutional protection of rights. It has instead been argued that the model of rights protections found in the Human Rights Act can be justified through the way in which it facilitates democratic dialogue. In addition, the book does not provide an argument that Dicey's conception of parliamentary sovereignty should be preserved as a form of constitutional arrangement that is superior to other constitutional arrangements. Instead, Dicey's theory has been regarded as the prevailing conception of sovereignty. The book has touched on its weaknesses and explored possible alternatives, but has neither fully justified, nor fully rejected, its accepted position as a dominant and perhaps defining characteristic of the English, if not the United Kingdom, constitution.

The conclusion aims to explore this last issue further, advocating a new defence of continuing parliamentary legislative supremacy. It will be argued that continuing parliamentary legislative supremacy is a better conception than self-embracing parliamentary legislative supremacy on constitutional grounds. This defence of continuing parliamentary legislative supremacy does not provide a conclusive argument against the establishment of a written, entrenched constitution for the United Kingdom. It does, however, provide an argument for ensuring that the process by which a constitution is entrenched is different from that used to enact legislation.

I. A MODEST DEFENCE OF CONTINUING PARLIAMENTARY LEGISLATIVE SUPREMACY

A. Sovereignty v Supremacy

The distinction between continuing and self-embracing theories of parliamentary sovereignty is often referred to in terms of entrenchment. Self-embracing theories of parliamentary sovereignty permit entrenchment. Continuing theories of parliamentary sovereignty do not. The book has argued that entrenchment is possible, if difficult to achieve, within theories of continuing parliamentary sovereignty. This entrenchment occurs through the modification of the rule defining validly enacted legislation—a rule which is not capable of being modified by Parliament acting alone. However, this recognition of the possibility of entrenchment poses a further difficulty for Dicey's conception of sovereignty, in addition to that of the possible blurring of the distinction between continuing and self-embracing conceptions of sovereignty. It calls into question whether Dicey's theory is really a theory of parliamentary sovereignty. Sovereignty refers to absolute power: it is the recognition that a particular institution possesses absolute power.[1] Yet, Dicey's theory, arguably, does not describe Parliament as holding absolute power. Parliament, if it enjoys sovereign law-making power, does so by virtue of the rule describing Parliament as possessing such power. This rule also establishes the definition of the legitimate law-maker and its successors, and the procedures the law-maker must use to enact legally valid legislation. The power of the law-maker derives from this rule, not from its own hands. Sovereignty vests not in Parliament, but in those who have the power to make and alter the rule determining the identity of validly enacted legislation.

---

[1] See ch 1, pp 15–17.

Consequently, Dicey's theory may be better understood not as a theory of parliamentary sovereignty, but of parliamentary legislative supremacy. Parliament is not sovereign, but it is supreme. As such, it determines the limits of its own law-making power. These limits cannot be challenged or overturned by any other institution. Yet, Dicey's theory of continuing parliamentary legislative supremacy places a limit on the law-making capacity of the Westminster Parliament that does not stem from Parliament itself—the inability of Parliament to bind its successors. This restriction stems from the very definition of continuing parliamentary legislative supremacy.

If Parliament were able to bind its successors, then it would enjoy self-embracing as opposed to continuing parliamentary legislative supremacy. Yet, the acceptance of this limit appears to lead to the inevitable conclusion that the Westminster Parliament does not enjoy legislative supremacy. To do so it would need to be in charge of all of the limits on its law-making power, including the restriction as to its inability to bind its successors. This would appear to suggest that Parliament can only enjoy legislative supremacy under a theory of self-embracing parliamentary legislative supremacy. Although future Parliaments may be bound as to the manner and form in which they pass legislation, these restrictions would stem from Parliament, not from the nature of sovereignty or supremacy itself, thus complying with our definition of legislative supremacy.

It would appear therefore, that self-embracing parliamentary legislative supremacy is a better theory than continuing parliamentary legislative supremacy. First, it can clearly be classified as a theory of legislative supremacy. The only limits on the law-making power of Parliament stem from Parliament itself. These limits are set by earlier incarnations of Parliament and bind future incarnations of Parliament. Secondly, Parliament can clearly be regarded as a sovereign law-making body. It has the power to pass legislation on any subject matter, save the restrictions that it placed on itself in previous incarnations. Parliament as a whole, taken across time, is sovereign. Thirdly, self-embracing theories of parliamentary legislative supremacy can accommodate criticisms aimed at the justification for granting sovereign law-making powers to Parliament. Parliament can legislate to entrench minority rights, enacting binding manner and form provisions that prevent future incarnations of Parliament from eroding human rights.

However, self-embracing legislative supremacy also suffers from logical contradictions and flaws when examined in greater depth. Jennings and Heuston are the main protagonists of self-embracing parliamentary legislative supremacy in English law. Their argument is founded on the recognition of sovereignty as a legal principle. As a legal principle, it could only be derived either from the common law or from statute. However, to vest the principle of sovereignty in a statute would require Parliament to have had the power to create itself—to pull itself up by its own bootstraps. Parliament does not have the power to confer sovereignty on itself. Hence, for Jennings and Heuston, sovereignty must be a principle of the common law. As a principle of the common law it can be modified by statutes enacted by Parliament, as statutory provisions override principles of the common law.

The recognition that sovereignty must derive from the common law gives rise to two problems. First, as Goldsworthy argues, the same 'bootstraps' argument can be applied to the courts.[2] If rules determining sovereignty stem from the common law and were made by the courts, then we need to investigate the source of the power of the courts to make the common law. Yet, this gives rise to the same element of circularity. The courts have the power to make the common law, including the rules relating to the identity of the sovereign law-making power and the rules relating to the creation of valid legislative acts. But, this power to make the common law itself stems from the common law. Courts have this power because courts have determined that they have this power. To vest the rules determining sovereignty in the common law, therefore, is subject to the same criticism used by Jennings and Heuston to explain why the rules relating to sovereignty cannot vest in statute law, leaving common law as the default position. Their error is to fail to recognise that there are other possible sources of rules relating to sovereignty. Continuing theories of parliamentary legislative supremacy do not fall foul of this criticism because the source of sovereignty is not found in either common law or statute. It stems from political facts which cannot be changed either by the legislature or the courts acting alone.

Secondly, if the common law is regarded as the source of the rule describing the identification of the sovereign law-maker, there is a danger that self-embracing theories of parliamentary sovereignty will collapse into theories of judicial sovereignty. If the rules concerning the identity of the sovereign law-making power, the processes by which this sovereign law-making power is exercised and the transfer of sovereign power from one incarnation of the sovereign to the next are found in the common law, then it is open to the judiciary, as well as the legislature, to modify these rules. It may also be open to the judiciary to modify the common law provision that statutory enactments override the common law. The judiciary alone could determine whether to grant legal validity to legislation according to its own determinations, modifying the common law.

Our analysis has failed to provide clear reasons to adopt a theory of continuing or self-embracing parliamentary legislative supremacy. Both may give rise to apparent paradoxes and contradictions and both may appear to have damaging consequences for the United Kingdom constitution. While continuing parliamentary legislative supremacy appears to prioritise democracy over human rights, self-embracing theories of parliamentary legislative supremacy could lead to the sovereignty of the judiciary as opposed to that of Parliament. However, our analysis has helped to clarify the differences between the two conceptions and to provide further support for the conclusion that the distinction

---

[2] For further discussion, see J Goldsworthy, *The Sovereignty of Parliament: History and Philosophy* (Oxford, Clarendon Press, 1999) 240.

between the two conceptions derives from the way in which entrenchment can be achieved and the relative powers of the legislature and the courts.

Entrenchment is possible under continuing parliamentary legislative supremacy when the rule defining valid legislation is modified, such modification stemming from an acceptance of this modification by the officials of the legal system, including the legislature and the courts. Entrenchment is possible through self-embracing theories of parliamentary legislative supremacy when Parliament modifies the rule defining valid legislation, courts recognising that this common law rule can be overridden by legislative enactment. To understand these differences further, and to explain how they help to provide a modified defence of Dicey's conception of sovereignty, we need to revisit the paradox of sovereignty discussed in the first chapter.[3]

B. From Paradox to Justification

The paradox of sovereignty derives from an analysis of omnipotence. The paradox arises as an omnipotent sovereign, as all-powerful, must possess the power to limit her own power. Yet, if this is the case, then following an exercise of her power to limit her own power, she is no longer omnipotent, having successfully limited her own power. However, if she does not possess the power to limit her own power, then she is also no longer omnipotent. There is something that she cannot do, namely limit the scope of her own power.

When discussing the sovereignty paradox, reference was made to HLA Hart's analysis, which demonstrated that both self-embracing and continuing parliamentary legislative supremacy were logically possible ways of resolving the paradox. Either the sovereign body was seen as sovereign over time, having the power to limit her own competences as in self-embracing theories of sovereignty, or she was viewed as sovereign at each specific moment in time, therefore not having the power to modify her future powers, as in continuing theories of parliamentary legislative supremacy.[4]

A better understanding of the true nature of the paradox of sovereignty is found in the discussion of JL Mackie.[5] Mackie explains the sovereignty conundrum by distinguishing between sovereignty over first-order rules and sovereignty over second-order rules. First-order rules are those which govern the actions of individuals other than the legislature. Second-order rules are those which govern the legislature and the process of law-making.[6] A sovereign lawmaker may possess:

---

[3] See ch 1, p 16.

[4] See ch 1, pp 15–17.

[5] JL Mackie, 'Evil and Omnipotence' 1955 *Mind* 200. See, J Allan, 'The Paradox of Sovereignty: *Jackson* and the Hunt for a new Rule of Recognition' (2007) 18 *King's Law Journal* 1.

[6] This distinction is not to be confused with that drawn by HLA Hart between primary and secondary rules. Mackie's second-order rules are similar to Hart's secondary rules as both are broadly characterised as rules about rules. However, Mackie's second-order rules are both narrower and

Sovereignty (1): ie sovereignty over first-order rules, or
Sovereignty (2): ie sovereignty over second-order rules.

Having drawn this distinction, Mackie describes the paradox of sovereignty in the following manner:

> If we say that Parliament is sovereign, we might mean that any Parliament at any time has sovereignty (1), or we might mean that Parliament has both sovereignty (1) and sovereignty (2) at present, but we cannot without contradiction mean both that the present Parliament has sovereignty (2) and that every Parliament at every time has sovereignty (1), for if the present Parliament has sovereignty (2) it may use it to take away the sovereignty (1) of later Parliaments.[7]

Continuing parliamentary legislative supremacy recognises that it is not possible for a current parliament to bind its successors as to do so would remove the sovereignty of later parliaments. It grants sovereignty (1) to any parliament at any time. However, it does not grant sovereignty (2) to Parliament, given that to do so may result in future parliaments not possessing sovereignty (1). Self-embracing parliamentary legislative supremacy grants sovereignty (1) and sovereignty (2) to Parliament, recognising that this means that future parliaments may not possess sovereignty (1).

When analysed in these terms, the paradox of sovereignty reveals a further difference between continuing and self-embracing conceptions of sovereignty. Self-embracing sovereignty vests sovereignty (2) in Parliament. Continuing parliamentary sovereignty does not. It will be argued that there are sound constitutional reasons to only grant sovereignty (1) and not sovereignty (2) to Parliament. These reasons are based on values inherent to constitutions, whether written or codified, predominantly legal or political, or which enable or forbid entrenchment.[8]

C. A Constitutional Defence of Continuing Parliamentary Legislative Supremacy

Although it is possible to define constitutions, it can be hard to determine values that adhere to all constitutions, regardless of whether they are codified, written, legal, political or historical, entrenched or otherwise. In one sense, constitutions merely delineate the organs of government, determining their identity and relative powers. It would be wrong, however, to equate a constitution with the rule of recognition. A rule of recognition determines valid law in a

---

broader than Hart's second order rules. They are narrower in that they only concern the nature of the legislature and the way in which the legislature is to enact valid legislation. They are broader in that they are not merely power-conferring rules.

[7] Mackie, above n 5, at 211–12.

[8] NW Barber, 'Against a Written Constitution' [2008] *Public Law* 11; D Feldman, 'Courts, Constitutions and Commentators: Interpreting the Invisible' (1993–4) 16 *Holdsworth Law Review* 37, 39–44; D Feldman, 'None, One or Several? Perspectives on the UK's Constitution(s)' (2005) 64 *Cambridge Law Journal* 329.

particular legal system. It has a narrower reach than a constitution. Constitutions have value not only in the way in which they delineate power, but also have intrinsic virtues that help to distinguish between good and bad constitutions. The defence of continuing parliamentary legislative supremacy rests on a claim that, in the current incarnation of the United Kingdom constitution, these values are best achieved by continuing as opposed to self-embracing parliamentary legislative supremacy.

First, constitutions need to strike a balance between stability and flexibility. Stability promotes constitutionalism by providing certainty and consistency, helping constitutions to achieve their objectives of identifying the institutions that constitute the state and the legal system, distributing their relative powers and governing the way in which these institutions relate to each other and to the citizens that they govern. Flexibility is needed to allow constitutional arrangements to change as the society that they govern changes. Flexible adaptation to change enables constitutions to evolve, avoiding the need for abrupt and disruptive constitutional change.

Secondly, constitutions may perform a legitimising function. Constitutions aim to justify the claim to the legitimate exercise of political power by those in authority. The need for legitimacy is illustrated, at least in part, by the debate concerning the balance to be drawn between the protection of human rights and the preservation of democracy. Those preferring a legislative protection of human rights do so from a standpoint of legitimacy, regarding a judicial protection of rights as undermining the legitimate law-making powers of a democratically representative and accountable legislature. Those preferring a constitutional protection of rights have a different perspective of a legitimate law-making power. Democratic lawmakers only enjoy legitimacy when their powers are not used to undermine human rights, particularly those rights underpinning democracy or those that protect minorities from the tyranny of the majority.

Thirdly, constitutions create checks and balance mechanisms through which to distribute power between different institutions, ensuring that institutions do not abuse their powers or usurp the functions of other institutions.[9] These mechanisms facilitate legitimacy and the balance between stability and flexibility. Checks and balances can be designed to ensure that no one institution obtains more power than it is legitimate for it to possess. In addition, checks and balances may provide a means by which constitutional crises can be avoided, facilitating necessary constitutional change that does not undermine constitutional stability.[10] Checks and balances also serve a separate function, promoting

---

[9] This checks and balances function is related to the doctrine of the separation of powers. However, it requires a more sophisticated analysis than the traditional tripartite distinction between legislative, executive and judicial powers.

[10] These mechanisms were referred to by Nick Barber and me as mechanisms of constitutional self-defence in an earlier article, see NW Barber and AL Young, 'The Rise of Prospective Henry VIII Clauses and their Implications for Sovereignty' [2003] *Public Law* 112.

efficiency through the allocation of power to the institution best suited to its exercise and by ensuring that institutions do not stray from their particular areas of expertise.[11]

To understand how continuing parliamentary legislative supremacy best serves these values, we need to return to the differences between continuing and self-embracing theories of parliamentary legislative supremacy. Continuing parliamentary legislative supremacy vests sovereignty (2) in a logically pre-requisite rule. We referred to Hart's theory of the rule of recognition as an example of such a logically pre-requisite rule, although adherence to Hart's theory is not necessary for the justification of continuing parliamentary legislative supremacy. What is required is the recognition that (i) rules relating to the identity of the sovereign (both at a particular point in time and as to possible future successors) and (ii) the identification of the law-making process by which the sovereign enacts legally valid legislation, cannot be changed either by Parliament or the courts alone. Their modification requires action by officials representing different branches of the legal system. This includes the law-maker, the courts and those administering the law, although it is hard to pin-point in practice precisely how many officials are required.

Self-embracing theories of parliamentary legislative supremacy vest sover-eignty (2) in Parliament. Parliament alone can modify the rules relating to the identity of the sovereign law-making body and its successors, as well as the process of enacting valid legislation. However, as argued above, theories of self-embracing legislative supremacy also describe the rules relating to the identity of the sovereign and validly enacted legislation as vesting in the common law.[12] Parliament retains sovereignty (2) as it can enact legislation to change sover-eignty (2)—and the courts will adhere to this change, given that the common law dictates that statutory enactments override principles of the common law. However, it is possible for the courts to modify these principles of the common law, potentially transferring sovereignty (2) from Parliament to the courts.

When analysed in these terms, we begin to understand the justification for preserving Dicey's theory of continuing parliamentary legislative supremacy. Placing sovereignty (2) in Parliament, as required by self-embracing theories of parliamentary sovereignty, appears to strike an effective balance between flexi-bility and stability. Flexibility is provided by Parliament's ability to entrench constitutional principles merely by passing an ordinary act of legislation. Stability is provided as these entrenched principles cannot be overturned by ordinary legislation.

The problem with self-embracing theories is that it may be harder to justify the legitimacy of the particular principles chosen by the Parliament exercising sovereignty (2) to achieve entrenchment. First there may be no difference

---

[11] NW Barber, 'Prelude to the Separation of Powers' (2001) 60 *Cambridge Law Journal* 59; J Jowell, 'Judicial Deference: Servility, Civility or Institutional Capacity?' [2003] *Public Law* 592.
[12] See ch 3, pp 68–75.

between this Parliament and any other future parliament, giving rise to criticisms as to the justification for future parliaments to be bound by the wishes of an earlier parliament. Secondly, even if there is agreement concerning the legitimacy of those principles that are entrenched, new principles may emerge that require entrenchment in the future, or old principles may lose their legitimacy in the face of changing theories of morality or political theory.

This need for change in sovereignty (2) rules may be satisfied by the judiciary, through the use of creative interpretation. In addition, the courts could modify the common law to overturn the will of the legislature,[13] should the legislature be unwilling or unable to modify the content of those provisions entrenched by an earlier incarnation of Parliament. Rather than encouraging stability, this tension between granting sovereignty (2) to Parliament, while also regarding the source of sovereignty (2) as being the common law, could lead to a series of constitutional crises between Parliament and the courts, threatening constitutional stability.

Such constitutional crises are less likely to occur under continuing parliamentary legislative supremacy that vests sovereignty (2) in a logically pre-requisite rule, possessing the qualities both of a rule of the legal system and a political fact. As described earlier, the content of this rule can change to entrench principles that are deemed to require greater protection. But this entrenchment does not occur through the actions of Parliament alone. Although this may be initiated by Parliament, modification requires acceptance by officials in the system: this need for acceptance by officials helps to preserve the legitimacy of those principles entrenched in this manner.

Moreover, as this logically pre-requisite rule is both a political fact and a rule of the legal system, its modification normally occurs through gradual evolution, avoiding a series of constitutional crises. This avoidance occurs because the checks and balances mechanisms between the different governmental institutions are not found solely in legal powers, but are also part of the political domain. Neither the courts nor Parliament have the sole legal power to modify the rules relating to the identification of the sovereign and the enactment of valid legislation.

When determining whether a purported modification of these rules is valid, officials of the legal system will have regard to political factors. Not only does this help to promote the legitimacy of such changes, it may also prevent either institution from trying to modify the content of this rule purely to enhance its own power in relation to the other institution. Such modifications may prompt a constitutional crisis that may result either in Parliament or the courts gaining legal ascendancy over the other institution through a modification of our current constitutional arrangements. As such, comity between the two institutions may help to enhance healthy checks and balances between Parliament and the

---

[13] Perhaps by changing the rule under which statutes, and therefore Parliament, always takes priority over rules of the common law.

courts. Neither can gain ascendancy without running the risk that this will also result in a loss of their current powers.

D. The Example of *R (Jackson) v Attorney-General*

Parallels can be drawn between the defence of continuing parliamentary leg-islative supremacy and the development of legal pluralism, both to explain the European Union,[14] and the law relating to the privileges of Parliament in the English legal system.[15] Legal pluralism arises where two different institutions each claim to have *kompetenz-kompetenz*—the aspect of sovereignty that grants the power to determine the scope of your own competences. In the European Union, for example, both national courts and the European Court of Justice claim to have the power to determine the scope of application of European Community law. This, in turn, creates two possible parallel rules of recognition. National courts claim to recognise the validity of European Community law according to provisions of national law. If European Community law is recognised as a valid source of domestic law, whose directly effective provisions override contradictory provisions of national law, it is because national law grants it this validity and force. The European Court of Justice claims that European Community law has validity in and of itself, regardless of the provisions of national law. European Community law deter-mines the validity and force of directly effective provisions of European Community law in the domestic legal systems.[16]

The existence of two parallel rules of recognition creates instability in the legal system where there is the possibility that the rules of recognition would recognise two different and contradictory propositions of law as legally valid. If, for example, English law were to recognise that directly effective European Community law only overrode contradictory provisions of English law enacted prior to the European Communities Act 1972 and European Community law were to recognise directly effective Community law as overriding all contradic-tory provisions of national law, regardless of the date of their enactment, then a

---

[14] See, M Kumm, 'Who is the Final Arbiter of Constitutionality in Europe?: Three Conceptions of the Relationship between the German Federal Constitutional Court and the European Court of Justice' (1999) 36 *Common Market Law Review* 351; N McCormick, *Questioning Sovereignty: Law, State and Nation in the European Commonwealth* (Oxford, Oxford University Press, 1999); M Poaires Maduro, 'Contrapunctual Law: Europe's Constitutional Pluralism in Action' in N Walker (ed), *Sovereignty in Transition* (Oxford, Hart Publishing, 2003) 501; DR Phelan, *Revolt or Revolution: the Constitutional Boundaries of the European Community* (Dublin, Round Hall Sweet and Maxwell, 1997); C Richmond, 'Preserving the Identity Crisis: Autonomy, System and Sovereignty in European Law (1997) 16 *Law and Philosophy* 377 and JHH Weiler, 'The Reformation of European Constitutionalism' (1997) 35 *Journal of Common Market Studies* 97.

[15] See, NW Barber, 'Legal Pluralism and the European Union' (2006) 12 *European Law Journal* 306.

[16] No claim is made here that the UK constitution is best understood from a perspective of legal pluralism.

contradiction would arise. The existence of contradictions creates instability in the legal system, creating a conflict whose outcome is determined when one rule of recognition is accepted as having validity within a particular legal system, overriding the claims of the competing rule of recognition.

For legal pluralism to exist beyond mere temporary situations, mechanisms are required to reduce possible conflicts, which in turn facilitate stability. This occurs in two ways. First, institutions avoid conflict because of the negative consequences that may arise should such conflict occur.[17] Secondly, mechanisms may exist to facilitate inter-institutional comity, providing a stronger incentive for co-operation to avoid conflict.[18] Continuing parliamentary legislative supremacy facilitates inter-institutional comity as well as raising the spectre of negative consequences should such comity fail. Self-embracing parliamentary legislative supremacy does not facilitate comity in the same manner. This can best be explained by means of an analysis of *R (Jackson) v Attorney-General (Jackson).*[19]

Jackson concerned the validity of the Hunting Act 2004, which was enacted without the consent of the House of Lords according to the provisions of the Parliament Act 1949. The Parliament Act 1949 was itself enacted without the consent of the House of Lords, under the provisions of the Parliament Act 1911. Jackson questioned the validity of the Parliament Act 1949, claiming that the Act was invalid as it could not have been enacted through the procedure of the Parliament Act 1911. Their lordships concluded that both the Parliament Act 1949 and the Hunting Act 2004 were legally valid Acts of Parliament, as the Parliament Act 1911 would not be contradicted by the enactment of the Parliament Act 1949.

In reaching this conclusion, using the provisions of the earlier 1911 Act to determine the validity of the later 1949 Act, their lordships appeared to contravene continuing parliamentary legislative supremacy. If the Parliament Act 1949 had contravened the Parliament Act 1911, then its provisions should have impliedly repealed the provisions of the 1911 Act. Therefore, the 1949 Act would have been legally valid regardless of whether its provisions fell within the scope of those permitted to use the 1911 procedure.

There are two possible explanations of *Jackson*. First, the Parliament Act 1911 can be interpreted as triggering a shift in the rule of recognition. This shift would occur only when it had been accepted as a political fact, with officials in the system accepting that the rule of recognition now included the ability to enact legislation without the consent of the House of Lords, provided that this was done in the manner proscribed by the Parliament Act 1911. Secondly, the Parliament Act 1911 can be interpreted as triggering a change to a self-embracing theory of parliamentary sovereignty. By enacting this legislation,

---

[17] Weiler, above n 14, at 124–7.
[18] Walker, above n 14, at 375–8; Maduro, above n 14, at 522–24; Kumm, above n 14, at 281–307.
[19] [2005] UKHL 56, [2006] 1 AC 262.

Parliament altered the manner and form in which legislation is passed, binding its successors to follow these provisions if it wished to enact legislation without the consent of the House of Lords. Therefore, courts have to examine the provisions of the Parliament Act 1911 to determine whether legislation enacted under its provisions is legally valid.

The first interpretation can be supported by Lord Hope's judgment. Lord Hope recognises that sovereignty is a political fact.[20] His conclusion that the Parliament Act 1949 is valid is based not only on an examination of the provisions of the Parliament Act 1911, but on the way in which the procedure established by the Parliament Acts 1911 and 1949 has been followed by the House of Commons in order to enact other statutes prior to the enactment of the Hunting Act 2004. For Lord Hope:

> The political reality is that of a general acceptance by all the main parties and by both Houses of the amended timetable which the 1949 Act introduced. I do not think that it is open to a court of law to ignore that reality.[21]

To interpret the validity of the Parliament Act 1949 in this manner facilitates comity between the legislature and the courts. Courts analyse political reality, determining whether purported modifications in the rule of recognition have indeed been accepted by the executive and the legislature. Evidence of this acceptance occurs not only with regard to the way in which the provisions of the Parliament Acts 1911 and 1949 have been used without challenge, but through the way in which the existence of these Acts has influenced debates surrounding other legislation. In recognising the validity of this legislation, the courts modify the common law, such that the modification of the rule of recognition is also recognised as a legal fact. Courts are not legally bound to accept the purported modification of the rule of recognition. Consequently, the legislature will need to consider the possible reaction of the courts to a purported modification to the rule of recognition.

Comity between the legislature and the courts not only furthers stability, but also instigates a form of checks and balances between the legislature and the courts. As Lord Hope remarked:

> In the field of constitutional law the delicate balance between the various institutions whose sound and lasting quality Dicey . . . likened to the work of bees when constructing a honeycomb is maintained to a large degree by the mutual respect which each institution has for the other.[22]

These checks and balances operate in the background, limiting actions on the basis of the prospective reaction of the legislature or the courts. They are reinforced by the awareness of the consequences, should such comity breakdown. Lord Hope remarks that the principle of parliamentary sovereignty is 'built

---

[20] [2005] UKHL 56, [2006] 1 AC 262, at [120].
[21] *Ibid*, at [124].
[22] *Ibid*, at [125].

upon the assumption that Parliament represents the people whom it exists to serve'.[23] Where the courts feel that legislation does not reflect the wishes of the people whom Parliament exists to serve, then the possibility remains not only that the population will not follow the law, but also that the courts, recognising this fact, fail to enforce legislation enacted by Parliament. Such a move would challenge the legitimacy of both the legislature and the courts, forcing a constitutional crisis. The constitutional crisis occurs not as a result of a power struggle between these two institutions, but because of a perceived challenge to the legitimacy of the legislature. Its resolution will depend, at least in part, on the wishes of the people Parliament is intended to serve, stressing the relational aspect of the sovereignty granted to Parliament.[24]

The second interpretation of *Jackson* can be supported by Lord Steyn's judgment which clearly adopts a self-embracing theory of parliamentary legislative supremacy.[25] By enacting the Parliament Act 1911 the legislature modified the manner and form under which legislation is to be passed, binding its successors. The 1949 Act is valid because it complies with the manner and form requirement established by Parliament. As such, the courts are bound to recognise the legislation as legally valid. This leaves little room for comity. Parliament is aware that its alteration of the manner and form in which legislation is to be passed will be accepted by the courts, enabling it to bind its successors. There is no need for Parliament to consider the potential reaction of the courts. Courts accept the validity of the alternation to the manner and form under which legislation is passed as a matter of law. As a legal principle, comity may only occur through principles of interpretation, restricting or expanding the scope of manner and form provisions. However, the scope of interpretation may be smaller in relation to such technical provisions of the law as compared with broader substantive protections of human rights.

This is not to deny that checks and balances may still occur within self-embracing parliamentary legislative supremacy. However, they occur in a different manner. This can be illustrated by the judgment of Lord Steyn. Lord Steyn recognises that, under 'strict legalism' it may be possible for the government to use the Parliament Acts 1911–1949 procedure to alter or abolish the House of Lords.[26] The procedures of the Parliament Acts 1911 and 1949 could also be used to 'introduce oppressive and wholly undemocratic legislation'.[27] In these circumstances, the courts may modify the principle of parliamentary sovereignty itself, which Steyn regards as a 'construct of the common law', created by the judiciary[28]:

---

[23] *Ibid*, at [126].
[24] See, M Loughlin, *The Idea of Public Law* (Oxford, Oxford University Press, 2003) 83–7.
[25] [2005] UKHL 56, [2006] 1 AC 262, [81]–[86].
[26] *Ibid*, at [101].
[27] *Ibid*, at [102].
[28] *Ibid*.

In exceptional circumstances involving an attempt to abolish judicial review or the ordinary role of the courts, the Appellate Committee of the House of Lords or a new Supreme Court may have to consider whether this is constitutional fundamental [*sic*] which even a sovereign Parliament acting at the behest of a complaisant House of Commons cannot abolish'.[29]

Checks and balances instituted in this manner threaten to replace parliamentary sovereignty with judicial sovereignty. It may indirectly restrict the power of the legislature, but the focus of the legislature may be to avoid conflicts which appear to remove the powers of the judiciary, as opposed to focusing on whether to modify the rule of recognition in a manner that will be accepted by the judiciary and ultimately the electorate. It provides the judiciary with a mechanism of constitutional self-defence[30] without the same facilitation of comity, which may potentially damage the stability and legitimacy of parliamentary sovereignty.

II. CONCLUSION

Our argument has come full circle. We have defended Dicey's conception of continuing parliamentary legislative supremacy through the manner in which it facilities inter-institutional comity. The Human Rights Act has been defended as facilitating dialogue between the legislature and the judiciary, a further example of inter-institutional comity designed to protect human rights. This is not to argue that Dicey's theory of continuing parliamentary legislative supremacy is the best form of constitutional arrangement that should remain the key principle of our constitution in perpetuity. Nor is it argued here that the Human Rights Act provides the only justifiable means of protecting human rights. Rather, it is to recognise that, in a constitutional system that seeks to place law-making power in a supreme Parliament, whose powers are not limited by an entrenched constitution enacted through a process different from ordinary statutory enactment, there are advantages to adopting continuing as opposed to self-embracing parliamentary legislative supremacy. Continuing parliamentary legislative supremacy provides a better means of evolution without constitutional crisis, facilitating a system of checks and balances and helping to give legitimacy to the current constitutional arrangement.

Our defence of continuing parliamentary legislative supremacy is modest. However, despite its modesty, it is robust to some of the more recent criticisms of Dicey's theory of continuing parliamentary legislative supremacy. Preserving continuing parliamentary legislative supremacy need not amount to a preservation of democracy over a protection of rights. This is illustrated both by our discussion of how entrenchment can be achieved without undermining continuing

---

[29] [2005] UKHL 56, [2006] 1 AC 262, [102].
[30] See, Barber and Young, above n 10.

parliamentary legislative supremacy and also through our analysis of the Human Rights Act. Nor is this preservation a perpetuation of Dicey's hold on the English constitution, or a desire to cling to outmoded constitutional principles.[31] Rather, it rests on its relative ability to promote values of constitutionalism. It also illustrates a paradox: continuing parliamentary legislative supremacy is valuable because, in one sense, Parliament is *not* sovereign. Continuing parliamentary legislative supremacy does not grant the power to Parliament to determine the definition of validly enacted legislation. This is vested instead in a rule whose modification requires the acceptance of both Parliament and the courts.

---

[31] See, JWF Allison, *The English Historical Constitution: Continuity, Change and European Effects* (Cambridge, Cambridge University Press, 2007) esp pp 103–84.

Index